AUSTRALIA 1942

IN THE SHADOW OF WAR

In 1942, the shadow of modern war reached Australia's shores for the first time. In this compelling volume, leading historians explore why 1942 was such a pivotal year in Australia's history, and explain how the nation confronted some of its greatest challenges. This broad-ranging study covers key issues from political, economic and home-front reform to the establishment of a new partnership with the United States; the role of the Air Force and the Navy; the bombing of Darwin; as well as the battles of Kokoda, Milne Bay, the Beachheads and Guadalcanal.

Australia 1942 provides a unique and in-depth exploration of the controversy surrounding the potential for invasion. Japanese and Australian historians offer perspectives on Japanese military intentions and strategies towards Australia and the South Pacific. Generously illustrated, it is essential reading for anyone interested in one of Australia's most decisive and critical years.

Peter J. Dean is the Director of Studies at the Strategic and Defence Studies Centre, the Australian National University and a Senior Lecturer at the Australian Command and Staff College. He is the author of *The Architect of Victory: The Military Career of Lieutenant-General Sir Frank Horton Berryman* (2011), a contributing editor to the Second World War journal *Global War Studies* and a managing editor for the journal *Security Challenges*.

AUSTRALIA 1942

IN THE SHADOW OF WAR

EDITED BY

PETER J. DEAN

CAMBRIDGE
UNIVERSITY PRESS

CAMBRIDGE UNIVERSITY PRESS
Cambridge, New York, Melbourne, Madrid, Cape Town,
Singapore, São Paulo, Delhi, Mexico City

Cambridge University Press
477 Williamstown Road, Port Melbourne, VIC 3207, Australia

Published in the United States of America by Cambridge University Press, New York

www.cambridge.org
Information on this title: www.cambridge.org/9781107032279

First published 2013
Reprinted 2013

Cover design by Anne-Marie Reeves
Typeset by Integra Software Services Pvt. Ltd
Printed in China by C & C Offset Printing Co. Ltd

A catalogue record for this publication is available from the British Library.

*A Cataloguing-in-Publication entry is available from the catalogue
of the National Library of Australia at* www.nla.gov.au

ISBN 978-1-107-03227-9 Hardback

For Sarah

FOREWORD

The Hon Kim Beazley, AC,
Ambassador to the United States of America

On 8 May 1942, John Curtin riveted the House of Representatives with an adjournment speech on the naval battle then raging in the Coral Sea:

> As I speak, those who are participating in the engagement are conforming to the sternest discipline and are subjecting themselves with all that they have – it may be for many of them the last full measure of their devotion – to accomplish the increased safety and security of this territory.

Given the critical character of the battle, the uncertainty then as to its outcome and the spontaneous nature of the Prime Minister's words, I would argue that in Australian political discourse this comes in character as close to the great brief orations (greatest of all being Lincoln's Gettysburg address) as Australian politics has ever come.

For the political class in Australia, one utterly steeped in the powerful grip of the logic of British Imperial Defence, the emotional shift Curtin's words captured was probably more important in broadening the Australian strategic mind than any cold calculation. In 1942 we learned the language of both self-reliance and new alliances in planning for our survival, even if, as fear of a threat to our national security receded, the traditional commitment to the United Kingdom was revived in later years in modified form.

In the First World War, the vigour, toughness, resilience and fortitude of Australia's volunteer army had created a consciousness of an individual Australian type and character. However, it was a character burnished in the bosom of what was to be that war's validation of the effectiveness and value of the system of Imperial Defence. Only a couple of months before Curtin spoke, confidence in that structure crashed on land with the Japanese capture of Singapore, at sea with the sinking of British warships *Prince of Wales* and *Repulse*, and at the front door with the bombing of Darwin and the fall of Rabaul.

It is impossible now to recreate in our minds the sense of vulnerability, shock and anxiety felt by the political leadership in Australia and many in the population, particularly in early 1942. Subsequent historical analysis disproves the theory of a Japanese intention to occupy Australia. No such confidence in Australia existed when the battle of the Coral Sea took place and as the long struggle along the Kokoda Track commenced. Curtin understood that defeat in the Coral Sea would likely terminate the Australian position in New Guinea – a position established consciously decades earlier with the intention of locking Australia's strategic front door. Without the strategic victories at Coral Sea and Midway, Australia's war would have become immensely complicated and a Japanese thrust to control the island chain dominating the easiest connection between the United States and Australia, entirely possible. As it happened, Coral Sea, Midway and the successful conclusion of the dual and related struggles in Papua and on and around Guadalcanal, had clearly secured Australia's position by early 1943.

Australia's near-total mobilisation in 1942 is a fascinating and admirable story. It is well told here. With civil conscription for single Australian women and, for the South Pacific battlefronts of 1942, civil and military conscription for men, and the direction of Australian industry, Australia was one of the most (arguably the most) mobilised belligerents in the Second World War. The story, and the associated battles, is deservedly inspirational, impelled in part as it was by the sense that for our allies we were a strategic backwater. Churchill and Roosevelt fashioned a priority for the struggle against Hitler – a fight in which thousands of Australian airmen participated throughout the war. Another battle in which Australian soldiers played a critical role in 1942 was the battle of el Alamein, described by Churchill as 'the end of the beginning' in the Western European theatre. In that fight the Australian Army provided 10 per cent of the troops for almost a quarter of the casualties.

A little too much can be made of the 'beat Hitler first' strategy. General Douglas MacArthur, sent to command in the South West Pacific Area, was the only identifiable American heroic general (deservedly or not) at the time. Even though he did not have more US soldiers than Australian under his command until 1944, he was sent with the intention of conducting offensive operations. More important, the leadership of the United States Navy was determined that an effective retaliation against the Japanese would be conducted immediately, with Australia at one end of an axis anchored at the other in Hawaii.

The man responsible for this policy was Admiral Ernest King, who features little in Australian history. He conceded that the general strategy of the focus on Hitler left the Pacific theatre forces with 'very few lines' of military endeavour but the most important of these in his mind was support for 'Australasia'. This meant securing the island chain between Australia and Hawaii. 'Such a line', he said, 'would be offensive not passive'.[1] His offensive was envisaged for the Solomon Islands but came to include Papua.

It was no accident then that, despite the vulnerability of Hawaii and an anticipated carrier struggle in June at Midway, half of the US Navy's carriers in the Pacific was committed against a superior force, part of which was on its way to Port Moresby, in the Coral Sea in May. At the time, Admiral Nimitz's Hawaii headquarters estimated the Japanese to be superior in carriers, battleships and shore-based air strength. Further, King had little confidence in Admiral Frank Jack Fletcher, the man in charge of US forces for the battle. This was high-order risk taking. We are used to the Americans as an ally in times of American superiority. In 1942 they proved a useful ally when they understood they were not. There was no querulous concern to concentrate around Hawaii until American mobilisation in 1942 would enable a push in 1943 or 1944. From the outset the Australian–Hawaii axis had to be held and the Japanese kept off balance.

Nevertheless 1942 is Australia's story. Whatever our allies thought, we believed we could and had to make a stand for ourselves. Papua dominated our thinking. Milne Bay and Kokoda rapidly became iconic. Only in recent times have we really appreciated the interrelationship between those struggles and the largely American effort in the Solomons (not exclusive: Australian coast watchers were vital in that fight and Australian naval units were also engaged). At home joy and frivolity were frowned upon, though Curtin obtained distraction and relief watching Aussie Rules games in Canberra. Australians lost lives in numbers as our year of living dangerously unfolded, and memory lingers in many families. In my own, my Uncle Syd, captured in Rabaul, was killed when an American submarine sank the *Montevideo Maru* on its way to Japan.

We remember our greatest generation. We remember too our friends. Over 1 million American service personnel passed through Australia during the war: 100 000 of them in 1942. An American, Douglas MacArthur, commanded our troops. He was an ambiguous figure then and subsequently both in Australia and the United States. For members of the Curtin government he was less so. To them he was a hero with our nation's best interests at heart. Arthur Calwell, then Minister for Information and Opposition Leader at the time of MacArthur's death, said of him:

> Now he is dead. There is neither rank nor station nor prerogative in the democracy of the dead or the republic of the grave. For us, however, Douglas MacArthur belongs to the immortal dead. But he belongs forever in the hearts and history of the Australian people. In the words of the poet, this country, as does his own, owes him 'the debt immense of endless gratitude'.[2]

Something like that is owed 'our greatest generation', and 1942 was the year it was tested.

Notes

1   Walter R. Borneman, *The Admirals*, Little, Brown & Company, New York, 2012, pp. 258–9.
2   Arthur Calwell, *Be Just and Fear Not*, Lloyd O'Neill Publishing, Melbourne, 1968, p. 106.

Contents

Photos

MAPS

CHARTS

ACKNOWLEDGEMENTS

The initiative for this book developed out of a conversation with Andrew Kilsby from Military History and Heritage Victoria (MHHV) in mid-2011. With Andrew's support, the idea was soon backed by the Society's president, Marcus Fielding. It was Andrew and Marcus who first brought together this fine collection of scholars and it is because of them and the MHHV that the foundations of this book were laid. I am very grateful to them that they entrusted me with turning their original concept into a book.

The work of developing this project largely resides with the remarkable collection of historians who have authored the chapters of this text. They have been tremendous to work with and they have made my job of editing a pleasure. Their breadth and depth of knowledge, their commitment to their research areas and their support for getting this book into print has been splendid. For readers who are familiar with Australia's military, social and political history during the Second World War, the list of authors in this book represents the some of the finest scholars in the country. I am particularly pleased that this book is also able to bring the perspective of the 'other side of the hill', through the work of Australian historian and Japanese language expert Steven Bullard and Japanese scholar Hiroyuki Shindo.

Particular thanks must go to David Horner who, as always, generously provided me with his sage advice and continues to encourage me in my endeavours, and to Kim Beazley, Australian Ambassador to the United

States of America, who kindly agreed to write the foreword. A special thanks to Steven Bullard, who provided some rather timely and erudite guidance on the organisation of the text just when I had hit a mental blank on where to turn next, and to Karl James for his assistance in developing the conclusion.

The production of this text would not have been possible without the support of the Strategic and Defence Studies Centre (SDSC) at the Australian National University (ANU). The head of SDSC, Brendan Taylor, has been exceptionally supportive of this work since I first mentioned it to him on my arrival at SDSC in September 2011. My thanks also extend to my colleagues at SDSC. They have proven to be wonderful colleagues to work with and the type of people that you would definitely want 'in the trenches' with you when things get tough. Special thanks also goes to Jenny Sheehan and Kay Dancey at the College of Asia-Pacific cartography unit (ANU) for turning scribbles on a page into excellent and erudite maps and charts, and to Kerry Neale for her help with the manuscript.

I would also like to offer thanks to Isabella Mead and the team at Cambridge University Press who have showed great enthusiasm and support for this work, and to Lily Keil, who brought the final elements of the manuscript together and has been a pleasure to work with.

Finally, I would not have been able to complete this project without the encouragement, patience, guidance and support of my family – Sarah and Flynn. During the course of this project they have borne the burden of a change of job, two moves of house, my numerous absences overseas and interstate, and the loss of evenings and weekends as I have toiled away – thank you.

CONTRIBUTORS

STEVEN BULLARD is a historian at the Australian War Memorial. He is Director of the Australia–Japan Research Project (AJRP). Being a Japanese speaker, he has translated several seminar and symposium papers including extracts from Japan's official account of the Second World War. He is also the author of *Blankets on the Wire: The Cowra Breakout and its Aftermath* and is currently writing Volume V of the *Official History of Peacekeeping, Humanitarian, and Post–Cold War Operations*.

KATE DARIAN-SMITH is Professor of Australian Studies and History at Monash University. She has been Director of The Australian Centre (1998–2005 and since 2010). Since 2000 she has been Deputy Dean, Associate Dean (International and Graduate Studies) and in 2010 was Acting Head of School of Historical Studies. She is the author of numerous books and articles, including: *On the Home Front: Melbourne in Wartime 1939–1945; Stirring Australian Speeches: The Definitive Collection from Botany to Bali*; and *Memory and History in Twentieth-Century Australia*.

PETER J. DEAN is the Director of Studies at the SDSC, the Australian National University and Senior Lecturer at the Australian Command and Staff College. He is the author of *The Architect of Victory: The Military Career of Lieutenant-General Sir Frank Horton Berryman* (2011), a board member and contributing editor to the Second World War journal *Global War Studies* and a managing editor for the journal *Security Challenges*. In 2011 he was Visiting Fellow at Georgetown University (Washington, DC) and Research Associate at the United States Studies Centre (Sydney University). He is currently writing a book on US–Australian joint military operations in the South West Pacific Area during the period 1942–5.

DAVID HORNER is Professor of Australian Defence History in the SDSC at the Australian National University. He is the author or editor of over 30 books on Australian military history, strategy and defence, including *High*

Command (1982), *Blamey: The Commander-in-Chief* (1998), *Strategic Command, General Sir John Wilton and Australia's Asian Wars* (2005) and *Australian Military History for Dummies* (2011). In 2004, David was appointed the Official Historian of Australian Peacekeeping, Humanitarian and Post–Cold War Operations. He is the general editor of this six-volume series and is writing two of the volumes, the first of which, *Australia and the 'New World Order'*, was published in January 2011. In 2009, David was appointed Official Historian for the Australian Security Intelligence Organisation.

KARL JAMES is a Senior Historian at the Australian War Memorial, Canberra. Completing his PhD at the University of Wollongong, he has specialised in Australia's involvement in the Second World War. His first book, *The Hard Slog: Australians in the Bougainville Campaign, 1944–45*, was published by Cambridge University Press in 2012.

MARK JOHNSTON is Head of History at Scotch College. He is the author of six books and numerous shorter publications about the Second World War, including *Alamein* and *Whispering Death: Australian Airmen in the Pacific War* (2011).

ROSS MCMULLIN is Senior Fellow at the School of Historical Studies at the University of Melbourne. His main research interests are Australian political history, Australia's role in the Second World War, and sport. Coverage of 1942 was a feature of his commissioned centenary history of the ALP, *The Light on the Hill: The Australian Labor Party 1891–1991*. His other publications include *So Monstrous a Travesty: Chris Watson and the World's First National Labour Government*. His biography *Pompey Elliott* was awarded the Melbourne University Press Award for Literature and also the Christina Stead Award for Biography, Autobiography or Memoir. His biography *Will Dyson: Australia's Radical Genius* was shortlisted for the National Biography Award. His most recent book is a multi-biography about the First World War, entitled *Farewell, Dear People: Biographies of Australia's Lost Generation*.

PAM OLIVER is Adjunct Research Associate in the School of Philosophical, Historical and International Studies at Monash University, and a professional historian. She has published and lectured widely on the Australia–Japan relationship, with special focus on Japanese immigration and business activity in Australia, espionage, wartime and Japan's intentions in the Second World War. Her books include: *Allies, Enemies and Trading Partners: Records on Australia and the Japanese* (2004);

winner of the Northern Territory Chief Minister's History Book Award for
2007, *Empty North: The Japanese Presence and Australian Reactions,
1860s to 1942* (2006); and *Raids on Australia: 1942 and Japan's Plans
for Australia*, (2010).

ALBERT PALAZZO is a historian with the Directorate of Army Research
and Analysis. He has written widely on warfare in the modern age and on
the Australian Army in particular. His many publications include: *Seeking
Victory on the Western Front: The British Army and Chemical Warfare
in World War I*; *The Australian Army: A History of its Organisation,
1901–2001*; *Defenders of Australia: The Third Australian Division*; *Battle
of Crete*; *The Royal Australian Corps of Transport*; and *Australian Military
Operations in Vietnam*. His current project is a history of the Australian
Army in the war in Iraq.

IAN PFENNIGWERTH previously spent 35 years in the Royal Australian
Navy. He researches, writes and promotes Australian naval history, and is
the editor of *Journal of Australian Naval History*. He is the author of
A Man of Intelligence: The Australian Cruiser, Perth, 1939–1942, and
*Tiger Territory: The Untold Story of the Royal Australian Navy in
Southeast Asia from 1948–1971*.

ALAN POWELL is Emeritus Professor of History and Political Science at
Charles Darwin University and is a former Dean of the Arts Faculty. His
teaching interests include classical history and Northern Territory history.
He has published extensively in military history, including *The Shadow's
Edge: Australia's Northern War* and *The Third Force: ANGUA's New
Guinea War*. He is the recipient of many research awards. Alan is currently
completing a book on the maritime history of the Australian north coast
and an article on the US Navy in Darwin during the Second World War. He
is Editor of the *Journal of Northern Territory History* and Publications
Editor for the Historical Society of the Northern Territory.

HIROYUKI SHINDO is currently Senior Researcher at the Centre for Military
History, National Institute for Defence Studies in Japan. He has an LLB from
Kyoto University, a LLM from Kobe University and is a graduate of the Ohio
State University PhD coursework program. His special areas of interest are
Japanese military strategy and operations during the Second World War and
US–Japan diplomatic and military relations in the 1930s. He is author of
numerous studies on the Second World War in English, including 'Japanese
air operations over New Guinea during the Second World War'.

ABBREVIATIONS

5SNLP	5th Special Naval Landing Party
AAF	Allied Air Forces
Adv GHQ	Advanced General Headquarters; MacArthur's headquarters in Brisbane/Port Moresby
Adv NGF HQ	Advanced New Guinea Force Headquarters (Corps HQ-subordinate to NGF)
AIF	Australian Imperial Force
AJRP	Australia–Japan Research Project
AMF	Australian Military Forces
ANGAU	Australian New Guinea Administration Unit
ANU	Australian National University
ARP	Air Raid Precautions
ASW	Anti-Submarine Warfare
AWM	Australian War Memorial
CCC	Civil Construction Corps
CGS	Chief of the General Staff
C-in-C	Commander-in-Chief
CMF	Citizen Military Force
CO	Commanding officer
FRUMEL	Fleet Radio Unit Melbourne
GHQ	General Headquarters, SWPA
HQ	Headquarters
IJA	Imperial Japanese Army
IJN	Imperial Japanese Navy
MHHV	Military History and Heritage Victoria
NGF	New Guinea Force (Corps, later Army level command based at Port Moresby)
NOIC	Naval Officer-in-Charge
RAAF	Royal Australian Air Force
RACAS	Rear Admiral Commanding the Australian Squadron

RAN	Royal Australian Navy
RSL	Returned Services League
SDSC	Strategic and Defence Studies Centre
SWPA	South West Pacific Area
USAHEC	United States Army Heritage and Education Centre
VDC	Voluntary Defence Corps
WRANS	Women's Royal Australian Naval Service

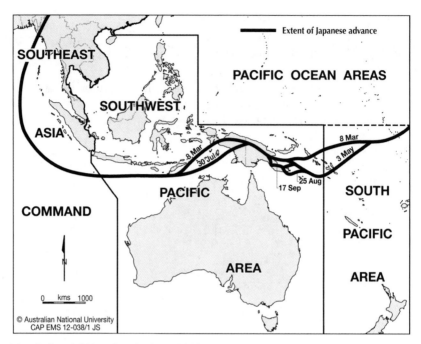

Map 1   South West Pacific Area, 1942–5

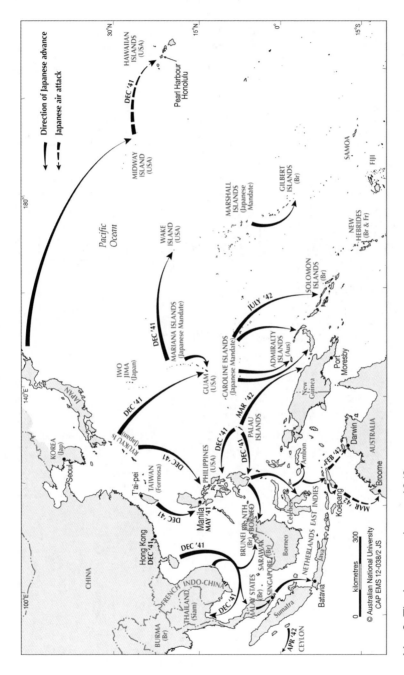

Map 2 The Japanese advance, 1942

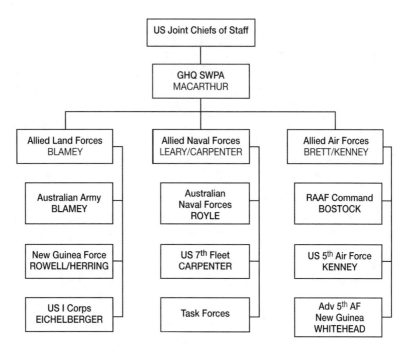

Chart 1 Command organisation in the SWPA, 1942

INTRODUCTION

The year 1942 represents the first time that the shadows of war from a great power conflict touched the shores of Australia. The bombing of Darwin and the Japanese air offensive against northern Australia, the attack on Sydney Harbour and the battles for the air, land and sea gap to Australia's north occurred within a critical period of Australia's history. This critical year is the focus of this text. Specifically, it concentrates on Australia after the fall of Malaya and Singapore through to the end of the battle for the Beachheads at Gona, Buna and Sanananda in January 1943. This period was described by the then Prime Minister, John Curtin, as the 'battle for Australia' and includes the creation of the South West Pacific Area (SWPA) under US General Douglas MacArthur, the defence of the air and sea approaches to Australia, the mass arrival of US forces in Australia and the campaigns in Papua and the Solomon Islands.

Australia 1942: In the Shadow of War is a military history but the need to contextualise and provide for a broad understanding of the events of this year means that its coverage often roams beyond the strict confines of time, location and discipline, at times taking in such perspectives as politics, social relations and cultural experience. The book is written for a general audience, as well as students of history and scholars. The intention is to be both accessible and scholarly – never an easy task, but one that I believe has been achieved. This edited collection of work is designed to provide a coherent story of Australia's experiences in 1942. However, the whole is only a sum of its parts and in order to appease the reader who desires to read chapters in order of interest rather than number, each chapter has been designed, where possible, to provide a comprehensible stand-alone piece of the wider story.

As noted, 1942 was a challenging time for Australia. In the face of a modern great-power conflict the nation had to navigate unprecedented challenges without the support of its traditional protector, the British Empire. In forging a new alliance and setting new directions Australia matured as a nation. The events also helped to cement the role of the Anzac legend in Australian society.

The Anzac legend, however, preferences the First World War and battles in far-off Turkey, France, Belgium and the Middle East over the events that occurred on Australia's doorstep in the Pacific during 1942–5. While commemorative activities around the 50th Anniversary of the end of the Second World War in 1995 were heavily supported by the Australian government, there is little evidence of their impact or resonance. With a change of government soon after the Australian Remembers Campaign, the new Prime Minister, John Howard, used his family links (via a grandfather in the Royal Naval Division) to the campaign at Gallipoli and his devotion to ties with Great Britain and the monarchy to help shift the focus of the Anzac legend back toward the landing at Anzac and the experiences on the Western Front.[1] This has meant that, aside from the prisoner-of-war experience,[2] the only area of the Second World War that has retained any sense of public consciousness is the battle for the Kokoda Trail.[3] Beyond this campaign, 1942 does not seem to resonate with the Australian public. So should it hold a more important place in the already crowded space of the history of war in Australia?

The key to answering this question is to establish just how important this year is in Australia's history. In response, Australia's pre-eminent military historian, David Horner, AM, argues convincingly in Chapter 1 that 1942 is in fact a 'pivotal' year in Australian history. While Gallipoli in 1915 might be firmly in the national consciousness as the birthplace of the Anzac legend, or even Australian national identity, it is in the shadow of Australia's relationship with Great Britain. 1942, as Professor Horner notes, is the year in which, devoid of the traditional reliance on Great Britain, Australia faced the threat of invasion for the first and only time since European settlement. In response Australia mobilised; industrialised; fought a number of vital battles; ratified the Statue of Westminster; forged a relationship with the United States of America; shifted power to the Commonwealth through legislative and taxation reform; and set the stage for postwar migration. Other than being the birthplace of Anzac, 1915, as a year, pales in comparison to the influence of these events and reforms on Australia's history.

David Horner's chapter forms the foundation for this work. It is the
very trunk from which the following chapters branch out to cover the
critical events and issues of 1942. From Horner's comprehensive outline
of the importance of 1942 in Chapter 1 it would be very easy to delve right
into a key battle or political reform. While such events are exceptionally
important, when faced with the threat of attack or possible invasion it is
critical to reflect on how the 'enemy' looked to Australians at the start of
the Pacific War. What type of relationship did Australia have with the
Japanese? How did this change over time?

Few of us know about the considerable number of Japanese citizens
who made Australia home in the years before the war and that, despite the
White Australia Policy, many were fully integrating into Australian society.
Nor is the extent of the commercial relationship between these two countries well known or understood. As Pam Oliver sets out in Chapter 2, this is
a complex and often misunderstood relationship that is much more
nuanced than our general understanding, shaped by war-time propaganda
and postwar antipathy, has allowed.

On 7 December 1941 Australia was not well prepared to defend itself.
The First World War was supposed to be the 'war to end all wars' and the
subsequent moves to limit armaments such as the Washington Naval
Treaty (1922) as well as the impact of the Great Depression had major
effects on the inter-war defence of Australia. The maintenance of
Australia's commitment to the system of Imperial Defence had seen the
AIF's infantry divisions deployed overseas, along with the ships of the
Royal Australian Navy (RAN) and aircrews of the Royal Australian Air
Force (RAAF) up to 1942. Home defence relied on a largely untrained
militia and a few tanks, guns and obsolete planes. As Albert Palazzo outlines in Chapter 3, Australia found itself in a 'desperate situation' in 1942.
This chapter explores how Australia got there, what the government did to
remedy the situation and how Australia was repositioned as a major Allied
base to support the defeat of Japan, while balancing the needs of self-
reliance and the machinations of great and powerful friends.

These were just some of the far-reaching decisions that Australia had to
make in 1942 in order to bolster its defences. It moved swiftly to mobilise the
population from what Blamey called a bunch of 'grazing gazelles' into a
society organised on an effective war footing. These moves caused a
number of major changes to the home front. As Kate Darian-Smith reveals
in Chapter 4, this was part of the government's move to encouraging
an 'All-in' war effort. These moves affected the role of women in the work
force and the domestic sphere, saw the introduction of widespread rationing

and civil-defence measures. But one of the most significant changes in Australian society from 1942 was the arrival of mass numbers of US service personnel. This new partnership and the decision to establish Australia as major base of operations against the Japanese meant that some 1 million US servicemen were to make their way to Australia during the course of the Pacific War, with 100 000 arriving in 1942. These troops, with their different culture and language, were to have a major effect on Australian society.

These changes had to be managed by an inexperienced minority government. John Curtin became Prime Minister not long before the Japanese assaults on Pearl Harbor and Malaya, and in Chapter 5 Ross McMullin explains how the Curtin government responded to the crisis of 1942. Critical to assessing its performance is an understanding of Labor's background leading up to its ascension to power. From this rocky platform Curtin and his ministers were able to forge a new partnership with the US C-in-C General Douglas MacArthur; recall the AIF to Australia; negotiate new conscription laws; institute austerity; and place a renewed emphasis on the war effort. As McMullin outlines, it is an impressive record.

The second half of the book turns its attention to more strictly military matters. In chapters 6 and 7 Hiroyuki Shindo and Steven Bullard provide us with the exceptionally important perspective of the 'other side of the hill'. Japanese plans for the South Pacific and Australia have been major points of contention and debate in Australia. After the fall of Singapore Curtin announced the 'battle for Australia', but did the Japanese really have designs to invade the continent? How did Japanese plans for the South Pacific unfold? As Hiroyuki Shindo argues, it would be a grave mistake to assume that the plans of the Japanese Imperial General Staff were set well in advance and that they were undertaking a long and considered plan for their conquests. What emerges is a General Staff split along service lines, with the Imperial Japanese Navy dragging its very reluctant Army colleagues into ventures in the far corners of the South Pacific.

This divergence in views is even more evident when it comes to Japanese plans for Australia. As Bullard notes 'it is impossible to find among Japanese military planners a coherent and simple policy in regards to Australia'. Most of the debate within the Japanese command was, in the end, academic, as Fleet Admiral Isoroku Yamamoto focused his command on drawing the US Navy into a major fleet action, and an invasion of Australia could only have resulted from an impossible number of 'counterfactual turns of history'.

The Japanese did, however, strike Australian soil and their air campaign against northern Australia started on 19 February 1942 with the attack on Darwin. The impact of this attack sent reverberations across Australia far beyond the 230 deaths caused by the raid. But as Alan Powell lays out in Chapter 8, while we know a great deal about the bombing of Darwin we are still left with a legacy of unanswered questions. Why was such an overwhelming force used for a mere tactical operation? Why were Darwin's critical and vulnerable oil tanks not targeted and why did such a considerable attacking force leave behind so little damage relative to their numbers? Beyond these intriguing questions is the legacy of history, memory and commemoration. Here, Professor Powell explores the contrasts between the 'reality of the raids and the evolving image of them'. He reveals our changing interpretations of this event through the written history and the phases of commemoration that have culminated in Prime Minister Julia Gillard calling in 2012 for 19 February to become a 'new national day of commemoration'.

The RAN and RAAF are often overlooked in the Anzac legend and Australia's history of war. The Army dominates, not just through sheer enlistments, size and battles, but also by the powerful legacy of evocative landscapes. Gallipoli and Kokoda allow commemoration and pilgrimage to flourish where the remembrance of air battles and naval actions cannot. This should not, however, diminish the importance of the contributions of the Air Force and Navy to the war effort and to the defence of Australia and its mandated territories in 1942. The key to defending Australia and defeating the Japanese in the SWPA was a maritime strategy and key to implementing that strategy was the role of the Air Force in establishing air superiority and the Navy in projecting force throughout the vast SWPA and landing troops on its hostile shores. These were not easy objectives to achieve in 1942.

As Mark Johnston reveals in Chapter 9, the RAAF was in a pitiful state in 1942. Its twin problems were a lack of modern aircraft and the European Air Empire Training Scheme, which sent a high number of recruits to the European theatre. The lack of modern aircraft was to prove devastating to the RAAF's aircrews. Fighting Zeros with Buffalos, Wirraways and Hudsons was a virtual death sentence. But the RAAF would fight back. Improved aircraft such as the P-40 and truly modern aircraft such as the Beaufighter would allow the RAAF, in collaboration with the US Army Air Corps, to make a substantial contribution to the air defence of Australia and to victory in the campaigns in Papua.

Australia's Navy may well have fared best of the three services in the inter-war period but its position at the beginning of 1942 was not enviable. The protection of Australia's 60 000 kilometres of coastline with an exceptionally small number of ships was a near impossible task. But as Ian Pfennigwerth reveals in Chapter 10, when it was placed under MacArthur in 1942 the US inherited a small but highly effective and combat-proven force. Despite the loss of the cruisers *Sydney* and *Perth*, and in the latter half of the year the *Canberra*, the RAN proved itself to be an effective and resilient organisation that forged an excellent working relationship with its new ally. It provided an essential service to the nation, and the foundation laid in 1942 in the Pacific was to see it remain on the frontline of Australia's war effort to the very end.

The last two chapters of this book cover the three largest ground operations in the SWPA that the Australian Army was involved in during 1942. The battle of the Kokoda Trail has taken on mythological status that arguably sees it rank second only to Gallipoli in the Parthenon of Australian military campaigns. In Chapter 11 Karl James explores the nature of this campaign and the equally important operation at Milne Bay. Despite the heroic struggle along the Kokoda Trail and the decisive victory at Milne Bay, 1942 would not end on a high for the Australian and US armies in Papua.

The optimism resulting from these two victories was to deteriorate in the malaria-ridden swamps of Papua's northern shore. As Peter Dean explains in the final chapter, the battles for Gona, Sanananda and Buna were the worst, in terms of casualties, in the whole South Pacific in 1942. The stubborn Japanese defences, assaulted by ill-trained and poorly supplied Australian and US forces cast a dark shadow over the successes of 1942. Borne from a combination of poor pre-war preparedness, failures in intelligence and an incorrect strategy forced on the SWPA's senior commanders, these battles and the reasons for their conduct remain controversial.

The end of 1942 looked very different from its beginning. The victories and Coral Sea, Midway, Kokoda, Milne Bay, Guadalcanal and the Beachheads had swung the balance of the war in the South Pacific firmly towards the Allies. But this outcome was not preordained in early 1942. It was to be a long, tough and bitter year with challenges at every turn.

Notes
1   This is not to overlook the commemorative activities and memorial construction undertaken during the Howard government era, which included the Hell Fire Pass Memorial in Thailand (opened on 24 April 1996), the

memorials at Sandakan, Borneo (dedication 18 March 1999) and Isurava, Papua New Guinea (dedication 14 August 2002).

2   This area of history has, more often than not, focused on POW experiences in the Pacific over those in Europe during the Second World War.

3   As judged by the number of popular histories and documentaries, a feature film and the number of trekkers that have visited the Kokoda Trail.

PART I

AUSTRALIA IN 1942

CHAPTER 1

AUSTRALIA IN 1942

A PIVOTAL YEAR

David Horner

In October 1941 the new Australian Labor government, led by John Curtin, recalled General Sir Thomas Blamey, Commander of the Australian Imperial Force (AIF) in the Middle East, to Australia for discussions. Since he had arrived in Palestine some 16 months earlier, Blamey's forces had fought in North Africa, Greece, Syria and at the siege of Tobruk. So he was well aware of the seriousness of the war against Germany and Italy. On 15 November 1941, after he had returned to Australia, Blamey delivered a nationwide radio broadcast in which he described the fighting in the Middle East. He continued:

> And to come from that atmosphere and its scenes back to Australia gives one the most extraordinary feeling of helplessness. You are like – here in this country – a lot of gazelles grazing in a dell on the edge of the jungle, while the beasts of prey are working up toward you, apparently unseen, unnoticed. And it is the law of the jungle that they spring upon you, merciless.[1]

Blamey's apprehension proved to be well founded. Less than a month after his address, Japan attacked in the Pacific. Less than two months later Japanese aircraft began attacking Rabaul in the Australian territory of New Guinea, and three months later the troops of the 8th Australian Division marched into captivity in Singapore.

Blamey, however, was not completely prescient. Although he had been distressed by observing the peacetime garrison mentality in Singapore, as he was returning to the Middle East in early December he discounted the possibility of an imminent Japanese attack. He was sipping drinks in Karachi as he continued his journey when he was stunned to hear about the attack on Pearl Harbor.[2]

This story gives some feeling of the shock that struck Australia when the Japanese attacked Pearl Harbor and other places in the Pacific on 7 and 8 December 1941. Within a few months, for the first time, modern Australia faced the prospect of foreign invasion. By any calculation, 1942 would prove to be a year of significant events: the fall of Singapore; the return of troops from the Middle East; Japan's invasion of New Guinea; the attacks on Darwin and Sydney; the mobilisation of military and civilian resources; and the battles of the Coral Sea, Milne Bay, Kokoda and el Alamein.

But if we are to describe 1942 as a pivotal year in Australia we need to take a broader view. The year is pivotal not just because of the string of significant events that took place within it, but because the events caused a long-term change in Australian history. And if we are going to talk about how Australia changed, we need to look briefly at what Australia was like before this allegedly pivotal year.

This chapter discusses six crucial issues, and along the way, where appropriate, describes the longer-term effect of these issues. These issues or questions are:

– How was it that Australia was so exposed to invasion in 1942?
– What was the effect of the events between December 1941 and March 1942?
– Did Japan plan to invade Australia and how did Australia respond to this threat?
– What were the pivotal battles of 1942?
– What was the impact of the arrival of the Americans?
– What was the role of the Australian government?

How was it that Australia was so exposed to invasion in 1942?

From the earliest times the Australian settlers were concerned about their security. Clinging precariously to a foothold on a vast continent across the other side of the world from Britain, the early settlers, who were few in number, knew that their security and safety could be affected by conflicts elsewhere. The colonists feared that foreign warships would suddenly appear and threaten to bombard their cities.

The Australian colonies achieved their security through their membership of the British Empire. But with the rise of Japan at the end of the 19th century, and Japan's victory over Russia in 1905, Australians feared that if Britain was preoccupied in Europe, Australia might be exposed to attack by Japan. There was an element of racism in these concerns. Soon after Federation in 1901 the Australian Government introduced immigration policies to exclude non-whites from Australia, broadly described as the White Australia Policy, and many Australians were concerned about the so-called 'yellow hordes' to the country's north.

As loyal members of the British Empire, in the late 19th century the Australian colonies sent volunteers off to fight in New Zealand, Sudan and South Africa. It was in the colonies' best interest to maintain the integrity of the British Empire.

After Federation in 1901 the Australian Government perceived that Australia would need to look out for its own security. So the government introduced conscription for home service (but not for service overseas) and also established the RAN. As we know, in 1914 the new nation sent volunteers to fight with Britain and its Empire in the First World War. It was not just a case of blindly following Britain. The Australian politicians believed that if Britain were defeated in Europe, Japan would be free to exercise greater power in the Pacific. And if Germany were to win the war it too would have been able to operate more freely in the Pacific, where it already possessed colonies.

After the First World War, Australian politicians and military leaders identified Japan as a possible enemy, but the government faced a dilemma. Australia had a small population; it was only 5 million at the end of the First World War. The Australian economy was weak, based more on primary industries than on manufacturing. Australia had only a limited industrial capacity. Further, it was hurt very badly by the Great Depression. So even if Australia had wanted to build a strong Army and a capable Air Force it had little capacity to do so. Instead, Australia decided to go along with a strategy that was based on defence within the umbrella of the British Empire (see Chapter 3).

The centre-point of defence policy was a scheme known as the Singapore Strategy, which was agreed in 1923. Britain undertook to build a major naval base at Singapore, to which it would send its main fleet in time of threat to deter the Japanese fleet. There were several problems with this scheme. It was unlikely that Japan would strike unless Britain was preoccupied in Europe, and in that case, Britain might not be able to spare its fleet to go to Singapore. This is, indeed, what happened in 1941–2. Another problem was defending the Singapore base until the main fleet arrived.

Photo 1 The cornerstone of Australia's inter-war defence policy, the Naval Base, Singapore, refitting a British warship, September 1941 (AWM 007748).

The Australian Government's blind optimism about the strategy was demonstrated by Prime Minister Stanley Bruce's comments in London in 1923: 'While I am not quite as clear as I should like to be as to how the protection of Singapore is to be assured, I am clear on this point, that apparently it can be done'.[3] The falseness of this hope was to be demonstrated in 1942.

Under the Singapore Strategy, Australia built up its Navy, but the Army was required merely to deal with small-scale raids against the Australian mainland and was starved of funds. Australian Army generals did not agree with this strategy, but the RAN's leaders supported it. When presented with conflicting views, the Australian Government sought advice from Britain, which, naturally, advocated the Singapore Strategy.

When the likelihood of war increased in the mid-1930s the Australian Government belatedly tried to build up its military forces, but it was constrained by lack of money, and by the difficulty of purchasing armaments overseas. Relying on the Singapore Strategy, the government concentrated on building the Navy, which by 1939 had two heavy cruisers, three light cruisers, an old cruiser, five old destroyers and two sloops. As the Defence Act did not allow for a large regular Army, the government sought to boost the part-time militia, which by March 1939 had a strength of 70 000.

It was poorly trained and equipped, lacking tanks and modern artillery. The regular Army was pathetically small – fewer than 4000 in number.

With a Regular and Citizen Force strength of 3600 personnel, by mid-1939, the RAAF had twelve squadrons, but its newest aircraft were already obsolescent. More modern aircraft were on order, but even the best, the Wirraway, was only a trainer, not a modern fighter. At this stage Australian industry did not have the capacity to build modern aircraft (see Chapter 9).

Some historians have claimed that with a weak and faltering economy the government had no option but to rely on Britain and the Singapore Strategy, and have noted that the government should be given some credit for making a start on manufacturing munitions.[4] There is some truth in this claim, but there was no easy solution to the lack of modern aircraft.

After the outbreak of the Second World War Australia formed the Second Australian Imperial Force and the 6th, 7th and 9th Divisions fought in the Middle East in 1941. Australian ships served in the Mediterranean, and Australian airmen were trained (as part of the Empire Air Training Scheme) and formed squadrons that operated out of Britain. The aircraft were provided by Britain. Contrary to some claims, the Menzies government was aware of the possible threat from Japan, but assessed that on balance it needed to support Britain in the Middle East. With regard to Japan, the best that Australia could do was to send the main part of the 8th Division to Malaya to help defend the naval base at Singapore.

Thus, when Japan attacked in December 1941 most of Australia's full-time soldiers were serving overseas. The Army in Australia consisted primarily of the part-time militia. Even when the ships of the Navy returned to Australian waters (and most were in Australian waters in December 1941), they were relatively few in number. The Air Force at home was extremely weak.

WHAT WAS THE EFFECT OF THE EVENTS BETWEEN DECEMBER 1941 AND MARCH 1942?

The broad outline of the events between December 1941 and March 1942 is reasonably well known. Although the Japanese landed in Malaya on 8 December 1941, and some Australian aircraft were involved immediately, the two brigades of the 8th Division did not get into action until mid-January 1942. After some intense and costly battles the brigades withdrew to Singapore Island on 31 January. Then on 8 February the Japanese attacked the island and the Commonwealth garrison surrendered on 15 February. Almost 15 000 Australians became prisoners of war.

An ad hoc Australian brigade also served in Java, and it too was captured, its 2700 members eventually joining the prisoners from the Malaya campaign in the Changi camp on Singapore Island. Australian battalions were deployed to Rabaul, Timor and Ambon, along with independent companies, which went to Timor and New Caledonia. Except for the independent company on Timor, most of these forces were also captured.

These disastrous campaigns had numerous outcomes. Strategically they isolated Australia, and if the Japanese had planned to invade Australia they would have had firm bases for their attack. Observing how the Japanese had advanced through the islands, the Australian defence planners began calculating how and when the Japanese might attack Australia. For example, on 27 February the Australian Chiefs of Staff advised the government that after its success in the Netherlands East Indies, Japan was 'now at liberty to attempt an invasion of Australia should she so desire'.[5] On 5 March the Deputy Chief of the General Staff, Major-General Sydney Rowell, advised the government that the Japanese might mount an attack on Port Moresby in the middle of March, on Darwin in early April, on New Caledonia in the middle of April and on the east coast of Australia in May.[6]

For the first time, Australian defence planners were facing the real prospect of a Japanese invasion. We need to remember that the Allied policy of 'Beat Hitler First', agreed by the British Prime Minister Winston Churchill and US President Franklin Roosevelt in December 1941, meant that Australia could expect no support from Britain and only limited support from the United States. There was an element of panic in the reactions of many Australians. Some Sydneysiders moved inland to escape a possible Japanese landing. The government developed scorched-earth policies in threatened areas. Certain groups planned to form guerrilla bands to harass the Japanese when they landed.

Australia's defence planners had to deal with the fact that a complete Australian infantry division – one quarter of Australia's well-trained AIF infantry divisions – had gone into captivity in Singapore and the islands to the north. This was a substantial blow to Australia's military capacity and morale. The capture of these troops resulted in three of the great tragedies of Australian history.

In June 1942 more than 800 military prisoners and about 200 civilians, who had been seized at Rabaul, embarked on the Japanese cargo ship *Montevideo Maru*, bound for China. When a US submarine sunk it en route, with no Australian survivors, it became the greatest single loss of Australian lives in the war. Out of 1050 prisoners in Rabaul in 1942,

Photo 2 All aboard were lost when the *Montevideo Maru* was torpedoed by the US Navy submarine USS *Sturgeon* on 1 July 1942 (AWM 303640).

only four were found alive there at the end of the war. Along with other Allied prisoners, about 13 000 Australian prisoners worked as slave labourers on the notorious Thai–Burma railway. About 2700 of these died from lack of food, tropical illness and maltreatment.

Australian prisoners found themselves in camps in Taiwan, Korea, Manchuria, Ambon, Hainan and Borneo. Those who went to Borneo had the worst experience. In January 1945 the prisoners in a camp at Sandakan, on the east coast, were ordered to march to Ranau, about 250 kilometres away. Many died from malnutrition, exhaustion, disease and ill treatment, and once they arrived at Ranau the survivors were shot. Six, who managed to escape and were looked after by local people, were the only survivors of 2500 Australian and British prisoners who set out on the march. All 292 prisoners who remained at Sandakan because they were too ill to march also died.

In total, about 22 400 Australians were captured by the Japanese during the war, and of those 14 340 survived to return to Australia. They had endured semi-starvation and often brutal treatment in labour gangs throughout the Japanese empire. The large numbers of Australian prisoners and their high death rate – almost one in five of all Australians to die in the war – became one of the defining features of Australia's experience in the Pacific War.

Perhaps there was one positive outcome from Australia's involvement in these ill-fated campaigns. For the first time Australia became properly aware of the strategic importance of the region. Thousands of Australians had lived and worked in the region and they knew that after the war Australia would not be able to ignore its neighbours. It was a true turning point in Australia's appreciation of these nearby lands.

DID JAPAN PLAN TO INVADE AUSTRALIA AND HOW DID AUSTRALIA RESPOND TO THIS THREAT?

One outcome of the Japanese advance was the effect on Australian defence planners, who in early 1942 began thinking seriously about repelling a Japanese landing in Australia. We therefore need to examine more closely whether the Japanese actually intended to invade Australia (see Chapter 7, and for a background on Australian–Japanese interactions leading up to 1942 see Chapter 2).

On the face of it, the threat seemed extremely real. On 19 February 1942 Japanese aircraft bombed Darwin, which was the first attack on Australia since white settlement (see Chapter 8). The attack came when the War Cabinet was considering a request from the British Government to divert a convoy carrying the 6th and 7th Divisions from the Middle East towards the Far East so that the troops could land and help defend Burma. Despite pressure from British Prime Minister Churchill, and US President Roosevelt, Prime Minister Curtin insisted that the troops return to Australia. The decision proved to be correct. If the troops had landed in Burma they would have gone into captivity. Instead, some of them helped defend Darwin, while most of them went to New Guinea and played a large part in winning the battles on the Kokoda Trail, at Milne Bay and at Buna, Gona and Sanananda (see chapters 11 and 12). Also, the Australian Government reaffirmed the principle that although Australia was part of the Allied coalition, ultimately it was for the Australian Government to decide where its troops would fight.

But while the Japanese threat seemed real, we know, and have known from soon after the war, that the Japanese never actually planned to invade Australia. Japan's rapid successes in December 1941 and January 1942 caught their planners unprepared (see Chapter 6). For example, on 5 January, when it looked as though they would achieve all their targets by the middle of March, the chief of staff of the Japanese Combined Fleet wrote in his diary: 'Where shall we go from there? Shall we advance into Australia, attack Hawaii; or shall we prepare for the possibility of a Soviet sortie and knock them out if an opportunity arises?'[7]

For the next two months Japanese Imperial General Headquarters debated this question. In the meantime, on 29 January, Imperial General Headquarters ordered the Commander-in-Chief of the Combined Fleet, Admiral Yamamoto Isoroku, to capture Lae and Salamaua and, at the proper time, Port Moresby and Tulagi in the Solomon Islands. The operational objective was 'to blockade the communication lines between the Australian mainland and the region, and in order to control the seas to the north of eastern Australia'.[8] Lae and Salamaua were seized on 8 March.

The Japanese Navy General Staff was keen to invade Australia, and in December 1941 calculated that they would need three divisions to secure footholds on the northeast and northwest coastlines. On 14 February 1942, one day before the fall of Singapore, a Naval Ministry official told a conference of Navy and Army staff in Tokyo that they had 'a good chance to make a clean sweep of Australia's forward bases'.[9] Again, on 27 February, after the successful strike against Darwin, and the landings in the East Indies, the Navy General Staff insisted on an invasion of the northeast coast of Australia.

The Japanese Army strongly resisted the Navy's plans, estimating that it would need at least 10 and perhaps 12 divisions to invade Australia. The Army did not believe that these divisions could be spared from China or Manchuria where they were located in case of war with the Soviet Union. If the Red Army collapsed before the German *blitzkrieg*, Japan might launch an invasion of Siberia. Even more crucial, a major assault on Australia would require one and a half to two million tons of shipping, but most of this shipping was required to transport the newly gained raw materials back to Japan from Southeast Asia.[10] Instead, the Army wanted an offensive in Burma and India.

Within the Navy there was no unanimity about the need to invade Australia. Admiral Yamamoto wanted to attack Midway Island, in the central Pacific, thus drawing the US Pacific Fleet into battle. Eventually a compromise was reached, and on 7 March the invasions of Australia and India were put aside.[11] On 15 March the Japanese agreed to capture Port Moresby and the southern Solomons, and 'to isolate Australia' by seizing Fiji, Samoa and New Caledonia.[12] The Japanese planned to form a defensive ring around their Greater East-Asia Co-prosperity Sphere. As Henry Frei wrote, 'Japan was now tightening the noose on Australia'. Rather fancifully, Japan hoped that Australia might withdraw from the war and become neutral.[13] Japan's main aim was to prevent Australia becoming a base for an Allied counter-offensive.

The security of Australia would therefore depend on the battle for Port Moresby, for if it were captured the Japanese could strike at will at the north coast of Queensland. Furthermore, if the Japanese extended their air and naval bases to Fiji they could interdict the lines of communication between Australia and the United States. That the Japanese high command never agreed to invade Australia does not detract from the crucial importance of the battles for Port Moresby in 1942. By itself, Australia could do little to interrupt these Japanese plans. But, as will be described later, Australian forces did play a role in helping to halt the Japanese advance.

For the moment, however, we should consider how Australia responded militarily to this threat. After the outbreak of the Pacific War the government had ordered all the units of the part-time militia to go to full-time service. The Army was then re-organised and General Blamey returned from the Middle East to become its C-in-C. Along with the 7th Division and part of the 6th Division that had returned to Australia, the Army in Australia soon had a strength of some eight infantry and three motorised or armoured divisions. In addition two US infantry divisions began to arrive in Australia. The problem was that Australia had insufficient naval or air forces to support large land forces if they were deployed to New Guinea. Initially, most of these forces were deployed in southern Australia, where they had been raised and trained.

Australia's confidence improved when General Douglas MacArthur, a famous US general who had previously commanded in the Philippines, arrived in Australia at the end of March 1942. MacArthur took command of the combined Australian, US and Dutch forces of the newly formed SWPA.

MacArthur later claimed that when he arrived in Australia he discovered that the Australians had a 'largely defeatist conception' of defending their country from the Brisbane Line. It was never his intention to defend Australia on the mainland. 'That was the plan when I arrived, but to which I never subscribed, and which I immediately changed to a plan to defend Australia in New Guinea.'[14]

MacArthur's claims were a distortion of the truth. There was never an intention to defend Australia only from a 'Brisbane Line'.[15] Certainly, defensive positions were established around the capital cities, and other provincial cities such as Townsville and Newcastle, and soldiers occupying the defences around Brisbane probably believed they were holding the Brisbane Line. These were sensible precautions, but they did not represent the government's complete plan for the defence of Australia. Both MacArthur and the Australians planned to move forces to northern Australia and New Guinea just as soon as trained troops were available and could be supported and supplied adequately. More generally, Australia went to a level of military preparedness never before reached in the country.

WHAT WERE THE PIVOTAL BATTLES OF 1942?

During 1942 the Australian forces were involved in a series of battles that helped shape the outcome of the war and had a long-term effect on the nation. At least three of these battles, Coral Sea, Kokoda and Milne Bay, have been given almost iconic status because, according to legend, they saved Australia from invasion. They have become the centrepiece of the 'Battle for Australia' promoted by the Battle for Australia Council.[16]

There is no doubt that these were important battles, but they need to be seen in context. The first battle to hold up the Japanese advance in the South West Pacific was not Coral Sea, but in fact took place two months earlier.

As mentioned earlier, the first step in the Japanese advance was to capture Lae and Salamaua on the north coast of New Guinea. On 10 March 1942 the US aircraft carriers *Lexington* and *Yorktown*, operating in the Gulf of Papua, launched their aircraft, which crossed the towering Owen Stanley Ranges to surprise the Japanese ships unloading at Lae and Salamaua. Four Japanese vessels were sunk and seven damaged – ships that were intended to support an invasion of Port Moresby. It was Japan's worst loss of vessels and men in one action since the war began. More important than these losses, the raid caused the Japanese to postpone their planned invasion of Port Moresby and Tulagi in the Solomons by a month. The Japanese now knew that their invasion forces would require the protection of aircraft carriers, thus setting the stage for the battle of the Coral Sea (see Chapter 10).

The Japanese were not able to resume their offensive in the South West Pacific until late April; they planned to land at Tulagi on 3 May, and Port Moresby a week later. The landing at Port Moresby was to be made by General Horii's South Seas Detachment, and the invasion convoy to be escorted by a small carrier, *Shoho*, four cruisers and a destroyer squadron. Nearby was a carrier division with two large carriers, *Shokaku* and *Zuikaku*, three heavy cruisers and seven destroyers.

Warned by signals intelligence, Allied naval forces, including *Lexington* and *Yorktown*, rushed to intercept the Japanese invasion force off the southeast tip of New Guinea. In air battles on 7 and 8 May US aircraft sunk the *Shoho* and damaged the *Shokaku*. The Americans lost the *Lexington*, while the *Yorktown* was damaged. An Australian cruiser was in the Anzac cruiser force commanded by Australian-born Rear-Admiral John Crace, RN, commander of the Australian squadron.

As a result, the Japanese called off their sea-borne invasion of Port Moresby, which would now have to await the conclusion of their next offensive, the attack on Midway in early June. Perhaps equally important, Japanese losses meant that Admiral Yamamoto's forces would be reduced for the Midway battle. The absence of one fleet carrier was perhaps crucial to the outcome of that battle. The battle of the Coral Sea gave the Allies vital breathing space in which to build up reinforcements in New Guinea. It was the end of an unbroken run of successful invasions.

Had the invasion fleet not been halted by the Coral Sea battle, Port Moresby would probably have been taken, and from there the Japanese air forces would have been able to attack northern Queensland. Certainly the war would have taken a different course.

Despite the success in the Coral Sea, Japan was still capable of threatening Australia. On the night of 31 May Japanese midget submarines entered Sydney Harbour. They tried to sink the US cruiser *Chicago*, missed, and sank an Australian barracks ship, HMAS *Kuttubul*, instead, killing 19 sailors. On the night of 7 June large Japanese submarines fired several shells into Sydney and Newcastle. Meanwhile Japanese submarines conducted an effective campaign off the Australian coast, sinking three merchantmen during a period of nine days. For the sake of public morale it was fortunate that this news was balanced by better news from the Central Pacific.

The next crucial battle in the struggle for the South West Pacific was the battle of Midway, fought well away from Australia in the Central Pacific in early June. The Americans surprised the Japanese carrier force, sinking four of their carriers for the loss of the *Yorktown*. The battle had an immediate effect on operations in the New Guinea area. Japan postponed plans to seize New Caledonia, Fiji and Samoa; instead, it was now even more urgent to capture Port Moresby. With the loss of the carriers, an amphibious operation was no longer possible, and General Hyakutake in Rabaul was ordered to plan an overland drive over the Owen Stanley Ranges to Port Moresby. The scaling down of the Japanese offensive plans indicated that strategically the tide of war was beginning to turn, but the Japanese were still capable of mounting a deadly offensive.

The battles of Kokoda, Milne Bay and Guadalcanal, which began in August 1942, all took place at roughly the same time and were closely connected. As noted earlier, the Japanese planned to take Port Moresby by an overland advance, and on 22 July they landed on the north coast of Papua to prepare for the advance. Papua was an Australian territory and technically Australia had been invaded. Then on 7 August the US Marines landed at Guadalcanal. The Japanese responded with a major operation to attack the American naval build-up and to eliminate the US troops on Guadalcanal. It was the beginning of a bitter six-month campaign.

In the first Japanese attack, on the night of 8–9 August, the Australian cruiser, *Canberra*, was sunk near Guadalcanal. The RAN had begun the war with five front-line cruisers. Three of them, *Sydney*, *Perth* and *Canberra*, had been lost in less than nine months. It was the biggest series of blows ever experienced by the RAN.

The Guadalcanal campaign had a major influence on Japanese operations in Papua. The Guadalcanal commitment caused the Japanese to delay their advance over the Kokoda Trail, but eventually they began a two-pronged offensive in Papua. They landed Special Naval Landing Forces at Milne Bay, at the eastern tip of New Guinea. There the garrison, mainly Australian infantry, defeated the Japanese. It was the first time that a Japanese invasion force had been forced to withdraw.

Photo 3 Guadalcanal, Solomon Islands, 18 August 1942. Australian Coastwatcher Captain W. F. Martin Clemens (left, with beard) being debriefed by Lieutenant Colonel Buckley, US 1st Marine Division. The Guadalcanal campaign had a major influence on Japanese operations in Papua (AWM P02803.001).

When the Japanese attacked on the Kokoda Trail on 26 August they were met by Australian infantry, who conducted a fighting withdrawal before the Japanese halted their advance at Ioribaiwa, about 50 kilometres from Port Moresby. The fighting on the Kokoda Trail has certainly gained iconic status in Australian military history. There is no doubting the courage and commitment shown by the diggers. But we need to remember that on 28 August, just as the Japanese were winning the battle at Isurava, because of pressure from the Guadalcanal campaign, they were ordered to restrict their advance through the Owen Stanley Range.[17] Several days after the Japanese reached Ioribaiwa on 16 September they were ordered to withdraw to the north coast of Papua.

These facts do not detract from the importance of the Papuan Campaign. There was much heavy fighting before the Australians regained Kokoda and, along with the Americans, defeated the Japanese beachheads at Buna, Gona and Sanananda in January 1943. Without that victory the counter-offensive of mid-1943 could not have even begun.

The Allied successes on the Kokoda Trail, at Milne Bay and on Guadalcanal ensured the security of Australia. But the victories were only possible because of the preceding battles, that is, the air attacks around Lae and Salamaua in March 1942, Coral Sea in May, and Midway in June. Australians played the principal role in only two of these six battles.

Australia was involved in two other pivotal battles in 1942. The first was the battle of el Alamein in Egypt in October–November 1942. This was the biggest battle in which Australians took part in the Second World War, and the 9th Australian Division played a crucial role in it. Forming perhaps one-tenth of the attacking force, the Australians suffered 22 per cent of the casualties. The battle was the turning point of the North Africa campaign.

The other pivotal battle, or more strictly, campaign, was the RAF's Bomber Command offensive over Germany. The campaign began in February 1942, with the appointment of Air Marshal Sir Arthur Harris as the C-in-C of Bomber Command. The campaign continued for the rest of the war, but its shape was determined by Harris and endorsed by the British War Cabinet in 1942. A total of 4050 Australians were killed while serving in Bomber Command, and this comprised more than 10 per cent of all Australian casualties in the war. Flying in Bomber Command was far more dangerous than fighting in the infantry. Alamein and the strategic bombing of Germany did not directly affect the Pacific War, but they certainly involved large numbers of Australian servicemen who, in 1942, were not available closer to home.

WHAT WAS THE IMPACT OF THE ARRIVAL OF THE AMERICANS?

The most important American was General Douglas MacArthur, who with the agreement of the Australian government, took command of all the Australian forces in the SWPA. Further, MacArthur became the chief military adviser to John Curtin's Labor Government. This was a substantial abrogation of Australian sovereignty. But perhaps in the circumstances Australia had no other option. Through MacArthur, the Australian Government was able to agitate for the United States to send additional troops, ships and aircraft to the theatre, despite the previously agreed Allied policy of beating Hitler first; although, of course, Australia had not been consulted.

From then on, to the end of the war, the Australian forces operated as part of MacArthur's command. For the Americans, this was a marriage of convenience. Australia furnished the Americans with a firm logistic base from which to mount its counter-offensive against the Japanese. Until at least the end of 1943, Australia provided MacArthur with the majority of his ground troops. Without these troops he would have been unable to win the battles in New Guinea in 1942 and 1943. Australian ships and aircraft also provided a useful supplement to MacArthur's US forces.

MacArthur did not always treat his subordinate Australian commanders, Blamey in particular, with the respect and consideration that they deserved. MacArthur was more concerned with his own advancement and the advancement of American national interests, than Australian interests. So Australia needed to learn how to look after its own interests. Nonetheless, the military alliance that was forged in 1942 continued, in different forms and after some hiccups, for the following 70 years. After the South West Pacific campaign, Australian forces fought alongside Americans in the Korean War, the Vietnam War, the First Gulf War in 1991, the 2003 invasion of Iraq and the Afghanistan War, which began in 2001. MacArthur's arrival was truly a pivotal event in Australia's military alliance relationships.

Domestically, the arrival of thousands of American servicemen had a huge influence on Australia. At the end of April 1942 they numbered 38 000, increasing to 200 000 by the end of June 1943. Under threat of invasion, Australians were delighted the Americans had arrived (see Chapter 4). US troops were based in most states, but the highest density of camps was in Queensland. At the peak of the war, Brisbane's pre-war population of 325 000 increased by more than 80 000 US troops. In northern Australia,

Photo 4 General Douglas MacArthur with Australian C-in-C General Sir
Thomas Blamey and Prime Minister John Curtin, 26 March 1942 (AWM 042766).

US bomber squadrons operated from air bases, often built by African-
American construction troops.

The American 'occupation' had some long-term effects. For example,
Australians were exposed to American culture, including music (played on
the radio to entertain the Americans), eating habits (cafés began selling
coffee and hamburgers) and sport, such as baseball and gridiron.
Australian girls were attracted to the well-paid, neatly dressed, polite
American servicemen. Between 12 000 and 15 000 Australian women
married and followed their husbands or fiancées to the United States at
the end of the war.

WHAT WAS THE ROLE OF THE AUSTRALIAN GOVERNMENT?

The year of 1942 saw momentous changes in Australia's government and
economy. Australia's industrial and human resources were fully mobilised
to maintain the war effort. In effect, the civilian workforce was conscripted
to work in factories as determined by the government.

The crisis of 1942 had a deep and long-lasting effect on Australia's
political life (see Chapter 5). Many historians consider that John Curtin

was Australia's greatest prime minister. In the interest of marshalling Australia's resources and defending the country he put aside his party's socialist ambitions for the duration of the war. He rallied the nation and was willing to take politically difficult decisions such as allowing conscripts to serve outside Australian territory.

Other historians have been less persuaded that Curtin was a great prime minister. He handed over control of Australia's military to a foreign general. He failed to repudiate fellow MP Eddie Ward's outlandish claims about the Brisbane Line. He could only take his political leadership so far. In the 18 months beginning in January 1942 Australia lost more than 900 000 working days due to industrial disputes. However, 1942 had fewer industrial disputes than in any other year of the war; the highest number was reached in 1945. In, short, despite the threat of invasion, not every Australian responded in a self-sacrificing manner. There was a vibrant black market. The crisis of 1942 revealed some less attractive aspects of Australian society.

Many other changes had a long-term effect on Australia. We can only touch on a few. Before the war Australia had a weak industrial base, but the war forced a rapid industrialisation that continued after the war. Before the war each Australian state levied its own income tax. In May 1942 the Government forced through a war measure that made the Commonwealth the sole collector of income tax. The measure was supposed to lapse one year after the end of the war; it was never revoked. The war caused an explosion in the size and influence of the Commonwealth public service. This continued after the war. The Government could only introduce many of these measures because of the extreme threat in 1942.

The threat of 1942 had one most important outcome. With a small population and a limited industrial base Australians knew that they could not withstand a powerful enemy without help from their allies, Britain and the United States. They also understood that Britain had not been able to come to their aid, and that there was no guarantee that assistance would be available in the future. Australia needed a larger population both to provide for larger armed forces and to build up a more substantial industrial base. Immediately after the war the Chifley Government launched a massive immigration program, and the first Minister for Immigration, Arthur Calwell, promoted it with the slogan 'populate or perish'.

Up to 1951, more than 180 000 refugees from Europe were settled in Australia. The immigration policy was maintained by successive governments over the next 60 years. By 2008 about 6.5 million people had immigrated to Australia, and this formed a significant proportion of the expansion of Australia's population from 7 million to more than 21 million. The postwar migration program completely transformed Australia in the second half of the 20th century.

Another, lesser known, but significant, result of the events of 1942 concerned Australian sovereignty. It is often assumed that Australia became an independent country at the time of Federation in 1901. In fact the British government retained many prerogatives. In 1926 Australia became a self-governing dominion in the British Commonwealth of Nations and in 1931 the British Parliament passed the Statute of Westminster, establishing legislative equality for the self-governing dominions of the British Empire. Australia failed to ratify the statute until October 1942, backdating it to September 1939. It was a significant step along the road to Australia's full independence.

In summary, before the end of 1942 the Australian community probably knew that the year had been a critical one in Australian history. Under threat of invasion, the nation had been mobilised and its armed forces had fought vital battles. The country had survived, and even if the government was reluctant to say so, it was clear that the tide of battle had turned against the Japanese. With the advantage of hindsight, however, we can see that the year was even more pivotal than it perhaps appeared at the time. Not since has the country been faced with the possibility of invasion. The long-term effects included the rapid industrialisation of the country, the initiation of a massive immigration program, and the continuing alliance with the United States. The dangerous year of 1942 was a pivotal one indeed in Australian history.

Notes

1   Script of radio broadcast, 16 November 1941, AWM 80, 1/36.
2   David Horner, *Blamey: The Commander-in-Chief*, Allen & Unwin, Sydney, 1998, p. 256.
3   Imperial Conference 1923, 'Stenographic Notes of Meeting', 22 October 1923, TNA: CAB 32/9.
4   See for example, A. T. Ross, *Armed and Ready: The Industrial Development and Defence of Australia 1900–1945*, Turton & Armstrong, Sydney 1995.
5   Chiefs of Staff Appreciation, 27 February 1942, NAA: A2760, 96/1942.
6   Report, 'Probable Immediate Japanese Moves in the Proposed New Anzac Area', 5 March 1942, NAA: A2684, 905.
7   Henry P. Frei, *Japan's Southward Advance and Australia: From the Sixteenth Century to World War II*, Melbourne University Press, 1991, p. 161.
8   *Japanese Army Operations in the South Pacific Area; New Britain and Papua Campaigns, 1942–43*, translated by Steven Bullard, Australian War Memorial, Canberra, 2007, p. 36. For another accessible, translated Japanese account see Sakuyi Mikami, , 'Eastern New Guinea Invasion Operations',

Japanese Monograph no. 96, prepared for the Military History Section, Headquarters Far East Command, in Donald S. Detwiler and Charles B. Burdick (eds), *War in Asia and the Pacific 1937–1949*, vol. 5, Garland, New York, 1980.
9   Detwiler and Burdick, *War in Asia and the Pacific 1937–1949*, p. 166.
10 The reasons for the Japanese Army's opposition are described by Hattori Takushiro, 'Statement Concerning Reasons for Opposition to Plan for Invasion of Australia', 16 August 1949, in Detwiler and Burdick, *War in Asia and the Pacific 1937–1949*, vol. 8. Colonel Hattori was chief of the operations section, Army Department, Imperial General Headquarters.
11 Frei, *Japan's Southward Advance*, p. 171.
12 S. Milner, *Victory in Papua*, OCMH, Washington, 1957, p. 13.
13 Frei, *Japan's Southward Advance*, p. 172.
14 MacArthur's statement of 18 March 1943 is reproduced in 'Notes of Discussions [by Shedden] with C-in-C SWPA Brisbane 25–31 May 1943', NAA: A5954, box 2.
15 The Brisbane Line has been discussed in a number of books, including D. M. Horner, *High Command: Australia and Allied Strategy, 1939–1945*, George Allen & Unwin, Sydney, 1982, reprinted as *High Command: Australia's Struggle for an Independent War Strategy, 1939–1945*, Allen & Unwin, Sydney, 1992. For a broad discussion see Paul Burns, *The Brisbane Line Controversy*, Allen & Unwin, Sydney, 1998.
16 Battle for Australia Council, 'Overview of the Battle for Australia', www.battleforaustralia.org.au/2900/Overview/, accessed 13 April 2012.
17 Japanese Army Operations in the South Pacific Area, p. 157.

FURTHER READING
Frei, Henry P., *Japan's Southward Advance and Australia: From the Sixteenth Century to World War II*, Melbourne University Press, 1991.
Horner, D. M., *High Command: Australia's Struggle for an Independent War Strategy, 1939–1945*, Allen & Unwin, Sydney, 1992.
Horner, D. M., *Inside the War Cabinet: Directing Australia's War Effort, 1939–1945*, Allen & Unwin, Sydney, 1996.
Horner, D. M., *Blamey: The Commander-in-Chief*, Allen & Unwin, Sydney, 1998.
McCarthy, D., *South-West Pacific Area – First Year: Kokoda to Wau*, Australian War Memorial, Canberra, 1959.
Milner, S., *Victory in Papua*, OCMH, Washington, 1957.

PART 2

RELATIONS, POLITICS AND THE HOME FRONT

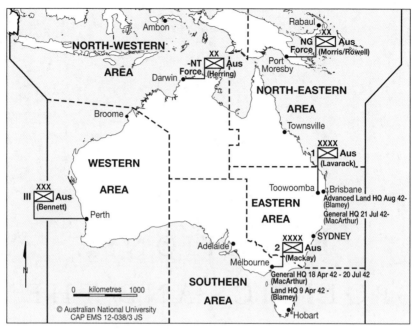

Map 3 The Australian theatre

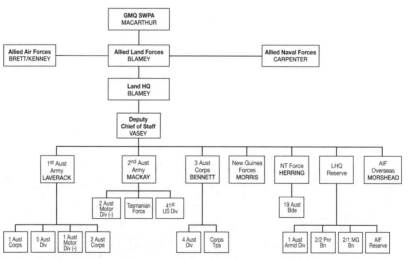

Chart 2 Command organisation: defence of Australia, 1942

CHAPTER 2

WORLD WARS AND THE ANTICIPATION OF CONFLICT

THE IMPACT ON LONG-ESTABLISHED AUSTRALIAN–JAPANESE RELATIONS, 1905–43

Pam Oliver

Actual warfare and the anticipation of conflict can alter the perspectives we form about other nations and their people. These tend to be lasting and can replace or bury previous perceptions. This is particularly so in the case of Australian perceptions of Japan in the wake of 1942 and subsequent wartime events.

Although Australian perceptions of Japanese people were not uniform prior to 1942, they were generally friendly. However, until at least 40 years after the war few would say: 'My mother worked for a Japanese firm in Melbourne during the 1920s and 1930s and had wonderful friendships with Japanese neighbours', especially when a family member, friend or close neighbour had died on the Thai–Burma railway. My own family's stories of interaction with Japanese are reflective of these mixed experiences. My mother never had a good word for the Japanese in the decades after the war. In the 1950s, she scared children half to death with wartime stories that ended: 'They nearly got us in the war – but for our boys in New Guinea'. Only in 2002 did we learn that her family's very survival during the Great Depression was due to employment linked directly to Japanese–Australian trade and Japanese import houses. It was 60 years after her marriage in February 1942 before she felt free to speak of Japanese people in a positive way, without a sense that she might be downplaying the horrific suffering of those she had known in the war.[1]

It is still inconceivable to many that Australians and Japanese were friends until late 1940. A common argument is that Australians were afraid of Japan and Japanese people for at least 50 years before 1942. Further, an enduring, but now contested, Australian belief remains that Japan planned to invade and include Australian territory within its empire in the Second World War.[2] However, evidence of a long friendship is incontestable. Hundreds of shelf metres of files on Japanese–Australian relations at personal, local and diplomatic levels within Australia are held at the National Archives of Australia. The magnificent collection of 3114 boxes of Japanese company records that were seized from offices and homes all over Australia on 8–9 December 1941 after the bombing of Pearl Harbor and Malaya forms only a small part of this record. The material is a time capsule from 1901 to 1941 of the work of Japanese-owned companies in Australia and their relations with large firms, like Myer and Dalgety, local shopkeepers and country farmers.[3]

Opinions vary considerably about how and when attitudes to Japan and Japanese people shifted; how widespread was a sense of friendship or enmity

Photo 5 Function at the Japanese Consul General's residence in the late 1930s (courtesy of Mrs Iida).

towards Japan within Australia at any given time? And how worried were Australians about Japanese activities and when? The continuous information provided by the records about Australians' views of the Japanese and Japan's valuing of a relationship with Australia clearly undermines the idea that the post-1940 antagonism existed for 50 years or more before that. The records contain evidence that we have read back into history the strong negative views of Japanese people held in 1941–2 but that they were not widespread before then. In many cases important pre-war events that were hailed at the time as friendship building were reinterpreted after 1942 as sinister beneath the surface. This change in the way Australia interpreted its relationship with Japan began on an official basis in 1942 with Australian Military Forces (AMF) reports and Department of Information writings for broadcasts.[4]

This chapter examines key aspects of the effect that war and the anticipation of war had on Australians' relationships with Japanese people and Japan's views of what it desired from the relationship. It details the shifts in expressed attitudes and interpretations of the others' actions over time from the 1890s. It examines the actual relationship with Japan; the nature of the friendships between the Australian and Japanese people at the personal and business levels; Japan's imperial intentions and Australian reactions to changes in Japanese activities. It traces how and why the friendship broke down and became buried. Finally, it looks at where Australia was placed in Japan's plans in the 1940s as a result of the long-standing friendship.

THE ACTUAL RELATIONSHIP

Australia and Japan were allies from 1894 to 1922 under various forms of the Anglo-Japanese Alliance. During the First World War, the Japanese Navy escorted Australian troop ships to the Middle East. Australia also had a good relationship with Imperial Japanese Navy (IJN) training ships, which visited all major Australian ports almost every two years from 1878 until 1936, with an average complement of 1500 officers and men. Apart from three diplomatic wrangles, the relationship was positive and beneficial for both sides until the late 1930s. From that time, suspicion characterised Australia's dealings and Japan became less satisfied with the trade and policy considerations it received as these were cut back. These difficult points were:

(1) The 1901–2 *Immigration Restriction Act* (or White Australia Policy), overcome in 1904 with special provisions enacted for Japanese merchants, tourists and students to enter Australia on passport;

(2) the discussions about the racial equality clause in the League of Nations Charter after the First World War, which Japan proposed but which was lost, with relations normalising especially after Australia provided substantial aid to Japan during the Great Kantoo Earthquake of 1923; and

(3) the 1936 Trade Diversion Dispute when Australia perversely decided to cut back trade with Japan, at a point when it was helping Australia in the Great Depression, in favour of an increased ratio of trade with Britain.[5]

Less damaging to relations were well-known events such as the Russo-Japanese War (1904–5) and Japan's military actions in China and Manchuria (1931–3 and after 1936). These wars were taken seriously but China was far from Australia. With the brutality of the Rape of Nankin in 1937, Australian attitudes to Japan altered. Some trade unions and the Communist Party began a campaign against Japanese goods, especially toys, because of Japan's bombing in China. This did not affect person-to-person relations within Australia. However, in 1940, when Japan signed the Tripartite Pact with Germany and Italy, friendship at the official level became very strained, but survived at other levels through the war and beyond. True hostility expressed against Japanese people, who were not personal or business friends, began in 1940 when some Australians hurled abuse at Japanese in the street for being traitors of the previous alliance.[6]

Apart from the naval visits, Australians had ample opportunities to meet Japanese people in daily life. The immigration of Japanese to Australia was substantial over time. Japanese residence before 1941 was concentrated around Sydney, the northwest of Western Australia and Thursday Island, with a fair representation in other cities and rural Australia. Most Japanese arrived of their own accord, often first travelling through China, Hong Kong, Singapore, Java or the US to Australian ports. They left Japan not only to seek adventure overseas but also to avoid the three-year national service faced by all young men in Japan. Many applied to remain and lived in Australia for decades.[7]

Unlike other countries to which Japanese people emigrated, for example, Brazil, the US and New Caledonia, Australia and Japan had no agreement regulating contract workers. Japanese who wished to work in pearling, cane cutting or on stations entered under the general provision in the Immigration Act that 'people of colour' could be hired to work north of the 23rd Parallel. This aimed to keep pearling and other industries supplied with labour and applied to all non-white nationalities.

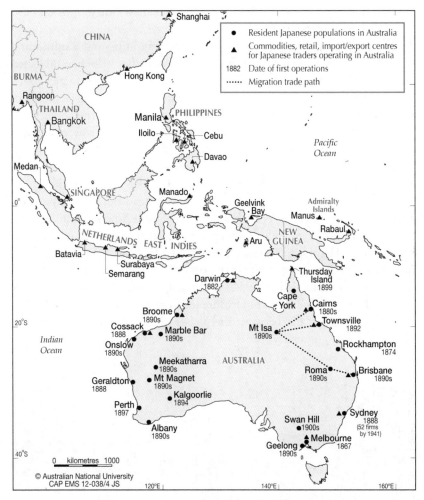

Map 4 Pre-war Japanese connections: Australia and Southeast Asia.

Most of Australia's Japanese pearl and sugar-cane workers were hired in Southeast Asia by Dutch, British and Australian businessmen. All Australian pearling crewmembers resided legally and were known to Federal and state governments. Crews could not contain more than 50 per cent of one nationality. No Japanese nationals ever owned Australian pearling fleets. Japanese-owned fleets sailed from Palau or Dobo to the Arafura Sea but never fished in Australian territorial waters. By 1936, the Japanese government centralised the licenses needed to hire Japanese labour overseas and only permitted six Australian pearling masters to hire Japanese expatriate labour.[8]

The 1904 amendments permitted business migration and a substantial trading-company network to blossom in Australia, which established enduring friendships and strong internal and external economic bonds from which many Australian families benefitted in the Great Depression. Firms owned by Japanese people in Australia, local firms owned by Japanese residents and branches of Japanese multinationals were concentrated in two hubs: Sydney and northwest Western Australia. Fifty-two firms operated in Sydney. The nine largest, including Mitsui Bussan Kaisha, Mitsubishi Shoji Kaisha, Okura Trading and Kanematsu, in Australia were multinationals or *zaibatsu* with head offices in Japan and branches in Europe, New York, South Africa, South America, China, India and Netherlands East Indies. These were branch networks in the Asia Pacific by 1941, of which Australia was a strong part.[9] A strategic connection is evident between places important to Japan before the war and the places first occupied in 1941. Our north is not of great interest but Sydney is. New Guinea does not feature much at all. There is a considerable disconnect in Australia between the places Japan bombed most and the places of greatest interest.

Photo 6 Staff of T. Iida & Co, Melbourne, 1930s (courtesy of Pam Herbert).

THE NATURE OF THE FRIENDSHIP WITHIN AUSTRALIA

Personal relationships included long-term individual, business and family friendships, intermarriage and membership of local clubs and societies. This friendly experience was reflected in the media, which was overwhelmingly positive when reporting on Japan and its people. The women's magazine *New Idea* regularly carried articles about Japan in the 1900s with competitions for trips to Japan and interviews with important visiting Japanese women such as the wife of Admiral Uryu Sotokichi. Japanese culture fascinated Australian women who shared the recent experience of their men going to war. Whenever there was an international incident involving Japan, media reporting was factual, lacking the xenophobic emphasis evident post-1937. Two exceptions were *The Bulletin* and *The Lone Hand*, which portrayed Japan as an ever-present threat after it defeated Russia in 1905. These articles were often part of an ongoing campaign to increase Australia's military capacity.[10] Archival files also contain sympathetic reports and letters in support of Japanese friends, neighbours and business associates. Many sought the release of Japanese friends from internment in the Second World War and remark that the person was 'as Australian as we are'.

Four stories show the diversity of occupations and mobility of the Japanese and their integration into Australian society. Many Japanese men arrived in Australia with no plans. Some had help from Australian or Japanese residents, who gave arriving Japanese men a start in life through prearranged jobs as station hands and houseboys, and English language classes. Even Dame Nellie Melba had a Japanese butler at one time.[11] The men progressed to better work in hotels, Australian trading houses and department stores. Some started their own laundry or trading businesses.

Ken Shimada came to Australia with the vaguest of plans. After finishing school, he started his own business with a partner trading with China in cotton yarn and straw but the quality of the goods was unreliable. He travelled through China to Hong Kong and read about Australia's gold rush. In 1896, he made his way to Townsville. He inspected a mine in Australia's Northern Territory but when the owner showed him the depth of the mine and how unhealthy it was he decided to open a laundry in Sydney instead. In 1916 he married an Australian widow, Mrs Craig, who had one daughter. They worked the Manly laundry living an Australian way of life until his internment in 1941.[12]

Warkichi Okamura, prompted by a 'youthful spirit', arrived in 1897. He mined guano for three years on the islands off Bundaberg and then cut cane. He opened a laundry in Brisbane and married Lily Williamson in 1910. They had six children. One son and one son-on-law served in the Army. Their daughters married Australians. His family was truly integrated into Australian life.[13]

From 1901, gentlemen like these who arrived in the 1890s were granted domicile status, equivalent to permanent residency. From 1904 onwards, merchants, tourists or students could enter Australia on a Japanese passport and reside legally for one year, after which they needed a Certificate of Exemption from the Dictation Test to remain for a further three years. Businessmen, if they were known to be 'in good standing' and still engaged in merchant activity, were granted unlimited extensions of stay enabling many to stay for decades. Generally, they married Australians and settled in suburbia like any other Australian resident. The laws conferred different rights in different states for Japanese people but security of stay excluded the right to vote and in some states excluded the right to own land. New South Wales was the state most favourable to Japanese people and to business. For example, one merchant, Hirokichi Nakamura, emigrated in 1897 because he was born illegitimate and had no future in Japan. He arranged to work as a houseboy for Mr Yasuda of Hunters Hill, a Japanese resident, who helped a number of Japanese men start out in Australia. Nakamura attended Ashmore Primary School to learn English. He then worked for Farmer & Co and learned the importing trade from its manager, John Pope, with whom he lived. He started his own firm in 1907 with a rented office, a phone and a secretary. He married Elizabeth Gerard in 1917. The couple owned a home in Mosman and had three daughters. He averaged £100 000 per annum profit by the 1920s. He hired an Australian maid and chauffeur and was a member of the local tennis club and Church of England.[14]

Rural Japanese also thrived. Kojiro Katsumata arrived in 1893, aged 14, to work on Andrew O'Keefe's station in Yarram, where he remained for 30 years. In 1923, he purchased a 14-acre farm property at Moama and worked it until his internment. He bought land and built houses in the town and set up a motor-repair shed. His houses accumulated £587–3–1d in rent during his internment.[15]

It may surprise that Australians and Japanese intermarried in White Australia. There was no stigma on marriage with Japanese people at this time. Women's magazines hailed the handsome sailors and officers during the training-ship visits. Crowds in their hundreds flocked to visit the ships

Photo 7 Hirokichi Nakamura, wife Bessie and their three daughters, Mosman, 1938 (courtesy of the Nakamura family).

during these large five-day events in major ports that included civic recep-tions. Australians invited the men to their homes, which often began decades of friendship. Women also regularly met Japanese businessmen at town-hall dances or at ballroom-dance classes and tennis clubs. The ladies thought Japanese men very polite and well turned out. Employees of trading houses earned more than Australian men and were considered good catches. They also spoke good English.[16]

The staff of Australian and Japanese firms built up longstanding per-sonal relationships. Any sub-manager of a section of Myer, for example, could ring up Mitsui & Co and talk about dinner services or the latest fabrics and fashions with their manager. The employees of these firms were at least on average 50 per cent Australians. Normally, only the managing director and department sub-managers were Japanese. This was necessary to communicate with Japan and visit factories in Japan to examine new products. The stability of staff favoured the development of long-term relationships. But such relationships were not confined to the cities. Trading houses regularly sent buyers to country areas for wool and wheat, developing friendships with farmers and livestock agents to organise enterprises such as the live sheep trade to Japan from 1920. The integration of these firms into the Australian economy was so extensive by the 1930s that it rivalled that with Britain. Large trading-house branches in Sydney were achieving profits of between £1–4 million a year by the 1930s. This extensive Australian–Japanese trade network, centred on Sydney, was connected to the worldwide Japanese trading network but integrated locally into the wider Australian economy. Japan was after all an ally and Australians did not forget that Japan had assisted Australian troops in the First World War.[17]

By 1931, Japanese residents were greatly trusted. Although police and customs checked the veracity of details in every application for extension of stay, from 1931, the Consul General in Sydney only needed to submit a list to the Commonwealth of those staying, those needing extension and those leaving. This meant that the consulates around Australia assisted in the actual administration of the Immigration Act.[18]

FRIENDSHIP AND JAPANESE 'IMPERIALISM'

It is obvious why pre-war friendship with Japanese people was buried after 1942 but not so obvious why its very existence is still challenged. Research demonstrates that our concept of Japanese 'imperialism' has played a large part. Many statements about Japanese imperialism, with the exception of those by Japan scholars like Sissons and Frei, assume that what was written, particularly after 1942, is accurate. What has been written since 1942 about Japan's intentions towards Australia has a tendency to take seriously the wartime *re-interpretation* of the friendly events and personal relationships that occurred between 1878 and 1940 as sinister rather than genuine in intent. However, when statements and reactions at the time of these events and friendships before 1940 are examined in their original context, these reveal overwhelmingly positive attitudes. Since the sudden attacks on 7–8 December 1941 and the deadly events that followed, we have assumed ulterior motives for Japan's pre-war friendship. We are still doing it. For example, because Japan's attacks were so quick and deadly, it is often argued that they must have been planned for a very long time before the war, perhaps using Japanese residents as spies. This argument was propagated by the Department of Information in prolific articles supplied to daily and regional papers for their information as wartime propaganda against Japan. In March 1942, 'Story of Japanese Aggression: Appetite grows with eating', in *The Canberra Times*, listed all Japanese actions from 1868 and argued that they formed one calculated, aggressive thrust.

In effect, the claim was impossible because there was no united Japan, even in the early 1900s. One document re-interpreted Japan's naval victory over Russia in 1905 as the precursor to Pearl Harbor, but it was a war that the Japanese saw as limited and very old fashioned by the 1930s. This practice of seeing one, distant, historic event and concluding that Japan was planning to attack Australia and dominate the world 'back then', obscured a much more complex and balanced reality.[19]

With imperialism, Japan's sense of its territory from the 1860s to the late 1930s differed from European concepts. For some decades after 1860, Japan was not a defined nation in our sense. Central control was hard-won and territory loosely defined as Japan consisted of concentric circles of diminishing control over warlords by the central authority. Japan was not united in its war against Russia in 1904–5. Coming after the Sino-Japanese War (1894–5) and the Boxer Rebellion, a war-weary public expressed opposition to the war, and divided loyalties between local areas and the newly developed concept of serving 'the state' were evident. Japan's fluid territorial concepts and the number of different statements circulated by a wide variety of Japanese politicians and military strategists made it impossible for Allied strategists to clarify what areas Japan included in Southern Expansion or Co-prosperity zones in the 1930s.[20]

Japan's desire for expansion until the 1930s, especially after the First World War, when Japan gained mandated territory north of the equator, stemmed from desires to plant the flag and obtain colonies like the great European powers had done. This process of economic expansion and trade coincided with Japanese emigration in hundreds of thousands. When Japanese documents use the word 'imperialism', it does not mean a narrow process of military conquest, occupation and colonisation. It is used mostly for doing business, trade in resources and cultural and information exchange. From 1922, Japan used newly mandated territories in the Caroline Islands and Marianas, to expand trade in the Pacific, but trade with Australia pre-dated this endeavour by two to three decades. Kanematsu opened in Sydney in 1890 and Mitsui in 1901.[21]

Japanese speeches contain different rationales and definitions of Japanese expansion or 'imperialism' at different times. Two statements that epitomise the formulation of a goal of Japanese expansion were made by men who had an intimate relationship with Australia: Vice Admiral Kobayashi Seizo, IJN, and Kawai Tetsuo, Japan's First Minister in Australia.

Vice Admiral Kobayashi lived through the period of Japanese naval expansion assisted by Britain in the late 19th century. His naval training ships visited Australia in 1902. He fought in the great naval battle against Russia at Tsushima in 1905. He was still a serving officer during the First World War and had developed a bond with Australian service personnel. Such was his standing that he was invited to lay the first wreath at the new Kings Park War Memorial in Perth in 1928. The reception of Kobayashi in Perth was close to vice regal. In his speech, he hailed the sacrifices of the heroes of Gallipoli. Kobayashi mention the tensions at the end of the Great War over racial equality, but stated that this was behind both nations. He described Japan, the US and Australia as keepers of the peace in the Pacific. In response, the Mayor and military speakers were glowing of Japan as 'saviour of Australia'. Although the formal alliance was superseded, there was no doubt that Australia and Japan remained close allies and partners in the Pacific.[22]

More hawkish in 1938, were Kawai's statements. A politician and diplomat, Kawai outlined three phases of Japanese expansion:
(1) early trade and shipping expansion before 1920;
(2) capital investment in Manchuria, the South Seas and South America, with emigration throughout Asia 'injecting fresh vitality and power into the community of Asiatic races'; and
(3) military action in China to prevent Russian invasion of Japan through Korea.

Kawai viewed the Axis Pact as a crusade against communism in Asia. Economically, Japan aimed to obtain additional mineral resources to manufacture and export goods. He envisioned peaceful expansion through tariff treaties and economic unification programs. However, differing from Kobayashi and many Japanese moderates, Kawai believed brute force was justified to forge a new Asian civilisation. Out of destruction, he argued, came new life. This rhetoric is familiar but belongs to the late 1930s.[23]

Speaking at the November 1940 congress celebrating the 2600th anniversary of the Empire's foundation, Prime Minister Prince Konoye, expounded the concept of 'eight corners under one roof', the spread of Japanese culture and empire throughout the world through limitless development. The AMF compared this concept to *Mein Kampf* because its grandiose vision included South America, Africa and Antarctica. Other delegates spoke of the Greater East-Asia Co-prosperity Sphere that Japan was establishing through trade. Japan's role for nations such as India and the Netherlands East Indies that wanted to throw off European colonial rule, was to realise its 'responsibility as the leader of East Asia'.[24] Konoye further warned that Japan would take action if blocked from achieving its objectives in Indochina.

By 1940, Australian authorities received increasing information about Japanese activities and centralisation. The speeches were no longer considered hawkish rhetoric after Japan signed the treaty with Germany and Italy in September 1941 and moved into Indochina. Information gathered from intelligence agents within Australia, the Pacific and Southeast Asia fell into three categories: military and espionage preparations, centralisation of business and trade, and patriotic calls on expatriates for support and funds.

Under the terms of the mandates, Japan was prohibited from building fortifications, but from 1938 military construction, new fuel and submarine depots were reported in the mandated territory. From November 1940 onwards, Australian intelligence received reports of Japan systematically collecting information through spy organisations such as F Kikan, Tokima Kikan and others operating in Lae, Salamaua, Rabaul, India, Burma and Malaya. During early 1941, Australian authorities watched visitors such as Major Hashida Sei very carefully and placed surveillance on all Japanese merchants and commercial activities within Australia. In July 1941, Australia joined the general freeze on Japanese funds instituted by the US and Britain in reaction to Japan's actions in Indochina. This crippled Japanese trade.[25]

By July 1940, Commonwealth intelligence organisations knew of plans to expand Japanese overseas Chambers of Commerce. The Japanese Ministry of Foreign Affairs allocated funds for trade mediation, information gathering and further introduction of Japanese goods for major centres in Burma, Siam, Indochina, Java and Australia. Business developed a political edge. A program of rapid centralisation in Japan had amalgamated thousands of firms into several hundred large businesses. In the South Seas, the Japanese government combined South Sea and Asian continental policies. The Foreign Office established two major companies, Formosa Development Company and the South Seas Development Company, to promote economic penetration of southern islands. All Japanese pearling fleets were amalgamated into one company.[26]

The Japanese government began to pressure all overseas Japanese after 1936 to complete questionnaires and raise funds for the war in China. On 25 November 1941 all consulates and local Japanese associations that existed around Australia were ordered to cooperate with their Italian and German counterparts.[27] This patriotic push was not always well received by resident Japanese. Such reports contradicted assurances made by Kawai in his interview with the *Adelaide Advertiser*, on 4 October 1941, during his first official visit to Adelaide as First Minister. He stated that, 'Just now the atmosphere is a little stiff' but he hoped to contribute to keeping up the past happy feelings between Japan and Australia, which had 'never yet been marred'.

Long before then the security services had planned the internment of Japanese people. In August 1941, in response to the reports detailed above, the AMF ordered all districts to await telegrams to intern Japanese, noting a rush by many to leave Australia. However, on 18 August 1941, the AMF noted that the 'invasion of Australia would be unnecessary. They would be able to force Australians to grow wheat and produce wool to be transported in their ships at their price'.[28]

BETRAYAL OF FRIENDSHIP

International events during the late 1930s gradually and unevenly began to change Australia's views of Japan across most sections of Australian society. The sense of suspicion in official circles was notable after 1937 but Japan's signing of the Axis Pact on 27 September 1940 changed ordinary Australians' attitudes overnight. For example, Mr Iida, Sydney manager of Okura Trading, had lived in Australia for 20 years and brought up his family with his Japanese-born wife. He arrived home that night shaken. He had been spat on by strangers in the street and called 'a dirty Jap'. He did not know why. His wife informed him that Japan and Australia were now enemies and life would be difficult from then on.[29]

After September 1940, the majority of Japanese in local communities did not experience any different treatment from Australians they knew. Their neighbours considered them 'as Australian as we are' and differentiated between Japanese they had known for decades and the government of Japan and its representatives. After Pearl Harbor and the internment of all Japanese regardless of age and gender, attitudes gradually hardened. Many documents from 1942 refer to the 'treacherous manner of Japan's entry into the war'.

The overwhelming majority of white women who had married Japanese men fought for their release from internment. Local communities who had Japanese residents did the same. Bessie Nakamura camped outside the offices of bureaucrats and politicians until her husband was released.[30] Very few examples exist of women distancing themselves from their Japanese husbands. Ken Shimada's wife at first supported him. She retained her British nationality and the laundry business. In June 1942, she wrote to him at Hay camp:

I know the feelings of the people here at present and have to stay quiet. It is hard for us all who have done nothing but time may sooth the ill feeling everywhere at present. That is why I think you are better ... up there you cannot imagine the state of Sydney just now. Everything scarce and everybody on each other's nerves ... Every family around here are suffering and that is why they are so bitter.

However, in July 1946, she had no objection to his deportation. He was devoted to his life in Australia but felt that he would have no life here after the war. He had given up seeking release despite being in terrible health with gastric ulcers and other complaints relating to his age (76 years). Shimada said: 'They won't let us go, you know what they call us: Bloody Japs!' The sense of betrayal of friendship was two-way.

Official attitudes hardened after the raids. For example, until May 1942 the Aliens Appeals Tribunal was prepared to release people like Shimada. It concluded:

We are satisfied that it is neither necessary nor advisable for the public safety, the defence of the Commonwealth or the efficient prosecution of the war that he [Shimada] should continue to be detained. We are further satisfied that his release would not be likely to occasion serious unrest in any Australian community ... and recommend that he be released.

Their attitude changed after the midget-submarine raid on Sydney. 'The release of Japanese nationals ... would be keenly resented by the public of Australia, even more so than the release of nationals of other enemy countries. They feared serious assaults on Japanese people "by irate citizens"'.

Some elderly Japanese men were released to home detention. Hirokichi Nakamura returned to Mosman because of his precarious health in 1944 and died in 1945. The president of the Brisbane Japanese Association, Taira Kashiwagi, a former silk shop owner who had arrived in 1895, was released in December 1943. His Australian-born wife, Marguerite, and their daughter, Mignonette, a physiotherapy student at the University of Queensland, were released before him to set up their home.[31]

The Deputy Director of Security in Queensland, Robert Wake, reported that: 'There is absolutely no evidence that [Kashiwagi] has ever shown himself to be disloyal to Australia'. Kashiwagi was trusted sufficiently to have a wireless set in his home once short-wave coils were removed. However, the Returned Services League (RSL) complained that he was seen working in his garden and neighbours were certain he was signalling the enemy because they heard him tapping in the chook shed. Security investigated the complaints in October 1944 and bemoaned the waste of investigation time to the Director of Security in Canberra. 'The foregoing [report] is merely submitted to demonstrate the number of man hours which will probably be spent on this and other cases in the future'. Kashiwagi had suffered two heart attacks. As Wake reported, under the terms of his restriction order he could not go more than half a mile from his home, 'even if his physical condition permits him to do so'.

Had there been spying? Were friendships a cover by Japanese for information gathering as postwar novels and other documents claim? Those who sought the release of Japanese friends from internment did not believe for a minute that their friend had spied. There was of course a small spy network from 1934, centred on Sydney. This, and the difficulty of interpreting Japan's intentions from 1937, led to surveillance dossiers being prepared on all Japanese people. Although all Japanese in Australia were interned, the fear of the enemy by 1942–3 led to reports of Japanese sightings all over the country.[32] This prompted the Commonwealth Security Service to write:

> A good deal has been written about enemy espionage during this war. We have seen official publications, newspaper and magazine articles, and an abundance of high romantic films. We have been overwhelmed with propaganda, some of which we felt was based on sound reasoning and acknowledged fact but a good proportion of which we also felt depended for appeal on lurid imagination.
>
> The main difficulty in any attempt to prove the existence of enemy espionage in a particular place is generally the inability to produce some outstanding fact, some disaster such as the sinking of a convoy, or sabotage of some highly important military installation ... Notwithstanding the lack of beautiful blond spies, ... there is in the hands of authorities sufficiently powerful evidence to prove the existence of enemy espionage in Australia. The evidence itself is not of the story book variety; it has been built up as the result of painstaking enquiry over a period of years.[33]

By the early 1950s, nearly every book that referred to Japanese people, whether a serious study or a novel like those by Ion Idriess, cast Japanese people as spies intent on invading Australia. This cemented the belief that Japan must have planned its attacks for decades and that Australians were fearful of Japanese people for 50 years or more before the war. This change in perception from friend to treacherous enemy meant many hid their views and friendships as they distinguished between the Japanese they had known and the ones that Australians were fighting. The re-interpretation of the friendship and the sinister intent placed on previous cooperation, especially by the Department of Information, alongside genuine worry about what Japan would do, cemented new interpretations of previous positive experiences.

THE RE-INTERPRETATION AND JAPAN'S INTENTIONS

Japanese friendship with Australians before 1942 was real but difficult to admit and maintain after the events of the Second World War. The fact that Japanese rhetoric in the 1930s also re-interpreted events, such as the Russo-Japanese war, and brought them into the realm of a heroic mythology used to stir up patriotic feeling in the late 1930s, may have influenced Australian re-interpretation during the war.[34]

Certainly, Japanese businesses expected to continue the good relations and input into government policy that they had always enjoyed. However, from 1940 they expected an intensification and extension of access through contracts to develop Australian mineral resources, wider trade deals and exemption from wartime regulations. Japanese multinationals had enjoyed extremely good relationships in the decades before 1940 with government departments and agencies, firms like BHP, Dalgety's, major primary producers in wheat, wool and milk, and export outlets into all areas of the Australian community. However, with the centralisation of business in Japan and the closer relationship between business and government that resulted, intensive policy approaches and demands to the Australian government in wartime damaged relations from 1940. Through 1940, major Japanese firms in Australia pushed very hard for exemptions from wartime regulations and new contracts almost to the point of threats. One firm even offered planes for wheat deals. Mitsui and Mitsubishi had reasonable expectations of deals because they held Australian government contracts to make parachutes and provide material for military uniforms from 1939. However, Australia became less cooperative as Japan pushed harder, through correspondence to government departments, to soften wartime restrictions on trade. As Konoye and Kawai said: Japan wanted peace but also control of resources. If denied what it needed it was prepared to use force.

The Australian–Japanese company record files contain plans for the wider centralisation of commerce, trade, transport, industry and finance of the type that already existed in Japan from 1937 but extended to Australia and other British territories. The aim was policy control and centralisation of resources and development, especially in minerals, food and agriculture within Australia to Japan's advantage as in other parts of Southeast Asia. Had Japan succeeded in gaining the ring of islands to the north, including New Guinea, as the AMF assessment of 1941 had suggested, such isolation and control of Australia without attack or military occupation would have been possible. Truly, 'They would be able to force Australians to grow wheat and produce wool to be transported in their ships at their price'. This was imperialism in its best Japanese style and what we were saved from during the battles of the Second World War.

The friendship was real. Espionage was also present later in the pre-war era. Those who spied for Japan were not those who befriended Australians in suburbia. Surveillance files confirm this. The unfortunate, but understandable, obscuration of the friendship under wartime re-interpretation of pre-war events and the shock of the change in perception from allies and friends to enemies, needs recognising so we can regain an appreciation of the full extent and significance of the friendship in our mutual history.

Notes

1 Yuriko Nagata, *Unwanted Aliens, Japanese Internment in Australia*, University of Queensland Press, St Lucia, 1996. Paul Jones & Vera Mackie, *Relations, Japan and Australia*, History Department, University of Melbourne, 2001.
2 See chapter 7.
3 Pam Oliver, *Raids on Australia, 1942 and Japan's plans for Australia*, Australian Scholarly Publishing, Melbourne, 2010, pp. 96–100. Pam Oliver, *Allies, Enemies, Trading Partners, Records on Australia and the Japanese*, National Archives of Australia, Canberra, 2004, pp. 62–71 for details of company records.
4 'Press Releases – Japan [transcripts] 1939–43', AWM80 11/96 and 'Japanese training ship visits series', National Archives of Australia (NAA), MP124.
5 David Sissons, 'Manchester v Japan', *Australian Outlook*, vol. 30. no 3, 1976. David Sissons, Senate Standing Committee – Japan, 1972.
6 Oliver, *Raids*, p. 213.
7 NAA, General and Classified Correspondence, series B13/0, Correspondence files, series A1/15, Second World War investigation dossiers, series C123.
8 Oliver, *Raids*, p. 147.
9 Ibid., pp. 149–61.
10 David Sissons, 'Attitudes to Japan and Defence, 1890–1923', MA thesis, University of Melbourne, 1956. *Lone Hand*, 1 February 1909 and 1 March 1911. 'Aliens Tribunal transcripts of evidence of objections against internment', NAA, MP529/3 TRIBUNAL 4.
11 'Thomas NAGAI, NAA, A367/1 C71179. Please note, Japanese residents in Australia adopted the Australian convention with surname last rather than the

Japanese practice of using surname first. Archival records are mixed in their practice of where to put surnames. This chapter uses surname first for residents of Japan and surname last for Japanese residents of Australia.
12 Transcript of evidence of objection by K. Shimada, NAA, MP529/3 TRIBUNAL 4 /56 and Shimada Ken, NAA,A367/1 C72449.
13 Okamura Warkichi, NAA, A367/1 C68978.
14 Oliver, *Raids*, pp. 61ff and pp. 162ff. Nakamura, Hirokichi, NAA, ST1233/1 N19133. Please note, the family pronounced their name 'nɔcámra'.
15 Katsumata Kojiro, NAA, A367/1 C23732.
16 Correspondence files, NAA, MP472/1 and Correspondence file, NAA, MP124/6 for training squadron visits.
17 Miscellaneous records, NAA, SP1098 series.
18 Japanese merchants' wives and assistants, NAA, A433 1940/2/2351.
19 Henry Frei, *Japan's Southward Advance and Australia from the Sixteenth Century to World War II*, 1991. Press Releases – Japan [transcripts], AWM80 11/96. Naoko Shimazu, *Japanese Society at War, Death, Memory and the Russo-Japanese War*, 2009, pp. 267 and 284.
20 See chapters 6 and 7. Shimizu, *Japanese Society*, p. 267.
21 See studies by Mark Peattie, *Nan'yo, The Rise and Fall of the Japanese in Micronesia, 1885–1945*, 1988. Frei, *Japan's Southward Advance* and William Wray, 'The 17th-century Japanese diaspora', web article.
22 Oliver, *Raids*, pp. 130–3. *The Age*, 29 June 1928. Visit of Japanese Training Squadron, NAA, MP124/6 603/203/347.
23 Tetsuo Kawai, *The Goal of Japanese Expansion*, 1938.
24 Japanese Activities in the South Seas, NAA, A1616/1 BS12/1.
25 Enemy Espionage, AWM, 54 627/1/3. Japanese Espionage, NAA, SP1714/1 N60621.
26 Oliver, *Raids*, pp. 213–14. Sandra Wilson, *The Manchurian Crisis and Japanese Society, 1931–33, 2002*. Japanese activities, NAA, D1915 SA19703.
27 Examination of Japanese material, NAA, A373/1 10298.
28 'Appreciation – War in the Pacific', AWM124 3/17. CO's Reports, AWM, 124 3/10. Overseas Views on Japanese Expansion, NAA, A373 11810. The Defence of Australia, A5954 769/.
29 Interview of Mrs Iida by Toshie Swift, 7 February 2004, used with permission.
30 Nakamura Hirokichi, NAA, ST1233/1 N19133.
31 Kashwagi, Tairo, NAA, A367/1 C34033.
32 Oliver, *Raids*, pp. 232–37.
33 SIC Plans, NAA, A8911 266.
34 Shimazu, *Japanese Society*, p. 284.

FURTHER READING

Frei, H., *Japan's Southward Advance and Australia from the Sixteenth Century to World War II*, Melbourne University Press, Melbourne 1991.
Jones, P. and Mackie, V., *Relations: Japan and Australia, 1870s–1950s*, History Department, University of Melbourne, Parkville, 2001.
Kawai, T., *The Goal of Japanese Expansion*, Hokiseido Press, Tokyo, 1938.

Nagata, Y., *Unwanted Aliens: Japanese Internment in Australia*, University of Queensland Press, St Lucia, 1996.

Oliver, P., *Allies, Enemies, Trading Partners: Records on Australia and the Japanese*, National Archives of Australia, Canberra, 2004.

Oliver, P., *Raids on Australia: 1942 and Japan's Plans for Australia*, Australian Scholarly Publishing, Melbourne, 2010.

Peattie, M., *Nan'yo: The Rise and Fall of the Japanese in Micronesia, 1885–1945*, University of Hawaii Press, Honolulu, 1988.

Shimazu, N., *Japanese Society at War: Death, Memory and the Russo-Japanese War*, Cambridge University Press, Cambridge, 2009.

Wilson, S., *The Manchurian Crisis and Japanese Society, 1931–33*, Routledge, New York, 2002.

CHAPTER 3

THE OVERLOOKED MISSION

AUSTRALIA AND HOME DEFENCE

Albert Palazzo

When Japanese bombs fell upon Darwin on 19 February 1942 the situation facing Australia appeared grave. Singapore had surrendered, much of the Netherlands East Indies had been overrun, the Japanese had occupied Rabaul and would soon land on New Guinea, and Australia's 8th Division was in captivity.[1] In addition, the US position in the Philippines had been effectively decided, although the defenders of Corregidor would hold out to 6 May. Making Australia's position appear even more desperate was that, as David Horner has noted, 'Most of its trained soldiers were overseas, mainly in the Middle East. The RAAF had few planes in Australia, many of the larger vessels of the small RAN were in distant waters, and the home defence force, the militia, was poorly trained and equipped'.[2] The Japanese advance had been so rapid and unchecked that fear of imminent invasion swept the country and panicky coast dwellers fled inland; even if today we know that the Japanese never had any intention to do so.[3]

This chapter will explore how Australia found itself in this desperate situation. First it will examine the assumptions and decisions that led to Australian territory being virtually bereft of military power as the Japanese threat neared. Second, it will discuss the measures initiated by Australia to remedy this deficiency and the steps taken to convert the country into one of the lines of Allied attack that would lead to Japan's defeat. In doing so, it will consider the interaction between two broad themes of Australian defence policy: the constant struggle to achieve an appropriate balance between a reliance on a great power protector and the requirements of self-reliance.

AUSTRALIAN UNPREPAREDNESS
FOR NATIONAL DEFENCE

That Australia found itself at war with Japan, and that its territory would soon come under attack from Japanese forces, should not have come as a surprise to the government's political and military leaders. After all, a succession of Australian governments, and their military advisors, had determined that Japan represented the country's primary security threat. This assessment was long-standing and was reached soon after the nation's founding in 1901. The Japanese victory over Russia in 1905 and its emergence as a great power confirmed Australia's perception of a deterioration in its security situation.[4] This found expression in numerous national security studies while senior military officers spoke openly and directly of the threat Japan posed to Australian territory and interests. For example, the members of a 1920 conference of the Army's senior officers were quite emphatic that Japan was Australia's only identifiable potential enemy. The conference also reconfirmed that Australia would not be able to resist Japanese aggression on its own but would require the assistance of a friendly great power.[5]

The post-First World War territorial settlement only served to reinforce Australia's fears. Japan retained control of the German island colonies it had seized in the Central Pacific and, because Australia had received a mandate over the former German territories in New Guinea and the Bismarck Archipelago, the two countries were now virtually neighbours, if still separated by sea.[6] The effect of the confirmation of the new boundary was that from Australia's perspective Japan no longer represented a distant menace but a near one.

Japan's actions in 1941 confirmed that there was nothing wrong with the rationality of Australia's national security policy and the objectivity of those responsible for its determination. Its designers had correctly deduced that Japanese militarism posed a real threat to the nation's welfare. What is at issue, however, is the linkage between the government's risk-assessment process and the design and implementation of a national security strategy by which to offset the danger Japan posed to the nation's security. In determining national security policy it is vital not only to determine the risks correctly, but also to provide for appropriate mitigations of these, if the process is to have legitimacy.

Robert Menzies, the Australian Prime Minister at the commencement of the Second World War, informed the Australian public that the country was at war soon after the expiration of the ultimatum that Britain and

France had given Germany following its invasion of Poland on 1 September 1939. Menzies had no hesitation in taking the step and he saw no leeway for Australia to pursue an independent path. Australia was a part of the British Empire and the Empire was at war.

Even though an imperialist, Menzies proved reluctant to dispatch any of Australia's admittedly limited military strength to the other side of the world. Despite the approaching crisis Australia's military capability was nearly nonexistent when the war broke out. The defence budget had suffered heavily over the preceding two decades and as a result the nation's military forces were unprepared for war. The Army was undermanned, poorly trained and largely equipped with leftovers from the First World War. Due to the restrictions of the Defence Act the existing part-time militia could serve only within Australia, and as a result the country would have to raise an expeditionary force from scratch for overseas service, as it had done in the previous conflict. The RAAF had suffered even more than the Army during the inter-war period and had barely survived as an independent institution. The aircraft it did have were largely obsolete and were no match for modern warplanes.[7] Of the three services, the RAN had fared the inter-war period the best, but the fleet was small, as were the majority of its ships.

Menzies' reluctance to send Australian forces to Britain's aid was not because of their modest capabilities, however. The Prime Minister displayed little enthusiasm for taking this step, mainly out of a concern for Japan's intentions. Japan had already demonstrated a preference for military expansionism, as the peoples of Korea, Manchuria and China well knew, and soon so would the inhabitants of the French colonies of Southeast Asia. The unknown was at what point Japan would become a sated aggressor, if at all. Before agreeing to dispatch Australia's military strength to Europe and the Middle East, Menzies sought reassurance from imperial authorities that Australia would not be left undefended if Japan decided to push southwards.[8] Britain needed to offer reassuring security assessments before Menzies agreed to London's demands.

In October the government decided to dispatch part of the Australian fleet to European waters and to the nation's participation in the Empire Air Training Scheme. But it was not until the end of November that Menzies acquiesced to demands to send ground forces and he did so only after receiving a promise that in the event of war with Japan the Admiralty would 'make such dispositions as would enable them to offer timely resistance either to a serious attack upon Singapore or to the invasion of Australia and New Zealand'.[9] At the end of November the government agreed to dispatch the newly raised 6th Division to the Middle East. The first contingent sailed in early January 1940.[10]

Australia reached this decision not specifically as a result of Germany's invasion of Poland. Rather, that act was only the catalyst that revealed two long-standing, but known and understood, potential problems in the government's conception of its national security policy. The government's security policy supported a navalist strategy that in turn rested on great power acquiescence. It was up to the Royal Navy to prevent an enemy from approaching Australia's shores and the policy downplayed the need for land forces. In addition, in doing so, it emphasised the defence of territory at the expense of interests, while still insisting on the security of Australia's interest within the imperial network. This was an incompatibility that the government chose not to reconcile, because to do so would have prevented it from achieving the second objective of its security policy: a desire to transfer the greatest possible share of defence responsibility onto the shoulders – and finances – of a great power.

After the end of the First World War Australia decided to base its security on what was to become known as the Singapore Strategy. In brief, the Singapore Strategy placed the defence of Australia in the hands of the Royal Navy. In case of war in the Pacific the Imperial Fleet would sail to the east where, from its base in Singapore, it would undertake operations to prevent a hostile country from attacking or invading Australia and New Zealand.[11]

In accepting the Singapore Strategy as the basis of its security policy the Australian government continued its reliance on a great power as the guarantor of national security. Yet, from the start the Singapore Strategy had a flaw; there was nothing to prohibit an aggressor from deciding to attack when the Imperial Fleet was distracted by other and more pressing demands. The Army's leaders made this point frequently to their civilian masters. For example, at a 1923 meeting of the Council of Defence General C. B. B. White questioned the ability of the Royal Navy to come to Australia's aid.[12] Senior Army officers insisted that it was unimaginable that the British government and people would consent to the dispatch of a major part of the fleet to the other side of the world. This was because 'command in the Atlantic is of vital importance to the British people, [whereas] command in the Far East is not'.[13]

However, the Singapore Strategy came with an implied obligation, one that reinforced the existing obligations of kith and kin. If Britain came under threat Australia would have no choice but to come to its aid. This was because if the mother country fell then Australia's security policy would unravel. Britain's survival was essential for Australia's security, although the inverse, it should be recognised, was not necessarily true.

Yet, instead of seeing the Singapore Strategy as requiring Australia to invest in defence capability, it was viewed by the Australian government as an endorsement of the massive cutbacks that it imposed after the signing of the Washington Naval Treaties in 1922. The onset of the Great Depression worsened the military service's position even further. Such savings resulted in a considerable reduction in the country's military establishment to the extent that the Army, for example, was essentially a 'mothballed' force that would require considerable re-animation in order to restore any degree of capability. Unfortunately, by the onset of the Second World War little had been done to restore the force's strength.[14]

This chapter is not minimising the problems the Great Depression created for the Australian government. These were indeed challenging times. But what must be remembered is that even in hard times governments do not reduce the spending of public monies to zero. Rather, the critical question facing governments in times of austerity is how monies are allocated. During the inter-war period the Australian government's adherence to the Singapore Strategy gave it a rational for a reduction of the defence estimate, far below levels that its military advisors thought wise. In doing so, the government reduced its own defence force's capability to impotence while devolving responsibility of the nation's defence to Britain. At the time, this may have appeared to be an efficient allocation of resources, but it was a decision that led to the implementation of a strategy that was incapable of meeting defence policy.

Perversely, once the war began, the government still continued to go slow on defence re-armament and it was not until June 1941 that Menzies called for an 'unlimited war effort'.[15] This contrasted with the casualness of the 'business as usual' mantra that had been his government's preferred catch-phrase up to that point.[16] Moreover, as the Army raised the 2nd AIF for overseas service the government continued to neglect the militia home-defence role. In fact, the militia's condition worsened as its best soldiers transferred to the AIF. In a denial of the true situation, financial considerations, more suited for peacetime conditions, still dominated the government's decision making. The treasury's attitude was that 'the war should not be an excuse for undue extravagance on the part of the services'.[17] Instead of intensive training, militia soldiers continued to report to all-too-brief camps at which they experienced limited training with obsolete weapons. As Jeff Grey has observed, the 'home army was in a dreadful shape'.[18]

A few days after Japan's entry into the war the Chiefs of Staff presented the government with the advice that it was 'necessary to establish and train now the force that would be required to prevent and to meet an invasion'. David Horner has observed, 'Clearly this would have been an admirable aim a year earlier'.[19]

In late January 1942 the Chiefs of Staff presented to the government a major appraisal of the force's readiness. The report was damning and highlighted the defence force's inability to defend the country. One of the report's conclusions was that the Army could make improvements at one point only by weakening a different point.[20] The air force was in a particularly dire state and it was no great exaggeration when a RAAF senior officer observed in February 1942 that the Air Force had 'hardly a feather to fly with'.[21]

Some of these ongoing liabilities can be explained by competing demands across the empire for scarce resources, such as modern guns, tanks and planes. After all, Australia had outstanding orders from overseas suppliers for all manners of equipment. But such an explanation is inadequate and, possibly, too kind. In preparing for war, time is unforgiving, and when allowed to slip away it cannot be regained. The government had neglected defence requirements throughout the inter-war years and commenced re-armament far too late. Once the war began the failure to bring the militia onto a war footing prior to the Japanese onslaught signalled the government's continued faith in the Imperial Fleet for the nation's defence, no matter the worsening situation in the Far East. This guaranteed that the militia would remain incapable when the threat did come.

In addition, this policy of national defence avoidance contains more than a suggestion that the Australian government believed military strength could be extemporised at will. Perhaps this reflects the nation's ongoing faith in the citizen soldier and the myth of the natural warrior ability of the Australian male.[22] Yet, what this belief fails to recognise is that armies, like navies and air forces, require long lead-times if they are to attain effectiveness and sustained maintenance if they are to retain skills. As is true for the sea and air domains, land power is more than the sum of the abilities of individual soldiers. Rather, it is the deep integration of individuals into a system of combined arms that creates combat capability. Just as the addition of a ship to a fleet needs considerable lead-time to allow for design, construction, trial and adoption, the same is true for land forces. If Australia wanted effective divisions in 1941 it needed to begin their creation in 1939, if not sooner.

Recalibrating national defence

Japan's entry into the Second World War completely changed Australia's strategic position. Whereas for the first two years the war seemed a distant disturbance, it was now in Australia's backyard. Civil defence suddenly took on a new urgency and coastal dwellers learned to live with a blackout, or considered fleeing inland. For the government the need to provide for the defence of the continent became a task that it could no longer ignore. Australia had two options: provide for its own defence by increasing its military forces and capabilities, or seek the additional assistance of a great power protector. The government chose to do both.

On 27 December 1941 John Curtin, only two months into the job as Prime Minister, issued a statement that formalised a shift in Australia's security focus from Britain to the US. Curtin said: 'Without any inhibitions of any kind, I make it quite clear that Australia looks to America, free of any pangs as to our traditional links or kinship with the United Kingdom'.[23]

In fact, Curtin was being disingenuous as the transfer in security affiliation had been underway for some months.

In early October 1941 – two months before the start of the Pacific War – Australia received an approach from the US (via Britain) seeking access to Australian bases by elements of the US Army Air Forces.[24] The US made similar approaches to Britain regarding access to Singapore and to the Dutch government in exile for access to military facilities in the Netherlands East Indies. In making these approaches the US was exploring ways to strengthen the air defence of the Philippines and adjacent territories. By opening its airfields Australia would enable the US to transfer air units between Hawaii and Manilla without them having to traverse Japan's Central Pacific territories. The Australian government replied to the US with an emphatic yes, stating that 'the Commonwealth government welcome[s] the US proposals ... and will do everything necessary to arrange for the facilities required in Australia and its territories ...'[25]

In November 1941 the commander of the Philippine-based US Far East Air Force – Major-General Lewis H. Brereton – made a secret visit to Australia.[26] More detailed and expansive requests for basing rights by the US soon followed. Australia agreed to give the US access to airfields at Rabaul, Port Moresby, Townsville, Darwin, Rockhampton, Brisbane and a variety of smaller fields in Queensland and the Northern Territory.[27] The US also agreed to provide Australia with the guns and equipment it needed to improve the defences of Rabaul. The US Navy sought these improvements as it hoped to use the harbour as a base for operations against Japanese forces in the Caroline Islands. The US agreed to provide Australia with 6–7-inch coast guns, 8–3-inch anti-aircraft guns, as well as radar sets, search lights, sonar buoys, anti-submarine nets and other equipment. Australia's part of the arrangement was to provide the personnel required to staff these enhancements, approximately 1600 additional personnel.[28] Again, Curtin readily agreed to these requests.[29]

At a conference held in Melbourne on 22 November 1941 the US broadened its request, from transfer rights to basing rights. This request was made in two parts: the basing of squadrons for the purpose of training and the basing of squadrons for the purpose of conducting offensive operations against the Japanese. Ultimately, Brereton hoped to operate up to 50 per cent of the Far East Air Force's strength from Australian bases. Locations identified were: Townsville, Charters Towers, Cloncurry, Batchelor, Port Moresby, Rabaul, Broome and Darwin. In addition, Australia gave the US permission to set up maintenance facilities at Alice Springs, Daly Waters, Longreach and Charleville and an engine repair workshop in Townsville. In total, the plan called for the basing of up to seven squadrons plus associated command, and administrative and support elements. In manpower terms this represented the basing of over 8000 US military personnel in Australia, at a time when Australia was not at war with Japan.[30]

Of course, events in the Far East moved far too quickly for the implementation of most of these plans, and few eventuated, at least in the form agreed upon. However, by mid-November at least 35 US B-17s had traversed Australia en route to the Philippines.[31]

Once the war in the Pacific began the new relationship between Australia and the US intensified as the two countries became formal allies. The catalyst for increased cooperation was the arrival of General Douglas MacArthur in Australia on 17 March 1942.[32] The US General saw Australia as a base from which to organise a counter-stroke against the Japanese, striking initially towards the Philippines and then on to Formosa and the enemy's homeland. MacArthur's desire to go on the offensive as soon as possible – a desire that was matched by Australia's land commanders – worked well with Curtin's hope to secure Australia with the help of the US. In a mutually beneficial arrangement MacArthur and Curtin worked together to draw US resources to the South West Pacific, a tactic in which they were largely successful.[33] By the end of 1942 there were

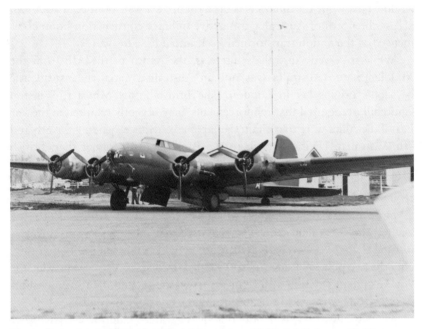

Photo 8 Archerfield, Queensland, November 1941. A US Army Air Corps Boeing B-17D aircraft, part of the group that traversed Australia en route to the Philippines prior to the commencement of the Pacific War (AWM P00264.011).

over 160 000 US personnel in Australia and New Guinea and MacArthur's command would eventually total in excess of 750 000.[34] As a result Australia would become a major base of operations for an Allied offensive against Japan.

However, in turning to MacArthur, Curtin did sacrifice some degree of the nation's sovereignty. MacArthur's influence over Australian military affairs became immense as he became Curtin's primary military advisor, rather than General Thomas Blamey, Australia's senior-most officer. Curtin would also place Australian forces under MacArthur's command, a privilege the US General retained until the war's conclusion.[35]

GALVANISING AUSTRALIAN STRENGTH

While seeking US assistance was vital in safeguarding the nation, the Australian government also undertook to increase the country's military and infrastructure capabilities. The AIF would be brought back from the

Middle East while the militia was brought up to a war footing. In addition, across the north of Australia, a massive military construction boon commenced as the nation transformed itself into a base for war.

While it served Australia's interests, the return of the AIF from the Middle East to Australia was not an Australian initiative. Instead, the decision's origins lay in London. The British Prime Minister, Winston Churchill, recognised that reinforcements were urgently required in the Far East if the Allies were to contain the Japanese advance. Sending the 6th and 7th Australian Divisions back to the Pacific theatre, rather than British troops, was a logical decision. Where Australia's influence was decisive, however, was in the AIF's ultimate destination. Churchill viewed military requirements from the centre of an empire and perceived the threat to Burma as more immediate than that which Australia faced. Consequently, he wanted the Australian troops to reinforce that theatre. Curtin, however, insisted that the Australians return home, which they did, although only after the two political leaders had exchanged strong words.[36] Eventually, the 9th Australian Division also returned to Australia, and the three divisions went on to play a critical role in turning the tide in New Guinea.

The AIF, however, was only one of Australia's land forces. The other was the long-neglected militia – or Citizen Military Force (CMF) as it would become known. As noted above, the militia had been ignored in favour of the AIF since the war's outbreak in 1939. By early 1942 it was more than 30 000 soldiers under full strength and still suffered from serious deficiencies in weapons and equipment and only a third of the force was on full-time duty at any one time.[37] The remainder rotated through three-month camps that provided little continuity and at best fragmented training.[38] In many ways the militia had become a basic training organisation for the AIF while it remained an inefficient force of part-time green soldiers.[39]

To make the situation worse, as the Japanese attack neared, the militia remained deficient in most categories of weapons and equipment. An inventory conducted in November 1941 showed that some critical categories, such as anti-tank and anti-aircraft guns were only at 50 per cent of requirements, while others, such as tanks, were virtually nonexistent. Mechanical transport was also well below requirements, with the force meeting less than half of its needs for trucks. It was only in basic weapons, such as rifles, that supply came closest to meeting demand, although shortages still remained.[40]

Bringing the militia up to strength was a chaotic activity that was carried out in necessary haste. The CMF underwent a series of reorganisations

Photo 9 November 1939, members of the 15th (Militia) Brigade undergoing bayonet training (AWM 000086/09).

as units were swapped between formations in order to provide some force that was combat ready, while others were broken up and its members transferred in order to bring surviving units up to strength. The militia also had to be reorganised at the unit-establishment level, due to its structure remaining on the pre-war pattern, whereas the AIF had been reorganised onto the British standard when it was in the Middle East. Thus the composition of the AIF and militia battalions was different, a situation that should have been addressed much earlier. The result was that by 1943 the militia bore little resemblance to its pre-war design.[41]

Of course, those in the militia continued to serve under the restriction of the Defence Act, which prevented their dispatch outside of Australia or its territory. Because of this Australia maintained what was in effect two armies for service in a single theatre. It was not until February 1943 that the government modified the Defence Act to extend the service obligation to anywhere in the SWPA. Yet, despite this extension, few militiamen were to serve beyond Australian territory.

Despite these impediments remarkable progress was made. In a mid-year report to the Advisory War Council it was admitted that the Army had been transformed from an ill-armed and ill-trained force to a sound and efficient one. One suspects, however, that this was an overly optimistic assessment as the report goes on to note that a further three months were required before the Army would be ready to undertake any task it might be called upon to perform. The RAAF lagged somewhat behind the Army due to difficulties in acquiring modern aircraft, as well as the continuing need to provide personnel to the Empire Air Training Scheme for service in the European theatre. As a result the report did not expect the Air Force to be completely ready before mid-1943. The Navy also suffered from handicaps, primarily related to its lack of integral air power; the report's writers believed that without carriers the Australian fleet would never reach its full potential.[42]

As the militia developed the Australian government also focused its efforts on improving other components of national power. The government continued to expand the nation's coastal defence and anti-aircraft system, the latter handicapped by a shortage of 3.7-inch anti-aircraft guns. Throughout the inter-war period coastal defence improvements had advanced at a torpid pace, largely due to underfunding. The commencement of the war had seen a big push to finish the planned defences. Now, to further protect the coast, the US provided Australia with a number of

Photo 10 A montage of pictures taken in 1942 of the Australian Women's Army Service, particularly some of its anti-aircraft artillery units (AWM P04428.007).

155-mm gun batteries. As the war was to be fought in the islands to the north the Australian Army raised an entirely new arm – Water Transport. Formed in September 1942 this arm would eventually include 1900 watercraft, ranging from workboats to ocean-going ships.

In 1942 the government further expanded its home defence force, the Voluntary Defence Corps (VDC). Its origin was as a privately formed body of enthusiastic Australians and it was formed under the sponsorship of the Returned Sailors', Soldiers' and Airmens' Imperial League of Australia. In May 1941 the VDC became a part of the Army and the following year a corps of the CMF.[43]

During 1942 the VDC grew rapidly and quickly exceeded its initial establishment of 50 000. By the end of the year it had doubled in size and the government sought a further expansion, despite Blamey's opinion that there was little military need. Its contribution to the nation's defence was mixed and the VDC's raising was not without cost. The force competed with the militia for scarce weapons, uniforms and other equipment, and the government struggled to prioritise requirements between the two services. Moreover, the need for the VDC passed quickly. After all, by mid-1942 the threat of invasion had passed but the home guard continued to grow. It was not until late 1943 that the government proved able to contract the scale of the organisation.

As the war progressed the government also made greater use of women in the military. Women began to replace male personnel in a large range of military tasks, including coastal and aerial defence positions, radar and radio operators, cipher and signal positions, as well as administrative and clerical roles. In 1942 the government called for a virtual doubling in the number of women serving in such tasks.

Simultaneously with improvements in its military capabilities Australia also had to address an inadequate infrastructure base, particularly in the country's north. Logistics are correctly known as the 'lifeblood of war', and without adequate support it is difficult, if not impossible, to project and sustain military power.[44] Viewed from the perspective of early 1942 the ability of the Australian countryside to serve as a base for war would not have looked promising to those tasked with taking the war to the Japanese.

When US military staff toured the north of Australia in late 1941 they were not impressed by what they found. After Brereton visited Batchelor, near Darwin, he described the airfield's condition as rudimentary – three US B17s had already been wrecked attempting to land there.[45] In early 1942 another US general commented that 'Australia is as undeveloped as the central United States was before the Civil War, or even more so.

Everything that is developed is on a miniature scale'.[46] This condition would not last long, however.

The need to transform Queensland into a base for war touched off a massive construction boom across the state, as well as the Northern Territory. Part of the work was done by Australian and US military engineers but the state construction authorities – such as the Queensland Main Roads Commission – were also critical. The Australian government formed a national body called the Allied Work Council, which raised its own labour force known as the Civil Constructional Corps (CCC). At its peak the CCC had an enrolment of more than 53 000 men and by the end of 1942 had completed over 750 jobs with another 1200 underway.[47]

The improvements these agencies implemented were profound. For example, by the war's end Queensland hosted over 200 airfields, with associated support facilities, and the Australian Army had built its critical Jungle Training Establishment in the Atherton Tablelands. The Allied Work Council laid 7500 kilometres of new roads while its workers improved many existing roads to a military traffic standard. New ports also appeared; the Brisbane River would host a US submarine base while Cairns became a major maritime trans-shipment hub. Without such infrastructure improvements the South West Pacific theatre would never have been able to serve as a line of counter attack against the Japanese.

CONCLUSION

Government defence thinkers had correctly assessed the risk Japan posed to the country. Yet, while identifying the correct policy objective a series of inter-war governments failed to adequately provide the means with which the nation's military forces might counter this threat. These governments took comfort in the false promise of the Singapore Strategy and they saw it as an opportunity to minimise defence capabilities and expenses in a period of increasing threat. When war came, the true nature of this 'peace dividend' was revealed to be a 'peace liability' and the nation's military forces had to struggle to regain capability that had been allowed to wane.

In the end Australia was never at a risk of invasion and the continent remained a minor theatre in the enemy's plans. This fact, however, should not forgive those who had reduced the nation's military forces to impotence. A national security policy that is based upon the kindness of your opponent is a hollow one.

Australia would muddle through in the end. It would reinvigorate its military strength and, in conjunction with the US, turn back the Japanese.

Yet, this re-animation of strength was left far too late. By the time the nation began to address the danger, the Japanese threat was real and immediate; a situation that could have been avoided – or at least made less grave – had the government enabled a more rational and honest defence policy.

Notes

1   The views expressed in this paper are the author's and do not reflect the official policy or position of the Australian Army, Australian Department of Defence or the Australian Government.

2   David Horner, 'Curtin and MacArthur at War: How Australia lost control of the war effort to an American general', *Wartime*, no. 2 (April 1998), p. 34.

3   Michael McKernan, *All In! Australia during the Second World War*, Thomas Nelson, Melbourne, 1983, pp. 103–4. For a refutation of the invasion threat see Peter Stanley, *Invading Australia: Japan and the Battle for Australia, 1942*, Viking, Camberwell, 2008.

4   Albert Palazzo, *The Australian Army: A History of its Organisation, 1901–2001*, Oxford University Press, South Melbourne, 2002, pp. 39–40.

5   See 'Report on the Military Defence of Australia by a Conference of Senior Officers of the Australian Military Forces', vols 1 and 2 (1920), AWM, item 20/7.

6   John McCarthy, *Australia and Imperial Defence 1918–39: A Study in Air and Sea Power*, University of Queensland Press, St Lucia, 1976, pp. 7–8.

7   George Jones, *From Private to Air Marshal: The Autobiography of Air Marshal Sir George Jones*, Greenhouse Publications, Richmond, 1988, p. 78.

8   David Horner, *High Command: Australia and Allied Strategy, 1939–1945*, Allen & Unwin, North Sydney, 1982, p. 23.

9   Quoted in ibid., p. 30.

10   John Robertson, 'The Distant War: Australia and Imperial Defence, 1919–1941', in Michael McKernan and Margaret Browne, *Australia in Two Centuries of War and Peace*, Australian War Memorial, Canberra, 1988, p. 227.

11   The Singapore Strategy is discussed in Ian Hamill, *The Strategic Illusion: The Singapore Strategy and the Defence of Australia and New Zealand, 1919–1942*, Singapore University Press, 1981; and McCarthy, *Australia and Imperial Defence*. See also Augustine Meaher IV, *The Road to Singapore: The Myth of the Great Betrayal*, Australian Scholarly Publishing, Melbourne, 2010.

12   'Minutes of the Council of Defence', 30 August 1923, National Archives of Australia, A9787, item 4.

13   'Appreciation of Australia's Position in Case of War in the Pacific', 23 March 1932, AWM 54, item 910/2/4, pp. 1–2.

14   Palazzo, *The Australian Army: A History of its Organisation*, pp. 106–8.

15   Paul Hasluck, *The Government and the People, 1939–1941*, Canberra, Australian War Memorial, 1956, p. 363.

16   Quoted in McKernan, *All In!* p. 25.

17   Gavin Long, *To Benghazi*, Australian War Memorial, Canberra, 1965, p. 41.

18 Jeff Grey, *The Australian Centenary History of Defence: The Australian Army*, Oxford University Press, South Melbourne, 2001, p. 121.

19 David Horner, 'Australia under Threat of Invasion', p. 248.

20 Hasluck, *The Government and the People, 1942–1945*, Canberra, Australian War Memorial, 1970, p. 38.

21 Jones, *From Private to Air Marshal*, p. 79.

22 The fallacy of this belief is addressed in Craig Stockings, 'There is an Idea that the Australian Soldier is a Born Soldier . . .' in Craig Stockings, ed., *Zombie Myths of Australian Military History*, New South, 2010, pp. 93–115.

23 John Curtin, 'The Task Ahead', *The Herald* (Melbourne), 27 December 1941.

24 'Cablegram – Secretary of State for Dominion Affairs to Prime Minister's Department', 5 October 1941, National Archives of Australia (NAA), A5954, item 555/7.

25 'Cablegram – Prime Minister Department to Secretary of State for Dominion Affairs', 11 October 1941, NAA, A5954, item 555/7.

26 'General Brereton's Visit', 13 November 1941, NAA, SP106/4, item SPCI/341.

27 'Air Defence in the Far East – United States Proposals', 13 October 1941, NAA, A2671, item 334/1941. See also, Lewis Brereton, *The Brereton Diaries: The War in the Air in the Pacific, Middle East and Europe, 3 October 1941 – 8 May 1945*, Da Capo Press, New York, 1976, pp. 25–30 and Douglas Gillison, *Royal Australian Air Force, 1939–1942*, Canberra, AWM, 1962, pp. 184–6.

28 'Minutes by Defence Committee held on Tuesday 7 October 1941, no. 142/ 1941', Defence of Rabaul, NAA, A2670, item 333/1941 and 'War Cabinet Minutes, 15 October 1941, Agendum no 333/1941, Defence of Rabaul', NAA, A2670, item 333/1941.

29 'War Cabinet Agendum, 344/1941, Air Defence in Far East – United States Proposals', 13 October 1941, NAA, A2671, item 344/1941.

30 'Notes on Conference at Victoria Barracks, Melbourne, 21 to 23 November, to discuss United States Projects', 23 November 1941, NAA, A2671, item 334/ 1941.

31 Brereton, *The Brereton Diaries*, p. 25.

32 Horner, 'Defending Australia in 1942', *War & Society*, vol. 11, no. 1, (May 1993), p. 6.

33 'Advisory War Council Minutes', 26 March 1942, NAA, A2684, item 967; and Horner, 'Australia under Threat of Invasion', pp. 259–60.

34 Hasluck, *The Government and the People, 1942–1945*, pp. 224–5.

35 Horner, 'Australia under Threat of Invasion', pp. 261–3.

36 'Notes for the Prime Minister's Statement on War Situation', 20 February 1942, AWM123, item 157.

37 'Strength and Present Dispositions of the Forces to Meet Scales of Attack', NAA, A2671/1, item 418/1941 and John McCarthy, 'The Imperial Commitment, 1939–41', *Australian Journal of Politics and History*, 23:2, August 1977, p. 181.

38 Frank Budden, *That Mob: The Story of the 55/53rd Australian Infantry Battalion, AIF*, Budden, Ashfield, 1973, pp. 1–2.

39 Russell Mathews, *Militia Battalion at War: The History of the 58th/59th Australian Infantry Battalion in the Second World War*, 58th/59th Battalion Association, Sydney, 1961, p. 1.
40 'Statement showing requirements of initial (fighting), training and 6 month reserve of certain items of equipment together with stocks available and percentage of those stocks in relation to the initial (fighting) requirements for AMF (order of battle) mobilisation, AIF in Australia and Armoured Division (AIF)', 30 November 1941, NAA, A2671/1, item 418/1841.
41 Palazzo, *The Australian Army: A History of its Organisation*, pp. 149–51.
42 'Advisory War Council Minutes', 17 June 1942, NAA, A2684, item 967.
43 Palazzo, *The Australian Army: A History of its Organisation*, pp. 186–8.
44 A reference to Julian Thompson, *Lifeblood of War; Logistics in Armed Conflict*, Brassey's, London, 1991.
45 Brereton, *The Brereton Diaries*, p. 25.
46 Quoted in Jeff Grey, *The Australian Centenary History of Defence, Volume 1*, p. 141.
47 See *The History of the Queensland Main Roads Commission During World War II, 1939–1945*, Government Printer, Brisbane, 1949 and 'Allied Work Council, Report June 1943', AWM70, item 233.

FURTHER READING
Hasluck, P., *The Government and the People, 1942–1945*, Australian War Memorial, Canberra, 1970.
Horner, D., *High Command: Australia and Allied Strategy 1939–1945*, North Sydney, Allen & Unwin, 1982.
Horner, D., 'Australia under threat of invasion', in M. McKernan and M. Browne, *Australia in Two Centuries of War and Peace*, Australian War Memorial, Canberra, 1988, pp. 245–71.
McCarthy, J., *Australia and Imperial Defence, 1918–1939, A Study in Air and Sea Power*, University of Queensland Press, St Lucia, 1976.
McKernan, M., *All In! Australia during the Second World War*, Thomas Nelson, Melbourne, 1983.
Meaher I. V. A., *The Road to Singapore: The Myth of British Betrayal*, Australian Scholarly Publishing, North Melbourne, 2010.
Oliver, P., *Raids on Australia: 1942 and Japan's Plans for Australia*, Australian Scholarly Publishing, North Melbourne, 2010.
Robertson, J., 'The Distant War: Australia and Imperial Defence, 1919–1941', in M. McKernan and M. Browne, *Australia in Two Centuries of War and Peace*, Australian War Memorial, Canberra, 1988, pp. 223–44.
Stanley, P., *Invading Australia: Japan and the Battle for Australia, 1942*, Viking, Camberwell, 2008.

CHAPTER 4

THE HOME FRONT AND THE AMERICAN PRESENCE IN 1942

Kate Darian-Smith

It was in the military context of early 1942 that the Australian government swiftly brought in comprehensive and far-reaching controls over all aspects of civilian life as a means of encouraging and enforcing an 'all-in' war effort and social unity across existing class, generational and political divisions. Although Australia had been at war since September 1939, with the 2nd AIF fighting in Europe and the Middle East, the home front had been geographically distant from the military theatre. With conflict now in Australia's immediate region, the relatively new Labor government of Prime Minister John Curtin was faced with the task of meeting the expanding requirements for labour and production so as to protect Australia in its 'darkest hour'.

This chapter outlines many of the changes on the Australian home front during 1942, as the nation experienced profound economic and social disruptions in a time of crisis. These upheavals included the unsettling of pre-war expectations about the role of Australian women in the workforce and domestic sphere, as the demands of war created new opportunities for women and publicly censured private behaviours deemed to be morally inappropriate. The 'friendly invasion' of thousands of US military personnel in Australia from 1942 until the end of the Second World War was to contribute to the aberrant and 'topsy-turvy' experiences of the Australian home front in ways that were often fleeting, but were also profound and long-lasting. Certainly, the bilateral relationships that developed between the two governments and on personal levels between the two peoples were to influence understandings of Australia's national identity and its sense of place within its region and the wider world in the postwar decades.

THE ALL-IN WAR EFFORT

With the entry of Japan into the Second World War, the Australian home front was visibly transformed as civil defence measures, particularly Air Raid Precautions (ARP), were accorded a new national urgency. Even before war was declared in September 1939, Prime Minister Robert Menzies had raised the importance of civil defence with the state premiers. By 1940, Australians were familiar via newsreel footage with the experiences of aerial bombing in Europe, particularly the German blitz on London and Coventry. British civil defence literature was widely circulated, and British training schemes were adopted with little regard for the vastly different conditions in Australia. Thousands of Australian men and women joined paramilitary organisations, often with their own distinctive uniforms, and trained in ARP work and first aid.

Photo 11 Sydney, September 1942. Air-raid practice at No. 113 Australian General Hospital. Members of the Voluntary Aid Detachment employed at the hospital don respirators before entering an air-raid shelter (AWM 026570).

In June 1941, the federal Department of Home Security was established to coordinate civil defence activities nationwide, and to standardise procedures such as warning signals, which varied across the states. In the aftermath of Pearl Harbor, Australians were advised to remain calm as national and local ARP drills were introduced, communal air-raid shelters erected, evacuation plans circulated and first-aid stations set up. By the end of 1941, dimmed or restricted night lighting – known as the brownout or blackout – was established as a protective measure in coastal Australian cities and in areas of strategic industrial and port activity. Australians busily hung black curtains or paper over their windows and dug hundreds of miles of air-raid trenches under the watchful gaze of ARP wardens.[1]

The brownout was a potent symbol of the crisis, and a constant reminder of the possibility of Japanese attack. The bombing of Darwin by the Japanese on 19 February 1942 was greeted with dismay throughout Australia. Although the censored account in daily newspapers grossly downplayed the 250 casualties, rumours were rife and tended to overestimate the damage. Barbed wire was strung along Australian beaches, and in remote Arnhem Land in Australia's north a special reconnaissance force of Yolngu men, under the direction of the anthropologist Donald Thomson, patrolled for signs of Japanese approach.[2] Plans for a scorched-earth policy in the case of invasion were in place, including the removal of signs at railway stations. When in May 1942 three Japanese midget submarines entered Sydney Harbour, shelling suburbs and sinking a converted ferry, this contributed to an ongoing sense of alarm among civilians.

The graphic thrust of government propaganda entreated civilians to be on the alert for signs of sabotage or suspicious behaviour among their neighbours and workmates. Those Australian residents of German or Italian origin had already been registered as 'enemy aliens' earlier in the war, suffering restrictions and in some cases internment. In December 1941, over 1000 Japanese living in Australia, mainly in northern pearling towns such as Broome, were all immediately interned. War in the Pacific also led to a higher internment rate for those Italians nationals, Australia's largest non-British group, who were living in north Queensland where there was a highly regional and extreme response to issues of national security.[3] By early 1942, the pool of 'refugee' and 'enemy' aliens in Australia was directed to work on building infrastructure under the CCC.[4]

Although there were occasional shortages of goods in Australia during 1939–41, most notably with the rationing of petrol, the onset of the Pacific War swiftly introduced a new 'austerity' approach to production and

Photo 12 Melbourne, June 1942. Crowds queue for their ration books in a suburban issuing centre (AWM 136476).

consumption on the home front. The mechanisms for comprehensive rationing and control of labour were swiftly enacted, supported by extensive official propaganda and enforced by coercive measures. At Christmas 1941, the Curtin Government banned annual leave for workers and festive advertising, encouraging Australians to contribute to austerity war loans.

The Rationing Commission controlled the supply of goods and services, and Australia was increasingly under pressure to meet expanding military requirements, exports to Britain and US Lend-Lease contracts. By June 1942, ration books were issued to all civilians. A system of coupons exchanged for clothing and household goods, based on the British model, was introduced. Tea and sugar were rationed, and later in the war this was extended to eggs and meat. There were also frequent shortages of fruit and vegetables, and of everyday household items ranging from sanitary napkins to clothes pegs, with luxuries such as chocolate, beer and cigarettes generally difficult to obtain. Not surprisingly, a black market operated. The comparatively higher wages of the US forces, and their access to goods such as cigarettes and chocolate through the lavishly supplied PX (Postal Exchange) canteens, meant that US military personnel were perceived as well-stocked and correspondingly generous in providing Australian civilians with gifts such as cigarettes and alcohol.

The home front was also transformed in 1942 by the control of labour, and the organisation of 'protected' or essential industries and occupations, under the Manpower Directorate. All Australians over 16 years of age were required to register with the Directorate and carry identity cards. Although the emphasis was on the regulation of labour, the Australian population had never been so occupationally and physically mobile: workers moved from rural areas for industrial jobs, from the cities to the country to undertake farm work, and from all around the nation to enlist in the military. Recruitment into the armed services was seen as the national priority, and the women's auxiliary branches played an increasingly prominent role in 'releasing' men from non-combat roles for active duty.

Moreover, war transformed the expectations of women's roles within the paid workforce. In the First World War, Australian women had been engaged in copious voluntary work, but unlike British women had not been mobilised into industry. By 1939, the Australian government recognised the economic importance of women's voluntary labour, officially registering those who were available for work in civil defence or with organisations such as the Red Cross. For women seeking paid work, the opportunities were open, and there were considerable benefits available through overtime and bonuses. Women were actively sought by the Manpower Directorate for essential munitions and factory work, and through the Women's Land Army into agricultural tasks. By 1944, the wartime employment of women in Australia peaked with 855 000 women in paid labour, representing 25 per cent of the total workforce.[5]

More significant than this numerical contribution, which represented in real terms only a 5 per cent increase in women's paid employment since 1939, was the high profile in the daily press and newsreels accorded to women who took over men's positions 'for the duration'. Only a few, such as women who replaced men as tram conductors, were awarded full male rates of pay by the Commonwealth's Women's Employment Board, which decided on whether women were performing exactly the same work as men. In some cases, married women were allowed to return temporarily to their pre-wedding employment as teachers or clerks. In other instances, including in the armed forces, women learned many new skills in communications, the operation of heavy machinery or management.

By 1942, a greater proportion of middle-class women was entering paid labour, which had gained a new respectability and alignment with feminine patriotism. Working-class women were moving from domestic service into other work, and would never return to work as servants in large numbers. Increasing tensions between the traditional roles of women as homemakers and mothers, and their new national importance as war workers were to be aired publicly in magazines such as the *Australian Women's Weekly*, and in newspapers and on radio. Underpinning these concerns were the more overt expressions of female sexuality and consumerism that had dominated popular culture and advertising in the inter-war years, and the historical reconceptualisation of a new and modern femininity that was to be strengthened during the Second World War – particularly with the arrival of the US forces on the Australian home front.[6]

THE ARRIVAL OF THE US FORCES

As the crisis following Japan's entry into the war unfolded, Prime Minister John Curtin's famous New Year message to the nation was published in the Melbourne *Herald* newspaper on 27 December 1941. It declared a refusal to perceive war in the Pacific as 'subordinate' to the fighting in Europe, and that 'The Australian government regards the Pacific struggle as primarily one in which the United States and Australia must have the fullest say in the direction of the democracies' fighting plans'.[7]

Australia was, of course, heavily and expediently reliant on the US presence in the Asia-Pacific, and although older loyalties to Britain were stretched they were by no means broken. Despite the disparities in military power, the promotion of Australia and the US as 'Pacific partners', sharing similar values and a democratic spirit, was to be the cornerstone of public relations exercises during the war.[8]

This was evident on 14 March 1942, when Curtin broadcast via radio networks across North America a heartfelt plea. His speech was delivered on the eve of a visit to the US by H. V. Evatt, Minister for External Affairs, to shore up additional resources for the Pacific theatre. Curtin told the 'men and women of the United States' that he spoke from one 'united people' to another:

> On the great waters of the Pacific Ocean war now breathes its bloody steam. From the skies of the Pacific pours down a deathly hail. In the countless islands of the Pacific the tide of war flows madly. For you in America; for us in Australia, it is flowing badly … We never regarded the Pacific as a segment of the great struggle. We did not insist that it was the primary theatre of war, but we did say, and events have so far, unhappily, proved us right, that the loss of the Pacific can be

disastrous ... Australia is the last bastion between the West Coast of America and the Japanese. If Australia goes, the Americas are wide open ... I say to you that the saving of Australia is the saving of America's west coast.[9]

Just days later, on 18 March 1942, the Australian press officially announced that substantial numbers of US soldiers were now in Australia. In actuality, thousands of US troops had been disembarking in Australia since December 1941.[10] The headquarters for the SWPA were established in Melbourne, primarily to be close to Australian Army and Air Force bases. MacArthur arrived in Melbourne on 17 March, after his dramatic flight from the Philippines via Darwin and Alice Springs and a train from Adelaide, and was greeted by a cheering crowd of thousands of people. He cut a dashing figure, with a showy style of leadership unknown in Australia that elicited much excitement. His black Wolseley limousine, with the number plate 'USA-1' became a familiar site on Melbourne's streets, and the press followed the shopping expeditions of his wife, Jean MacArthur, and their young son, Arthur MacArthur, in great detail.[11]

MacArthur found his troops already established at Camp Pell, in Melbourne's Royal Park, and further facilities to meet the US requirements were quickly erected. Public buildings, including the brand new Royal Melbourne Hospital and several schools, were requisitioned for US military use. Officers were accommodated in the city's most prestigious hotels. The US military authorities set up their Hospitality Bureau, and soon dances and other social events were organised in association with local church and community groups, and young Australian women were recruited to attend as dance partners. Clubs such as the Myer Emporium's Dug-Out provided facilities for US personnel on leave, and soon hamburger and hot dog stalls opened to cater to what were at the time considered exotic culinary tastes.[12]

The recreational facilities of Melbourne – and indeed of other Australian cities and towns – were soon found to be inadequate. This was mostly due to the heavy demand on cafés, cinemas and dancehalls in a city that was already bursting at the seams with an influx of war workers, and where there was much substandard and overcrowded housing. By June 1942 there were 30 000 US servicemen stationed in Melbourne. In the evenings, thousands of GIs and their civilian friends would wander through Melbourne's streets and parklands, down to the seaside pleasure strip at St Kilda. Soldiers, many in their teens, would be entertained in civilian homes, where they were 'adopted' by Australian families for the term of their stay.

Both Australians and Americans were ill-informed about each other's country, culture and history. The US troops were issued with a *Pocket Guide to Australia* when they disembarked, to explain social customs and language, and the Australian public was subjected to an official campaign to explain American sports, habits and food preferences. As the host nation, Australians eagerly took measures to make the Americans feel welcome, such as playing the 'Star Spangled Banner' after 'God Save the Queen' at the cinema, and through the inclusion of additional news about the US, including sporting scores, in the press.

On the whole, Australians knew far more about the US than Americans knew about Australia. The impact of the American 'invasion' of Australia in 1942 was part of a longer history of the flow of ideas, people and finance between the United States and Australia. American traders and seamen, and even the occasional American convict, were to be found in the early colonial period, and there was a strong American presence on the Australian goldfields in the 1850s. Recent scholarly work, particularly in transnational history, has explored the intellectual, technical and economic exchanges between the United States and Australia from the mid-19th century. The influence of American ideas in Australia among politicians, trade unions and intellectuals during the Federation period and beyond can be traced in relation to such matters as race, immigration and environmental management.[13]

In the 1920s and 1930s, economic ties between Australia and the US had strengthened. Ford, Chrysler and General Motors plants in Australia manufactured local replicas of American models. Sunbeam electrical goods, Heinz canned foods, Coca-Cola and Johnson and Johnson pharmaceutical products were widely available. More significantly, Australians typically went to the cinema two or three times per week, and US films dominated Australian mass culture, proving considerably more popular than 'highbrow' English alternatives. US films provided stereotypical representations of the American way of life, mainly of Hollywood or New York. The equation of American culture with commercialisation and popular consumption meant that Australian intellectuals were already discussing the Americanisation of Australian society, and contrasting this with the cultural values of Britain, well before the Second World War.[14]

By August 1942 there were 100 000 US troops located throughout the Australian continent. This number was to peak at 119 000 in September

1943, and to decline markedly in the later years of the war. Overall, between 1942–5, almost 1 million US troops passed through Australian towns and ports en route to military engagement in the Asia-Pacific region. For many, their time in Australia was transitory; for some, such as the men of the 1st Marine Division, it involved eight months' rest and recreation after intense fighting at Guadalcanal in the Solomon Islands.[15] The US military presence was perhaps to have the greatest impact in the remote areas of northern Australia, and in the Queensland towns of Townsville, Rockhampton and the state capital of Brisbane.[16] But the American 'invasion' was experienced in many other locations during 1942, as these two examples demonstrate.

On 22 February 1942, US troops arrived in Western Australia and by early March they had established a naval presence that was to continue until the end of the war. The port of Fremantle was established as the base for submarines and repairs to naval vessels for the SWPA. In Perth, the US Navy established a base for Catalina Flying Boats at Crawley Bay on the Swan River, with mess and other facilities at the University of Western Australia. By March 1942, US officers and enlisted men, as well as a small number of military nurses, had a notable presence at Perth's hotels, cinemas and as guests in the homes of many local people. On Independence Day, a large party to celebrate the American presence was organised at the Perth Zoo and public relations activities undertaken by the military authorities of both countries encouraged cross-national relations to proceed smoothly. It was, according to Anthony J. Barker, the 'confident self-sufficiency rather than numbers' that distinguished the Americans from the Dutch and British military groups also based in Fremantle and nearby Perth.[17]

The Victorian regional town of Ballarat, with a population of around 15 000 and a short train journey inland from the port facilities in Melbourne, was to host three distinct groups of US service personnel over the course of 1942. On 28 February, over 5000 men from the US Army Taskforce 6814 were billeted in private homes for a one-week sojourn. This initial encounter was to leave a lasting and favourable impression on Ballarat residents, and on 8 March they opened their homes again to almost 3000 men of the US Air Forces, who remained in the town until they departed for New Guinea in May. By this stage, the Americans had constructed a camp at Victoria Park on the town's western fringe, which accommodated over 2000 men from the 147th and 148th Field Artillery from July until October 1942.[18]

In Ballarat, the civilian experience of hosting US troops was, as in other regional towns, particularly intense. Ballarat resident Lorna Ellis remembered that in February 1942, US soldiers:

> ... came up Sturt Street with their big trucks ... and Ballarat grew up overnight. We turned from a little conservative country town into this surging rage of men. And they came down Lydiard Street, they came off the train ... and the brass band played, you know, an *American* brass band ... and all of us girls just *stood* there ... Everybody came out to welcome them. You know, we looked at all these men as though they'd come from outer space.[19]

Australian writer Henrietta Drake-Brockman set her wartime novel, *The Fatal Days*, in Ballarat during February to March 1942 at a time when the population was increasingly anxious about Australia's vulnerability from enemy attack.[20] Published in 1947, the book was regarded by the literary critic and novelist Miles Franklin as an informative account of the Americans in Australia during the Second World War.[21] *The Fatal Days* traces the arrival of the GIs to Ballarat, their warm reception and interactions with the local people. Drake-Brockman's narrative, however, is less concerned with understanding the GIs than ensuring that they (and her readers) learn lessons about Australia's environment, culture and history, including key historical events like the miners' rebellion at the Eureka Stockade and the Gallipoli campaign. In this way, the US military presence serves as a literary vehicle for exploring Australian nationalism and its achievements.[22] Other Australian home-front novels, such as Dymphna Cusack's and Florence James's *Come In Spinner* and Xavier Herbert's *Soldiers' Women*, were more confronting about the American presence, examining their romantic entanglements with Australian women and a society in the throes of wartime upheaval.[23]

SEXUALITY, RACE AND TURMOIL ON THE HOME FRONT

During 1942, the SWPA general headquarters was initially located in Melbourne, and the city was the first location to experience on a mass scale the arrival of the US force. With a population of 1 million people, and an important hub of the national munitions industry, the 'management' of relations between US forces and Australian civilians was tested in Melbourne.

With thousands of young Australian men away from home on active military service, the arrival of the US forces in Melbourne evened up the ratio between the sexes. The GIs, however, were perceived by the Australian people to differ from Australian men in their presentation and character. The media delighted in such stories, inviting Australian women to make cross-national comparisons and in doing so open up discussions about forms of masculinity. Existing Australian assumptions gleaned from the movies cast the American male as smooth, sexually sophisticated and comfortable in the presence of women.

The Australian obsession with American film stars was evident as US Headquarters was besieged with enquiries as to whether James Cagney and James Stewart were serving in Australia; one Melbourne woman insisted that she had seen Clark Gable in an officer's uniform. The stylish uniforms of the GIs certainly bolstered their glamour. While the Australian military forces were issued with a single uniform in khaki wool, US soldiers were allocated two sets of clothes, and the US Army encouraged regular laundering and stressed personal hygiene. All US soldiers wore a tie, an accessory only granted to Australian officers.

Photo 13 Melbourne. US sailors and soldiers on their arrival in Australia quickly made friends wherever they went. Here, two US servicemen are strolling arm-in-arm with Australian girls along the banks of the Yarra River (AWM 011543).

American masculinity was also popularly perceived to have a darker side: that of sexual deviance. Certain US military practices, such as displays of posters of pin-up girls in mess rooms, drawings of nude women on Air Force bombers and the widespread contraceptive advice offered through as military medical services contributed to an image of the US servicemen being 'oversexed'. So, too, did the American social practice of approaching women blatantly in the street, and a propensity to display physical affection such as kissing or embracing far more publicly than Australians were accustomed to.

The arrival of the US forces in Melbourne coincided with growing concerns expressed by the police, politicians, the medical profession and religious organisations about the role of women in wartime. Industrial growth and an open labour market had brought social and economic changes for women, and many young women were living away from home for the first time and earning relatively high wages. They were also getting engaged and married at a younger age than prior to the war, swept up in rapid courtships driven by what commentators referred to as 'war fever'. Oral histories reveal the uncertainties and emotional excitement experienced by young women during the Second World War, while newspapers and archival records reveal increasing concerns about women's immoral behaviour.[24]

With thousands of single males in the city of Melbourne in 1942, there was an increase in prostitution. However, the city's moral vanguard was more concerned with monitoring the activities of what were referred to as 'good time honeys', young women who openly enjoyed themselves with US servicemen at dances and in cafés and were seen fraternising with the soldiers at Flinders Street Station or at St Kilda beach.

In order to prevent the perceived immoral actions of women, the police developed a small bicycle squad who would patrol Melbourne's parks and the banks of the Yarra River at night, and urge couples to go home. The Salvation Army also organised a similar night patrol, which aimed to clear the darkened city streets. There were sermons from the pulpit and on the radio urging moral restraint. Several artists in Melbourne, including Albert Tucker, Arthur Boyd and John Percival depicted the wartime city as a world turned upside town. Tucker's famous series 'Images of Modern Evil' contains images of unchecked sexuality in city streets and cinema aisles, and his well-known 'Victory Girls' shows women in red, white and blue skirts in the company of leering Australian and US soldiers.

To restore order to the home front, both state and federal legislation was enacted during 1942 that sought to control the sexual behaviour of women, or more specifically, that of young working-class women, considered to be the most vulnerable social group. Women under 21 were prohibited from drinking alcohol, although the age of alcohol consumption for men remained at 18 years. This was based on the belief that women were more likely to be sexually active if drinking. The sale of condoms and other contraceptives was limited, a measure that sought to inhibit the sexual activity of unmarried couples and encourage married couples to have children; during the Second World War there was mounting public concern in Australia about increasing the birth rate as a national priority.

Not only were charges of vagrancy used to detain young women who appeared to be living with US soldiers, but new legislation – that disregarded civil liberties – meant that women who were suspected of carrying a sexually transmitted infection could be required by the police to undertake a medical examination. While such inspections were infrequent in Melbourne, similar powers were granted to the police elsewhere in Australia, and were enforced in some instances in Queensland.[25] US military authorities were particularly outspoken in supporting the introduction of such restrictive legislation, and exerted pressure on the police to raid hotels and dance palaces to 'catch' young women with no fixed address. Their major concern was the growing rates of sexually transmissable infection among the troops; before 1944, when penicillin was available, syphilis was a debilitating affliction, requiring on average about 60 days in hospital and the loss of many 'fighting hours'. Sex education was offered to Australian and US soldiers who were going on leave, although the advice given by the US medical service was more detailed. It was claimed that it was 'ordinary' women, rather than prostitutes, who were more likely to be at risk of spreading disease; men were seen as the 'victims' in these circumstances. Posters in Melbourne's public male toilets, and at the military camps, warned that one hour of pleasure 'could last a lifetime' and entreated 'Don't Risk it Feller, Use a Sheath'.[26]

In May 1942, with 30 000 US soldiers based in Melbourne, the serial murders of three women appeared to confirm perceptions of American sexual depravity and contributed to growing tensions in US–Australian relations on the home front. The police were at a loss when the partially clothed bodies of the women were found in public places. The civilian reaction, particularly that of women, was widespread, and directed towards the Americans as responsible. On 23 May it was announced that

US Private Edward Leonski, who had been stationed at Camp Pell, was in custody and had confessed to the murders. Curtin announced that members of the US forces breaching Australian civil law would be tried by a US military court, a radical departure from usual legal conduct. MacArthur insisted the trial proceed quickly, as a public relations gesture to curb anti-American sentiment. In July, Leonski was court-martialled and found guilty, and was hung at Pentridge Goal in November.

In the aftermath of the Leonski murders, some parents warned their daughters not to associate with US servicemen. In some instances, Australian women in the company of a US soldier would be viewed with some suspicion as promiscuous and even unpatriotic by betraying an Australian husband or boyfriend. This was a perception Australian soldiers were particularly keen to promote. The portrayal of Australian women as sexually aggressive and 'on the make' was to increase over the course of the war, including in the US. This was accompanied by growing reports of Australian civilians overcharging US soldiers for taxi fares, drinks and food, and the general growth of the black market.

On 21 July 1942, MacArthur and his staff and troops moved north to Brisbane to be closer to the fighting, and established a command hub in the AMP Building in Queen Street. Although MacArthur left Australia in 1944, never to return, some elements of his Headquarters remained until the Japanese surrender in September 1945. Brisbane was much smaller than Melbourne, with a population of around 300 000, but shared an absence of facilities and infrastructure to cope with thousands of US military personnel.

There had been a small US presence in Brisbane since the beginning of the year, and unlike Melbourne the city accommodated significant numbers of African-American soldiers. In the 1940s, Australia clung to the racially restrictive White Australia Policy in relation to immigration. Indigenous Australians had no citizenship rights, although this did not prohibit their enlistment in the Australian military; as many as 3000 Indigenous people did so.[27] The Curtin government had initially rejected the inclusion of African-American troops, but US military authorities were insistent they were an essential component of the racially segregated US Army. It was agreed that African-Americans, who were mainly in engineering and other supports units, would generally be dispatched to the Northern Territory and remote areas, away from the bulk of Australian civilians.[28]

In March 1942, prolonged riots erupted in South Brisbane between white and African-American GIs. At the heart of the riot was the resentment by white American soldiers that African-Americans were fraternising with

Australian women, and were allowed into the same dancehalls and even brothels as white US soldiers.[29] As a result, in Brisbane, and in other northern towns, segregated facilities and zoned areas for white and African-American GIs were put in place, though this was more at the insistence of American than Australian authorities. When these segregated areas were breached, as happened in September 1942 at Ipswich but also in several other recorded instances, further confrontations occurred within the US forces.

Brawls and rioting, often fuelled by alcohol and sparked by tensions over access to Australian women, were not uncommon between US and Australian soldiers. In November 1942, what has become known as the 'battle of Brisbane' erupted in that town over two nights, leaving one Australian soldier dead and many hundreds of US and Australian servicemen wounded. Similar incidents occurred in other cities and towns, including a 'battle of Melbourne' in early 1943. With large numbers of young men crowded together, it was probably inevitable that in a wartime climate national rivalries would emerge. In the latter years of the war these were not only about access to women but reflected tensions over MacArthur's deployment of Australian forces in the Asia-Pacific, and for both sides, an increased war-weariness.

CONCLUSION

Following Allied success at the battles of the Coral Sea and Midway Island in May and June 1942, and subsequently at Kokoda in New Guinea and the Solomon Islands, the military situation in the Pacific theatre improved. Civilian morale correspondingly followed. Civil defence drills were relaxed, and although the brownout was to remain in Melbourne until the end of the war, air-raid trenches soon filled with water and became a hazard. While Australian authorities remained focused on industrial expansion and the control of labour, by 1943 attention had also moved towards detailed planning for postwar reconstruction. Central to this was the emphasis on the rebuilding of family and domestic life after the turmoil of war, including the demobilisation of the military and the move of women from the paid workforce back to the home.

US forces continued to be based in large numbers in Australia until 1945, although by the latter years of the war this was primarily in Brisbane and northern Australia rather than in the southern states. There is no doubt that deep friendships developed between American soldiers and many

Australian families, and in some cases these were maintained via correspondence and into subsequent generations for several decades. For some Australian women, wartime romance turned into a more permanent union. Up to 15 000 Australian women were to marry Americans during or after the war, travelling in 'bride ships' to the US in 1946 and 1947, where they began new lives.

At a strategic level, relations between the US and Australia were marked in the immediate postwar years by disagreement over matters including trade and investment, Pacific air transport and the terms of the peace treaty with Japan. In 1951, however, the signing of the ANZUS Treaty between Australia, New Zealand and the United States cemented the defence alliance forged in the Second World War throughout the Pacific region.

In more general terms, the influence of US material products was to increase during the war, and was evident in Australian patterns of consumerism and the growth of US imports and economic investment in Australia in the postwar decades. While the GIs introduced new foods, customs, music and words to the Australian population, the mass media was probably more important in the circulation of Americanised popular culture. However, the American presence did force Australians to become more educated about themselves, with much public debate about Australian history and social patterns and why these differed from those in the United States.

It also opened up Australians to a more ethnically diverse national group, and the Italian and Polish names among the US servicemen arguably assisted in the preparation of Australians for the large-scale migration scheme of the postwar period. For some Indigenous people, the model of African-American soldiers was also to contribute to their later political activity. The upheaval of the social and economic position of women, and the meanings of femininity, masculinity and patriotism that occurred on the Australian home front during the Second World War went on to surface in new ways in Australian youth cultures of the later 20th century, and continued to shape public commentary on the American influences on Australian society.

Notes

1   For discussions of civil defence see J. Fisher, 'Civil Defence Organisation', Appendix 1, in P. Hasluck, *The Government and the People 1942–1945*, Australian War Memorial, Canberra, 1970, pp. 637–67; for a case study of Melbourne and Victoria, see K. Darian-Smith, *On the Home Front: Melbourne in Wartime 1939–1945*, Melbourne University Press, Melbourne, 2009, pp. 15–49.

2   D. Thomson and N. Petersen, *Donald Thomson in Arnhem Land*, rev. edn, Melbourne University Press, Melbourne, 2003.

3   See M. Bevege, *Behind Barbed Wire: Internment in Australia during World War II*, Queensland University Press, St Lucia, 1993; K. Neumann, *In the Interest of National Security: Civilian Internment in Australia during World War II*, National Archives of Australia, Canberra, 2006.

4   P. Hasluck, *The Government and the People 1939–1941*, Australian War Memorial, Canberra, 1952, pp. 593–8.

5   Statistics quotes from R. White, 'War and Australian Society', in M. McKernan and N. M. Browne (eds), *Australia: Two Centuries of War and Peace*, Australian War Memorial and Allen & Unwin, Canberra, 1988, p. 410–12.

6   See M. Lake, 'Female Desires: The meaning of World War Two', in J. Damousi, and M. Lake, *Gender and War: Australians at War in the Twentieth Century*, Cambridge University Press, Melbourne, 1995, pp. 60–80.

7   *Herald* (Melbourne), 27 December 1941.

8   See G. Johnston, *Pacific Partners*, World Book, New York, 1944 for an account of Australia at war written for an American audience.

9   J. Curtin, Broadcast to a Network of United States, Canadian and South American Radio Stations, 14 March 1942, National Archives of Australian (NSW), ABC Broadcasts Series SP300/1. Box 7.

10 See Chapter 3 for details on Australian–US military ties prior to 7 December 1941.

11 *Herald* (Melbourne), 21 March 1942.

12 The account of Melbourne during wartime in this chapter is drawn from K. Darian-Smith, *On the Home Front: Melbourne in Wartime 1939–45*.

13 See, for instance, H. Reynolds and M. Lake, *Drawing the Global Colour Line: Whiteman's Countries and the International Challenge of Racial Equality*, Cambridge University Press, Cambridge, 2008.

14 See P. Bell and R. Bell (eds), *Americanization and Australia*, UNSW Press, Sydney 1998; P. Bell, *Implicated: The United States in Australia*, Oxford University Press, Melbourne, 1993.

15 See exhibition website 'Over-Paid, Over-Sexed and Over Here? The US Marines in wartime Melbourne', City Gallery, Melbourne, 2010, curated by Darian-Smith, K. and Jenzen, R. http://history.unimelb.edu.au/overhere/indexmain.html

16 The most detailed account of the US wartime presence in Australia is E. D. Potts and A. Potts, *Yanks Down Under 1941–45: The American Impact on Australia*, Oxford University Press, Melbourne, 1985. See also R. Campbell, *Heroes and Lovers: A Question of National Identity*, Allen & Unwin, Sydney, 1989; J. H. Moore, *Over-Sexed, Over-Paid, and Over Here*, University of Queensland Press, St Lucia, 1981; and D. Phillips, *Ambivalent Allies: Myth and Reality in the Australian-American Relationship*, Penguin, Ringwood, 1988.

17 A. J. Barker, 'Yanks in Western Australia: The Impact of United States Servicemen', J. Gregory (ed), *On the Homefront: Western Australia and World War II*, University of Western Australia Press, Nedlands, 1996, p. 121.

18 See R. Jenzen, 'A Home Away From Home: American servicemen in wartime Melbourne, 1942–1943', unpublished Honours thesis, Department of

History, University of Melbourne, 1992. Around 5800 men from the First
Marine Division were also stationed in Ballarat from January to September
1943, following their evacuation from Guadalcanal.
19 Interview with L. Ellis, in R. Jenzen, 'A Home Away From Home', p. 7.
20 H. Drake-Brockman, *The Fatal Days*, Angus & Robertson, Sydney,
1947.
21 See M. Franklin quoted in *The Argus*, 21 February 1952; M. Franklin,
*Laughter, Not for a Cage: Notes on Australian writing, with biographical
emphasis on the struggles, function, and achievements of the novel in three
half-centuries*, Angus & Robertson, Sydney, 1956.
22 D. Coates, 'Damn(ed) Yankees: The Pacific's Not Pacific Anymore', *Antipodes*,
2001. pp. 123–9.
23 D. Cusackand F. James, *Come in Spinner*, Angus Robertson, Sydney, 1951;
X. Herbert, *Soldiers' Women*, Angus & Robertson, Sydney, 1961.
24 For example, see L. Connors, L. Finch, K. Saunders and H. Taylor, *Australia's
Frontline: Remembering the 1939–45 War*, University of Queensland Press,
St Lucia, 1992; K. Darian-Smith, 'War Stories: Remembering the Australian
Home Front during the Second World War', in K. Darian-Smith and
P. Hamilton (eds), *Memory and History in Twentieth Century Australia*,
Oxford University Press, 1997, pp. 137–57; R. Campbell, *Heroes and Lovers:
A Question of National Identity*, Allen & Unwin, Sydney, 1989.
25 K. Saunders, *War on the Homefront: State Intervention in Queensland 1938–
1948*, University of Queensland Press, St Lucia, 1993.
26 Such posters gave public health warnings about 'amateur' and professional
prostitutes, and included lurid images.
27 R. Hall, *The Black Diggers: Aborigines and Torres Strait Islanders in the
Second World War*, Allen & Unwin, Sydney, 1989.
28 Potts and Potts, *Yanks Down Under*, p. 14.
29 K Saunders, 'In a Cloud of Lust: Black GIs and sex in World War II', in
J. Damousi and M. Lake (eds), *Gender and War: Australians at War in the
Twentieth Century*, Cambridge University Press, Melbourne, 1995 pp. 178–90.

FURTHER READING
Barker, A. J. and Jackson, L., *Fleeting Attraction: A Social History of American
Servicemen in Western Australia During the Second World War*, University of
Western Australia Press, Nedlands, 1996.
Beaumont, J. (ed.), *Australia's War 1939–45*, Allen & Unwin, Sydney, 1996.
Damousi, J. and Lake, M. (eds), *Gender and War: Australians at War in the
Twentieth Century*, Cambridge University Press, Melbourne, 1995.
Darian-Smith, K., *On the Home Front: Melbourne in Wartime 1939–45*, 2nd edn,
Melbourne University Press, Melbourne, 2009.
Gregory, J. (ed.), *On the Homefront: Western Australia and World War II*,
University of Western Australia Press, Nedlands, 1996.
Hasluck, P., *The Government and the People, Volume 1: 1939–1941*, Australian
War Memorial, Canberra, 1952. www.awm.gov.au/histories/second_world_
war/volume.asp?levelID=67916

Hasluck, P., *The Government and the People, Volume 2: 1942–1945*, Australian War Memorial, Canberra, 1970. www.awm.gov.au/histories/second_world_war/volume.asp?levelID=67917

McKernan, M., *All-In! Australia During the Second World War*, Thomas Nelson, Melbourne, 1983.

Neumann, K., *In the Interest of National Security: Civilian Internment in Australia during World War II*, National Archives of Australia, Canberra, 2006.

Potts, E. D. and A., *Yanks Down Under 1941–45: The American Impact on Australia*, Oxford University Press, Melbourne, 1985.

Saunders, K., *War on the Homefront: State Intervention in Queensland 1938–1948*, University of Queensland Press, St Lucia, 1993.

CHAPTER 5

'DANGERS AND PROBLEMS UNPRECEDENTED AND UNPREDICTABLE'

THE CURTIN GOVERNMENT'S RESPONSE TO THE THREAT

Ross McMullin

What happened in 1942 remains central to Australians' perceptions of our leaders and their comparative performance. The widespread acceptance that John Curtin remains the greatest prime minister that Australia has ever had stems from how he responded to the crisis of 1942. Not so well known is the extent of the daunting challenges that he and his government had to overcome in order to provide effective national leadership.

For a start, Curtin and his government were inexperienced, and had a precarious hold on the reins of office. Also, Curtin's own background and personality hardly equipped him for the circumstances of 1942. Furthermore, he and his colleagues were all too aware of their party's history, which gave little basis for confidence that they would be able to govern effectively in the crisis.

THE BACK STORY

The Australian Labor Party (ALP), founded in 1891, had advanced so rapidly that it had become by far the most successful party of its type in the world. It formed the first labour government in the world – in 1899 in Queensland – which lasted for a week. It formed the first national labour government in the world – in 1904 under Chris Watson – which lasted about four months. It formed the first national labour government in the world with a majority in both houses of parliament – in 1910 under Andrew Fisher.

But the ALP became the victim of its own early success when, unlike any other party of its type, it was in government during the First World War, with the responsibility of administering the war effort in a conflict beyond anyone's expectation and experience. The pressures and stresses of being in government at such a difficult time resulted in a devastating rupture, which remains the biggest of all the various splits in the party's long history.

In 1929, long after the First World War split, the ALP was just emerging from this damaging experience, and had just regained office for the first time in 13 years, when the startling collapse of the United States stock market ushered in the calamitous Great Depression. Once again the federal Labor government disintegrated during the crisis, this time in a three-way split. When the prime minister of that government, Jim Scullin, was asked later if he would like to write a memoir of his time in office he replied: 'It nearly killed me to live through it. It would kill me to write about it'.[1]

Federal Labor was not in good shape for much of the 1930s. The split during the Depression had eroded confidence in the party's aims and even its fundamental purpose, its raison d'être. The continuing fallout from the split had left the party with a breakaway group of Langites, followers of the maverick state leader Jack Lang. Their leader in federal parliament was Jack Beasley, who after voting to bring down the Scullin government had acquired the nickname 'Stabber Jack'.

Curtin, who succeeded Scullin as leader in 1935, was widely criticised, including from within his party, for being diffident and ineffective as ALP leader and as opposition leader. An influential powerbroker in the party, Clarrie Fallon, put it this way: 'There are going to be difficult times ahead, and to have a Labor government in power then, with Jack Curtin at its head, would be a bloody calamity'.[2]

Curtin had a very difficult task. At one stage he was heard to grumble that he only ever seemed to visit New South Wales in order to participate in yet another unity conference that proved to be yet another failed attempt to build cohesion in the party's state branch. The disunity in NSW prevented the ALP from winning the 1940 federal election, when the party fell narrowly short of victory and gained two illustrious acquisitions in Ben Chifley and Bert Evatt. There was a hung parliament, and Robert Menzies, who had struggled to be convincing as a war leader, was now reliant on the support of two independent MPs.

With the Menzies government vulnerable, some Labor MPs, notably Evatt, were frustrated with Curtin's reluctance to press wholeheartedly for power. Curtin was wary of taking office without a majority in either chamber of parliament; as a backbencher he had seen firsthand how the Scullin government's difficulties had been increased by its lack of a Senate majority. His hesitancy was also influenced by his lack of confidence in his own ability to measure up as a war leader. But he also sensed, correctly as it turned out, that if as opposition leader he showed himself to be principled and measured rather than hungry for office at the earliest opportunity, this would help him attain the kind of political authority and legitimacy that would be vital later on if he did end up becoming prime minister in a minority government.

This back story is essential to any analysis of the Curtin government, because it critically influenced the perceptions and perspectives of the main players, Curtin especially, in the lead up to the crisis of 1942. One pleasing development for him was that in February 1941 reunification of the ALP and the Langites was at last accomplished. Later that year, in October, the independents in federal parliament switched their parliamentary support to Labor, and Curtin was sworn in as prime minister.

RESPONDING TO THE CRISIS OF 1941–2

The Curtin government began with impressive zeal, dedication and cohesion. All the accumulated frustration and rancour concerning the right approach in opposition vanished overnight now that there was important work to be tackled urgently. Suspicions about Evatt's craving for office became admiration for the astonishing 'Doc', who maintained a cracking pace during gruelling working hours, juggling numerous complex problems simultaneously as Attorney-General and Minister for External Affairs. Curtin was soon raving about Evatt's ability to dictate word-perfect legislative clauses and cable messages on complicated issues. Other senior ministers, including Eddie Ward, Norman Makin and 'Stabber Jack' Beasley, also began well, and Chifley toiled to such good effect as incoming Treasurer that he was able to unveil a revised budget before the end of October.

However, the minister most transformed in government was Curtin himself. His adjustment to the prime ministership surprised him and others aware of his wariness of office. His integrity, oratory and dedication had always been second-to-none; now, as well, he managed to muster the inner strength to sustain him through the momentous decisions and administrative grind he had to grapple with. He still worried terribly at times, but the doubts and diffidence of opposition days disappeared. Instead, he was soon demonstrating unexpected assurance in the top job. Curtin's genuineness, modesty

Photo 14 Studio portrait of Australian Prime Minister and Minister for Defence Co-ordination, John Curtin, the minister most transformed in government (AWM 003870).

and 'innate integrity'[3] appealed to Australians. To them he conveyed – in a manner that was beyond Menzies – a genuine concern for the nation and its people, and a willingness to ensure that in Australia's time of trouble his government would take the drastic measures that were appropriate.

Nevertheless, the new government was still adjusting to being in office when Japan launched the Pacific War with a devastating attack at Pearl Harbor, an invasion of Malaya, air-raids against Singapore and the destruction of a British battleship and battle cruiser that had just arrived in a blaze of publicity after being dispatched by Winston Churchill in response to repeated Australian entreaties that Singapore should be fortified. For many Australians, who had long feared Japan more than any other nation, this was a dire sequence of events.

Curtin reacted decisively. Appropriate emergency measures were swiftly taken, and Curtin made a national broadcast that was straightforward yet inspiring: 'Men and women of Australia', he began. 'We did not want war in the Pacific', but 'are now called upon to meet the external aggressor' in 'the gravest hour of our history'.

We Australians have imperishable traditions. We shall maintain them. We shall vindicate them. We shall hold this country, and keep it as a citadel for the British-speaking race, and as a place where civilization will persist.[4]

Curtin had for years had misgivings about the wisdom of relying on Singapore and the British Navy to safeguard Australia, and Japan's initial success had substantiated his assessment. His remarks to the Australian people acknowledged that there was a difficult fight ahead, but sought to counteract despondency as well. 'Enemy striking-power in the air has given to the enemy an initial momentum, which only a maximum effort can arrest', he said, 'but nobody worries about being a few goals down at half-time'.[5]

In view of the ominous progress of the Japanese forces, it was a priority for Curtin and Evatt to pursue support from Britain and the United States, especially with most of Australia's soldiers and airmen far from home helping Britain. Curtin and Evatt ploughed through the cable traffic assiduously, but felt that their progress was minimal. They concluded that Churchill, in particular, underrated the Japanese, overrated the strength of Singapore, and was inclined to give over-optimistic assurances that he could not fulfil.

Accordingly, Curtin decided that 'the stage of gentle suggestion has now passed'. He told Churchill bluntly that the measures proposed to bolster Singapore were 'utterly inadequate'. About this time he read a draft article prepared by his press secretary, Don Rodgers, in response to a request from the Melbourne *Herald* for a New Year message about the challenge facing Australians in 1942. Curtin amended and strengthened the draft, Rodgers sent it to the *Herald*, and a sentence in it was soon flashing around the world: 'Without any inhibitions of any kind, I make it quite clear that Australia looks to America, free of any pangs as to our traditional links and kinship with the United Kingdom'.[6]

This was highlighted as a dramatic shift in foreign policy, but Australia had in fact been looking to the US privately for some time. The much-quoted sentence drew attention away from Curtin's attempt in the same article to ensure that Australians were aware of the gravity of the situation, which 'far exceeds in potential and sweeping dangers anything that confronted us' in the First World War; 'Australia is now inside the fighting lines [and] Australians must be perpetually on guard … against the possibility, at any hour without warning, of raid or invasion'.[7]

Meanwhile the relentless Japanese advance showed no sign of faltering. Singapore fell on 15 February, and four days later the war reached

Australia itself. 'Stabber Jack' Beasley was in Sydney, engaged in top-level discussions, when he was called away to receive some information. He burst back into the meeting and blurted out 'The Japs have bombed Darwin!'[8] Hundreds were killed in this air-raid, and almost another hundred died in another major air-raid at Broome 13 days later.

It now seemed that the Japanese might well be about to invade Australia, as some Japanese strategists had been advocating. No prudent national government, naturally, could ignore the possibility. Curtin was exhausted, and was in hospital with gastritis when the main Darwin air-raid occurred; he left hospital prematurely, not fully recovered. Meanwhile, some of his ministers apparently became unnerved by the alarming turn of events. Nevertheless the Curtin government responded, on the whole, resolutely, rapidly and effectively to the critical situation facing Australia.

More men were called up into the militia. An Allied Works Council was established for the numerous construction projects urgently required, with E. G. Theodore, the highly capable former federal treasurer, in charge with sweeping powers. A CCC was created to become the workforce for these projects. The manufacture of various goods now deemed unnecessary was prohibited, so that those who had been producing them could be transferred to war work. An identity card for each citizen was introduced, taxes were increased and restrictions were brought in or tightened on trade and travel, employment and supplies.

In the emergency the deployment of the AIF became contentious. The acute anxiety that Curtin felt as he agonised over this issue had contributed to his hospitalisation in February 1942. He and his government wanted Australia's Army back home, understandably, and the transfer of the 6th and 7th Divisions from the Middle East to Australia was approved. But Churchill wanted the 7th Division diverted to Burma en route; Curtin and Evatt remained adamantly opposed to this, and made their view clear. Churchill nevertheless arranged for the 7th Division to be diverted to Burma anyway. Curtin and his senior ministers were appalled and enraged by Churchill's cavalier disregard of their explicit expression of Australia's desire, and made this clear too. Churchill reluctantly backed down and redirected the convoy to Australia.

What made this stressful period even more difficult for Curtin was that leading conservative figures sided with Churchill on this matter. No fewer than six influential men who at some stage held the office of prime minister on the conservative side of politics pressured the Curtin government to allow the diversion to Burma that Churchill wanted. In the circumstances it is hard

Photo 15 Night scene of a convoy at sea, during the voyage of AIF troops returning from the Middle East. Debate of the destination of the AIF was a major point of contention between Churchill and Curtin. The troops returned to Australia and went on to fight the Japanese in Papua in 1942 (AWM 025719).

to think of a more flagrant dereliction of Australia's national security in our entire history. With Australia imperilled as neither before nor since, it was surely appropriate to bring Australia's soldiers straight home; moreover, at the time the soldiers lacked air support and were detached from their arms and equipment, and they would have been slaughtered if they had been diverted on Churchill's wild-goose chase to Burma.

The strain continued to be acute for Curtin. He was terribly anxious about the safety of the troopships. It was an excruciating time for him. His sleep was disrupted for weeks – night after night he paced around the grounds at the Lodge. When he had to make an overnight train journey during this period, a journalist happened to get up in the middle of the night and found the prime minister staring out of the window with his hands shaking and sweat trickling down his face. When the journalist asked what the matter was, Curtin replied that he had just had a ghastly nightmare about the AIF troopships being torpedoed. He was immensely relieved when the troopships arrived home safely.

Curtin had further good news in March 1942 when he learned that Douglas MacArthur, a famous US general, had arrived in Australia after a secret journey from the Philippines, to take up the position of Supreme Commander of the South West Pacific Area, which President Roosevelt hoped Australia would endorse. Curtin agreed with the appointment, and he and MacArthur developed a highly effective rapport. Curtin came to rely on MacArthur's strategic grasp, which was fine in 1942 when their objectives were identical, although later, when Australia's interests and MacArthur's objectives did not always coincide, Curtin was criticised by some for being too subservient to the US general.

In May 1942 a Japanese naval force intending to attack Port Moresby was intercepted, and a vital engagement began in the Coral Sea. Parliament happened to be sitting at the time, and Curtin was notified that an important battle had started. He made some stirring, impromptu remarks that electrified the House of Representatives:

> The events that are taking place to-day are of crucial importance … As I speak, those who are participating in the engagement are conforming to the sternest discipline and are subjecting themselves with all that they have – it may be for many of them the last full measure of their devotion – to accomplish the increased safety and security of this territory … I put it to any man whom my words may reach … that he owes it to those men, and to the future of the country, not to be stinting in what he will do now for Australia. Men are fighting for Australia to-day; those who are not fighting have no excuse for not working.[9]

Some observers, including Don Rodgers, who saw Curtin deliver many speeches, and witnessed how his words moved hard-bitten journalists (as well as MPs) on this occasion, concluded that this was Curtin's finest-ever speech. The upshot at Coral Sea was that the Japanese attackers experienced their first significant setback in the Pacific when their force was turned away from a planned landing at Port Moresby. However, it was to become more significant in retrospect than it seemed at the time.

AUSTERITY AND DEDICATION

Curtin kept reiterating that austerity was appropriate in the crisis of 1942. He became frequently irritated when others demonstrated by their decisions or behaviour that the appropriateness of austerity had eluded them, especially when Curtin felt that they should have known better. He had a dedicated ally in John Dedman, his minister for War Organisation

Photo 16 Minister for War Organisation and Scientific and Industrial Research, John J. Dedman (AWM 010015).

of Industry. Dedman's department had been established months earlier under Menzies, but nothing had been done: when Dedman took over as minister, all he inherited – remarkably – were some sheets of blank paper and an otherwise empty office.

Dedman was utterly dedicated to the task of diverting Australia's non-essential resources to the war effort, but in public he was earnest and humourless. Public relations techniques were a closed book to him, and he had no one like Rodgers to polish his image. Curtin could proclaim, as he frequently did, the virtues of austerity, without losing his lustre as a noble war leader urging the unpalatable in the interests of eventual victory. It was altogether different, though, when Dedman, motivated by identical ideals, announced that women's clothing would be restricted to three basic sizes, men's clothing would be standardised to the 'Victory Suit' and shirts with shortened tails, and a variety of other commodities would be rationed or completely banned. Dedman was subjected to ferocious criticism, and became the most unpopular individual in Australia. Though inevitably bruised by the experience, he persevered, essentially undeterred, because of his dedication and determination.

Curtin's relationship with the press was very different. In fact, it was unique – no Australian prime minister has been more open with journalists than Curtin. He decided that the best way to handle highly secret wartime information was to take the journalists into his confidence, so that they could appreciate what could and could not be reported, and why. Curtin, having been a pressman himself, had a higher regard for journalists' trust-worthiness than most politicians did. He had regular informal gatherings with the senior correspondents of the major newspapers, often twice a day, when he would brief them about matters that other PMs would never have divulged. In the main his trust was vindicated, but there were occasions – relatively rarely – when he found to his disappointment that his faith in the journalists was not always justified.

One aspect of how the Curtin government met the challenge of the 1942 crisis resulted in a substantial change that stemmed from an initiative of Treasurer Chifley. With Australia endangered, the government was looking for ways to generate increased revenue to finance the war effort. It also wanted to remove the inequality and inefficiency created by the way the states independently collected varying rates of income tax. Chifley became convinced that a uniform system of centralised direct taxation was necessary; when the premiers refused to go along with a voluntary scheme, Chifley introduced legislation in May 1942 for a national takeover of all income tax. The legislation was not solely reliant on the defence power of the federal government, which is far-reaching in wartime; when opponents of the change challenged its constitutional validity in the High Court and failed, the upshot was that it became a reform with lasting significance.

Doc Evatt was another senior minister who continued to demonstrate dedication to the national interest in the difficult months of 1942. He kept pressing for an increased allocation of resources to the Pacific, and for Australia to have a greater role in the strategic decision-making affecting Australia.

Evatt saw his task as 'to bang on closed doors' to get Australia's message across. He hated flying, but he ran the Japanese gauntlet in the Pacific to press Australia's claims in the highest quarters. 'Stabber Jack' Beasley was full of admiration for him: 'poor bloody Evatt' would 'be crawling aboard those little planes at night, without lights, no heating, freezing to death, the stink of petrol everywhere, and sit for hours in a roar that would knock your ears off, with the plane trembling all around him'.[10] This of course is not to imply that Evatt's ordeal matched the battle experiences endured by soldiers and sailors and airmen, but it does confirm that Curtin and his senior ministers displayed unmistakable dedication to the national interest in the challenging days of 1942.

CONSCRIPTION

It was also in 1942 that Curtin and his party grappled with the issue of conscription. This was an extremely difficult controversy for the ALP; its leaders and most influential activists were acutely aware that the issue of conscription had ruptured the party a quarter of a century earlier. Curtin was determined to handle the issue in a less confrontational fashion than Billy Hughes had done in 1916, so that this time there would not be the catastrophic effect on party cohesion that had arisen from Hughes's belligerent, win-at-all-costs approach.

The issue of conscription arose in 1942 because Australia had two military formations, and their operational scope was different. On the one hand, there was the volunteer force known as the AIF, which could serve anywhere; on the other, there was the conscripted militia, which had a more limited role, since conscripts could only be directed to fight in Australia and its adjacent territories. During 1942 Labor's opponents kept emphasising that Australia should have one force, one army, which could be deployed wherever its leaders considered appropriate. They were well aware that this would necessitate the introduction of conscription, which had devastated the ALP in 1916, and were savouring the prospect of a repetition while piously declaring that of course the objective of an efficient defence force was uppermost in their thoughts. Actually, while Australia was intent on defending its territory against the menacing advance of the Japanese, the issue was irrelevant. But Curtin accepted that it would become a relevant consideration when the process of driving the Japanese back began.

He eventually decided that it was appropriate to extend the area into which the Australian militia could serve. It seems that MacArthur was influential in persuading Curtin that this decision was strategically worthwhile. Curtin reluctantly acquiesced, well aware that this would open up an explosive controversy within his party. After all, he and a number of his senior ministers had been strident opponents of Hughes's attempts to introduce conscription during the First World War.

Curtin was intent on a careful, nuanced approach that respected his party's traditions. Federal conference was the most senior decision-making body in the ALP's structure, and he unveiled his views at the party's conference in November 1942. He had discussed his intentions beforehand with Chifley, perhaps with Scullin, and possibly with no one else. Having been confined to bed with neuritis shortly before, Curtin told the conference that there was 'no argument against one army'; it was an anomaly that 'a man could be sent to Darwin, where he could be bombed, but not to Timor to save Darwin from being bombed'.[11]

However, he did not pursue the objective of one Army outright, knowing that this could well trigger a replay of the 1916 upheaval. Instead he asked conference to agree that in this war a larger region was vital to Australia's security than the area defined in the legislation that authorised conscription for home defence. Accordingly, he proposed that the Defence Act should be amended to encompass not only Australia and its territories, but also 'such other territories in the South-West Pacific area as the Governor-General proclaims as being territories associated with the defence of Australia'. When Arthur Calwell, a fervent anti-conscriptionist, objected that Curtin's motion was 'not properly before conference', and should be considered by the party's constituent state branches before federal conference voted on what in effect meant support for conscription, Curtin obligingly acquiesced. A spirited debate then began within the party.[12]

It was a difficult debate for the prime minister. Some of his closest supporters, both in his cabinet and beyond, opposed him vehemently on this issue; they had fought alongside him in 1916, but opposed him now. Other ALP identities, who were not closely aligned with Curtin, attacked him ferociously, which distressed him and did some harm to the government's cohesion.

Eventually, though, Curtin managed to obtain his party's endorsement of a limited adjustment. Though well short of his preferred homogeneous Army, it was a notable accomplishment from his perspective. He had succeeded in achieving the maximum possible change while maintaining ALP unity; although the angry debates inflicted some bruises on the party's cohesion, it remained essentially united. Curtin's achievement in getting this change through reflected his standing in the ALP. In contrast to Hughes in 1916, Curtin was respected and fundamentally trusted by his party.

He was also respected and fundamentally trusted beyond his party. This was confirmed by a remarkable opinion poll at the end of 1942. Curtin's performance as prime minister was rated as having been 'fairly good' to 'excellent' by nearly 90 per cent of Labor voters – no surprise there – but also by no fewer than 72 per cent of non-Labor voters. Only 5 per cent of the respondents considered that Curtin had not been a success.[13]

Conclusion

The Curtin government's response to the daunting circumstances it encountered was, overall, impressive, especially considering it had only just taken office and it lacked a majority in parliament. As Curtin pointed out, his government had provided stable leadership without a majority in either the House of Representatives or the Senate, whereas the conservatives had been unable to provide stable government with a majority in both parliamentary chambers. It is widely accepted today that Curtin remains Australia's finest-ever prime minister.

The federal election of 1943 gave the Australian people an opportunity to deliver a verdict on the Curtin government's performance, and also on the comparison of Curtin and Menzies as war leaders. During the campaign Curtin made the case for Labor:

> We faced an era of dangers and problems unprecedented and unpredictable. We met them unwaveringly. We had a trusteeship to and for Australia. Our country has now withstood the direct trials; it has lived through its darkest hour; it is now confronting the dawn of a victorious and a better day. The Labor Government has done its duty.[14]

The electorate's judgement was clear. Labor, having gone into the election without a majority in the House of Representatives or the Senate, had a thumping win that gave the ALP the numbers in both chambers of parliament. In the Senate Labor had not had a majority for over three decades. As for the House of Representatives – and this is a little-known electoral statistic – the 1943 result remains the ALP's biggest-ever victory at a federal election in the proportion of House of Representatives seats won.

Notes

1 Ross McMullin, *The Light on the Hill: The Australian Labor Party 1891–1991*, Oxford, Melbourne, 1991, p. 182.
2 Ibid., p. 209.
3 David Day, *John Curtin: A Life*, Harper Collins, Sydney, 2000, p. 487.
4 McMullin, *The Light on the Hill*, p. 215.
5 Ibid.
6 Ibid., p. 216.
7 Ibid.
8 Ibid., p. 217.
9 Ibid., p. 219.
10 Ibid., p. 220.
11 Ibid., p. 222.
12 Ibid.

13 Day, *John Curtin*, p. 494.
14 McMullin, *Light on the Hill*, p. 225.

FURTHER READING
Day, D., *John Curtin: A Life*, Harper Collins, Sydney, 2000.
Grattan, M., (ed.), *Australian Prime Ministers*, New Holland, Sydney, 2000.
Hasluck, P., *Australia in the War of 1939–1945: The Government and the People 1942–1945*, Australian War Memorial, Canberra, 1970.
McMullin, R., *The Light on the Hill: The Australian Labor Party 1891–1991*, Oxford, Melbourne, 1991.
Sawer, G., *Australian Federal Politics and Law 1929–1949*, Melbourne University Press, Melbourne, 1963.

AUSTRALIA UNDER THREAT

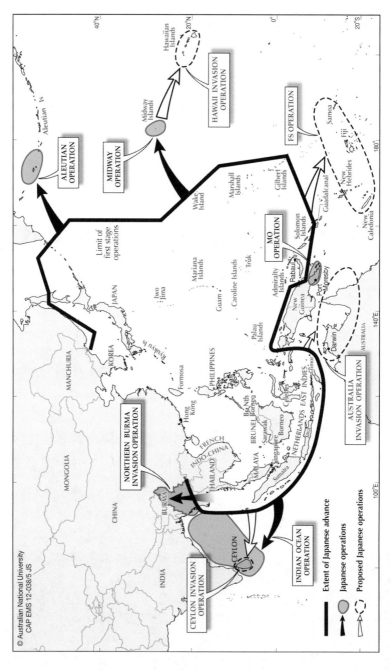

40°N

20°N

Hawaiian
Islands

HAWAII INVASION
OPERATION

0°

20°S

FS OPERATION

Samoa

Fiji

New Hebrides

New
Caledonia

180°

Aleutian Is

Midway
Islands

ALEUTIAN
OPERATION

MIDWAY
OPERATION

Wake
Island

Limit of
first stage
operations

Marshall
Islands

Gilbert
Islands

Guadalcanal

Solomon
Islands

MO
OPERATION

JAPAN

KOREA

Ryukyu Is

Iwo
Jima

Mariana
Islands

Caroline Islands

Trūk

Guam

Admiralty
Islands

Rabaul

New
Guinea

Port
Moresby

Palau
Islands

Darwin

140°E

AUSTRALIA

AUSTRALIA
INVASION OPERATION

MANCHURIA

Formosa

PHILIPPINES

Hong
Kong

Bn Nth
Borneo

Celebes

NETHERLANDS EAST INDIES

Timor

NORTHERN BURMA
INVASION OPERATION

MONGOLIA

CHINA

FRENCH
INDO-CHINA

THAILAND

BRUNEI

Sarawak

MALAYA

Singapore

Borneo

Java

Sumatra

100°E

BURMA

INDIA

CEYLON

CEYLON INVASION
OPERATION

INDIAN OCEAN
OPERATION

Extent of Japanese advance

Japanese operations

Proposed Japanese operations

Map 5 Japanese plans in the Pacific, 1942

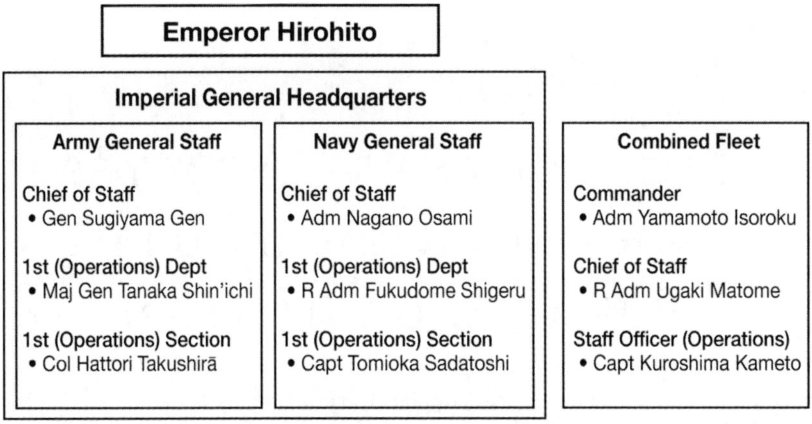

Emperor Hirohito		

Imperial General Headquarters

Army General Staff	Navy General Staff	Combined Fleet
Chief of Staff • Gen Sugiyama Gen	Chief of Staff • Adm Nagano Osami	Commander • Adm Yamamoto Isoroku
1st (Operations) Dept • Maj Gen Tanaka Shin'ichi	1st (Operations) Dept • R Adm Fukudome Shigeru	Chief of Staff • R Adm Ugaki Matome
1st (Operations) Section • Col Hattori Takushirā	1st (Operations) Section • Capt Tomioka Sadatoshi	Staff Officer (Operations) • Capt Kuroshima Kameto

Chart 3 Japanese Command organisation, Imperial General HQ

CHAPTER 6

THE JAPANESE ARMY'S 'UNPLANNED' SOUTH PACIFIC CAMPAIGN

Hiroyuki Shindo

The Japanese, Australians and Americans fought a long and difficult war in New Guinea and the Solomon Islands from early in 1942 through to the end of the Second World War. Unfortunately, in many ways it has become a forgotten campaign in Japanese and American histories of the war. In the case of the Japanese, this is largely because the New Guinea and Solomons campaigns were, with the exception of the battle for Guadalcanal, unglamorous and unspectacular.

From the Australian perspective, the New Guinea and Solomons campaigns were a vital part of Australia's experience in that war. In this chapter these campaigns shall be examined from the Japanese side, articulating what was happening 'on the other side of the hill' often enables one to gain a fuller understanding of what took place. The focus will be on the Japanese Army; more specifically, the Japanese Army's perspective of the Pacific War, the process by which the Japanese Army committed itself to the war in the South Pacific, and an overview of some of the problems this created for the Army.[1]

The term 'Pacific War' when used in this chapter means the war that was begun in December 1941 against the Americans, British, Dutch, and, of course, the Australians, and was fought in Southeast Asia and the Pacific Ocean. This is to distinguish that war from the ongoing war in China, which continued to be a major focus of the Japanese Army's attention until the end of the Second World War.

THE JAPANESE ARMY'S PERCEPTION OF THE PACIFIC WAR

In order to understand the difference in the views held by the Japanese Army and Navy regarding the Pacific War, one must first understand the historical differences in the missions of these two services.[2] Since no later than the early 20th century, the Japanese Army viewed Imperial Russia, and later the Soviet Union, as its primary hypothetical enemy. After Japan had defeated Russia in the Russo-Japanese War of 1904–5, the Army in particular feared Russia would want to fight a war sometime in the future to avenge its loss. In addition, Japan had gained certain economic interests in the Manchuria area as a result of its victory in the Russo-Japanese War, such as rights over the Southern Manchuria Railroad, and now had to think about defending those interests. The obvious and seemingly most dangerous military threat was Russia.

The Russo-Japanese War also had a major effect on the Japanese Navy's perception of its main mission. With the demise of the Russian Navy, the only remaining country that had the potential to pose a naval threat to Japan in the western Pacific was the United States. As a result, the Japanese Navy began to focus on the US Navy as its most likely opponent in any future war.

The services were not specifically limited to these missions in any official document, but thereafter the Army and Navy each concerned itself primarily with what each understood to be its own mission and hypothetical enemy. This does not mean that the Army completely ignored the United States. During the 1920s, the Army did undertake a serious study of the United States, particularly the US Army, because it had been impressed by the rapid and massive military mobilisation carried out by the US during the First World War.[3] However, these efforts were made by a minority within the General Staff, the vast majority of which remained focused on the Soviet Union.[4] Since the Pacific Ocean area was understood to be the responsibility of the Navy, the Army naturally did not have any plans for operations in the South Pacific, New Guinea or Australia prior to the Pacific War.[5]

By the late 1930s, Japan was deeply mired in its war in China, and, for various reasons, began to seriously consider a military expansion into Southeast Asia. The result of this was the adoption of a national policy in 1940 that approved a move into Southeast Asia. Around this time, a war with the Americans and British increasingly became a concrete possibility, and, from the fall of 1940, the Army began studying the problems that it would encounter in any operations in Malaya and other parts of Southeast Asia. This marked the first time that the Japanese Army seriously studied and planned operations on a major scale to take place in an area other than the East Asian mainland. Even at this time, however, the Army left New Guinea and Australia out of its operational planning.[6]

As far as the Pacific War was concerned, the Army felt that its role should be to concentrate on fighting the British in Malaya, Burma and India, and that it would leave the war against the US, in the Pacific Ocean, to the Navy, with the exception of the Philippines.[7] Again, there was no formal written agreement on such a division of responsibility, but the perception was reflected in the division of areas to be put under the military administration of the Army and Navy, as determined in the 20 November 1941 decision by the Imperial General Headquarters – Government Liaison Conference concerning the military administration of occupied areas.[8] The Army was assigned responsibility for the military administration of Hong Kong, the Philippines, Malaya, Sumatra, Java and British Borneo, while the Navy was assigned responsibility for Dutch Borneo, Celebes, the Moluccas, Lesser Sundas, New Guinea, the Bismarcks and Guam. While this did not mean that the Army and Navy's respective areas of operational responsibility were strictly divided into these areas, it did lead each of the services to think in terms of operations within their perceived 'areas of responsibility' when planning military operations.[9] Therefore, as far as the Pacific War was concerned, the Army would concern itself with operations in Southeast Asia, and operations to the east of a line drawn just eastwards of the Philippines down through Borneo and east of Java would be the business of the Navy.

The Army would continue its focus on the Soviet Union and China at least until early 1943, when it was finally forced to realise that the greatest present military threat to Japan was now the United States and the war in the Pacific Ocean. Even thereafter, in many ways the Army would not fully identify the Americans as the primary enemy. For example, it would not be until September 1943 that the Army's Inspector General for Education would state that education and research in the Army would henceforth be shifted to a focus on operations against the Americans.[10] Until then, of course, the focus of such research and education was on the Soviet Red Army.[11]

A comparison of the number of divisions deployed in Southeast Asia, China and Manchuria is another indicator of the relative weight assigned by the Army to the different theatres of war. At the opening of the Pacific War, the Japanese Army committed only 10 divisions to Southeast Asia, and only the brigade-sized South Seas Detachment to help the Navy take

Guam and Rabaul in the Pacific Ocean. In comparison, the Army had 21 divisions plus a cavalry group deployed in China, 13 in Manchuria, two in Korea and four in the Japanese home islands.[12] The distribution of divisions among these theatres would not be significantly altered until late 1942 and early 1943. While operational requirements and logistical capabilities were also important factors in determining the number of divisions to be deployed in any theatre, this comparison does show that China and the Soviet Union carried great weight in the minds of Army planners well into the Pacific War.

THE JAPANESE ARMY'S COMMITMENT OF MAJOR FORCES TO THE SOUTH PACIFIC

Despite the perception by the Army that the war against the US in the Pacific Ocean was the Navy's war, the Army became heavily committed to the war in the South Pacific by late 1942 and in 1943 and beyond. The process by which this happened may be understood by examining the Army's intentions regarding strategy and operations after the end of the 'Southern Area Operations', which were called the 'First Stage Operations' by the Navy. These operations were aimed at the occupation of Malaya, the Philippines, the Dutch East Indies and other areas at the start of the Pacific War. The Army intended to follow the strategy outlined in the Operations Plan of 5 November 1941, which called for the occupation and consolidation of the 'Southern Resources Area', and the establishment of a 'long-term, undefeatable condition', or a condition of self-sufficiency, in that area, which was considered necessary to fight a long-term war of attrition against the Western powers.

The Army's first priority, however, remained its war in China, and as a means of completing that war, it was considering a further advance westwards into Burma and India. The Army saw this not only as a means of tightening the encirclement of China, but also of defeating the British, which was one of the national objectives of the Pacific War as given in the 15 November 1941 Liaison Conference decision regarding the conduct of the war against the British, US, Dutch and Chiang Kai-shek.[13] Further, the Army wanted to get back to preparing for its war against the Soviet Union. In fact, by early 1942, the Army had decided to reduce the size of its commitment in the Pacific War over a period of months, by transferring a number of divisions from Southeast Asia to either Japan, where they would be partially demobilised and the manpower utilised in wartime industries, or to China or Russia, where they would reinforce the Army's ongoing

Photo 17 1942. Japanese Special Naval Landing Forces landing by boat on Buka Island in the Solomon Islands. It was the Japanese Navy that drove operations in the South Pacific, while the Japanese Army remained committed to its operations in China and preparations for war against the Soviet Union (AWM 129750).

efforts.[14] The Army had also agreed, before the war, to release 1.1 million tonnes of shipping that had been temporarily allocated to them for the 'Southern Area Operations'. This would take place over a number of stages, but by July 1942, the Army would be allocated only one million tonnes of shipping. This arrangement had been reached in the fall of 1941, and was intended to ensure that Japan's industries had an adequate allocation of shipping to enable Japan to fight a protracted war.[15] This would mean that the Army would not have enough shipping to carry out a major campaign in Southeast Asia or the Pacific after the summer of 1942, but that wasn't considered a problem, because the Army was not contemplating any such campaign beyond its 'Southern Area Operations' in Southeast Asia or the Pacific.

Despite these intentions, the Army became heavily committed against the Americans and Australians in the South Pacific by the end of 1942 because of, very broadly speaking, the Navy's efforts to expand the war into that area. From immediately after the Pearl Harbor operation, the Navy had studied its options for its 'Second Stage Operations'. While the Army wanted to consolidate Japan's gains in Southeast Asia and return to a focus on the mainland, the Navy wanted to continue aggressive operations against the US, to keep them on the defensive. Specifically, this would be realised through operations that would either neutralise Australia's capabilities as a base from which a US counter offensive could be launched, or which would force the remnants of the US's Pacific Fleet to fight a decisive battle with the Japanese.[16]

In early 1942, the neutralisation of Australia became an issue between the Army and Navy. In discussions on future strategy and operations with the Army, which lasted from January through early March, the Naval General Staff proposed that Australia be invaded. The Army baulked at this, because it would require as many as 12 divisions. More specifically, the Army opposed an invasion of Australia because it felt a strategic pursuit in the direction of Australia or Hawaii, which was also being proposed by the Navy, could be very dangerous and go beyond what should be Japan's culminating point of the offensive. The Army did agree that pressure should be maintained on the Americans, but felt that that should be accomplished through tactical offensives rather than a strategic offensive in the Pacific. The Army therefore advocated the adoption of a strategic defensive in the Pacific and the establishment of a 'long-term, undefeatable condition' as stipulated in Japan's original 5 November 1941 operations policy.[17]

Since the Army adamantly refused to agree to an invasion of Australia, the Navy proposed operations to cut the lines of communication between the United States and Australia, which became known as Operation FS. This would entail the occupation of the Fiji Islands, Samoa and New Caledonia. The Army was concerned about the possibility that a conflict with the Soviet Union might begin while FS was being undertaken; on the other hand, the Army did agree with the value of further operations against the Americans, provided that such operations would not interfere with the consolidation of the Southern Resources Area nor with preparations vis-à-vis the Soviet Union and the completion of the war in China. On 30 January, the Army made a de facto decision to proceed with FS, although formal approval would not come until later.[18]

On 16 February, Army Chief of Staff Hajime Sugiyama formally notified his counterpart, Chief of the Naval General Staff Osami Nagano, that the Army opposed the invasion of Australia on the one hand, but on the other could agree to an operation to cut the lines of communication between the US and Australia. As far as the Army was concerned, it had herewith finalised its position on the issue of invading Australia, although discussions with the Navy would continue until early March.[19]

The Army had agreed to FS not only because it recognised the danger Australia posed to the southeastern part of the newly expanded Japanese empire, but also because FS would require only a minimal additional commitment by the Army in the Navy's area of operational responsibility. More specifically, Operation FS as it was planned in March 1942 required only the following commitment by the Japanese Army.[20] The Kawaguchi Detachment would assault the Fijis. Samoa would be assaulted by the Higashi Detachment, and New Caledonia by the Aoba Detachment. Each of these detachments was approximately the size of a brigade. The Kawaguchi Detachment consisted of the 124th Regiment of the 18th Division and supporting troops, while the Higashi Detachment consisted of part of the 41st Regiment of the 5th Division. Both of these divisions had taken part in the Malaya Operation, and the Aoba Detachment from the 2nd Division had played a key role in the assault on Java, therefore this did not mean a new commitment by the Army to the Pacific War.

In the meantime, the South Seas Detachment, which had been standing by at Rabaul after its successful assault there in late January and would support the assaults on Lae and Salamaua in March, had been committed to an assault on Port Moresby. The decision to undertake the Port Moresby operation, which was on the initiative of the Navy, had been made in late January, 1942. It is important to note that the assaults of Lae, Salamaua and Port Moresby were all actions not included in the initial 'First Stage' operations, and represented an

THE JAPANESE ARMY'S SOUTH PACIFIC CAMPAIGN   113

expansion of the war by the Navy. Rabaul had been included as an objective to be occupied in the 5 November 1941 operational plan because the Navy believed that aircraft based there would pose a threat to Truk, its main base in the central Pacific.[21] Once Rabaul had been occupied, however, the Navy felt that aircraft based in Port Moresby would pose a threat to Rabaul.[22] Therein lay the perceived need for the occupation of Port Moresby.

The first attempt to take Port Moresby, Operation MO, was turned back by the US victory in the battle of the Coral Sea. The perceived threat of Port Moresby still remained, however, and the Army agreed to undertake an overland approach across the Owen Stanley Mountains to Port Moresby. The Army had initially opposed, in turn, the Navy's plans to assault Rabaul, Lae and Port Moresby, because of concerns over the over extension of Japan's forces. It is still somewhat unclear why the Army, which had been concerned earlier about the Navy's irresponsibility in expanding the geographical scope of the war and ignoring of the concept of culminating points of offensives, now changed its stance and decided to conduct a land offensive against Port Moresby. Colonel Kumao Imoto, a staff officer in the Operations Section of the General Staff, stated in his postwar memoirs that although the Army was not completely satisfied with the vague explanations the Navy gave for the aborting of Operation MO, it accepted the Navy's claims that it had sunk two US carriers and had achieved a victory in the Coral Sea battle. The Army therefore did not fully understand the extent to which the Navy had lost control of the seas in the Solomon and Coral Seas, and therefore did not feel that an overland approach to Port Moresby would be too difficult, especially in terms of the Japanese Navy's ability to maintain a naval line of communication between Rabaul and Buna. Therefore there seemed to be no reason another effort to assault Port Moresby should not be undertaken, and since the 2 February 1942 order to capture Port Moresby 'if possible' was still valid, the Army felt that the assault on Port Moresby had to continue, more or less on schedule.[23]

Another Army officer who took part in the operation has suggested that the Army–Navy rivalry may also have played a part in the agreement by the Army to try an overland assault on Port Moresby. In other words, the Army may have been eager to embarrass the Navy by successfully taking Port Moresby after the Navy had failed in its seaborne approach.[24] Another factor may have been the fact that the South Seas Detachment, which was the main unit tapped by the Army to undertake the overland approach to Port Moresby, was already in the area, standing by at Rabaul after it had taken part in the capture of Lae. In other words, an assault on Port Moresby relying mainly on the South Seas Detachment would not require the Army to commit another major unit to the South Pacific.

On 18 May, roughly two weeks after the Coral Sea battle, the Army activated the 17th Army headquarters, for the purpose of commanding both the overland Moresby operation and Operation FS.[25] However the 17th Army was allocated barely enough resources to undertake any major operation let alone an operation as ambitious as the occupation of such widely separated points as Port Moresby and Samoa. The 17th Army consisted essentially of the four brigade-sized detachments mentioned earlier: the South Seas, Kawaguchi, Higashi and Aoba detachments. It therefore had no divisions and no supporting Army air units attached. In summary, by May 1942, therefore, the Army had agreed to undertake assaults on Moresby, Fiji, Samoa and New Caledonia, but its commitment remained very minimal relative to the scope of the proposed operations.

The Japanese defeat in the battle of Midway forced the postponement of Operation FS, and later, on 9 July, its cancellation. The Army then decided to use the units freed from FS in its Port Moresby operation. The Army's plan, as mentioned above, called for an overland approach from Buna to Port Moresby via the Kokoda Trail, with the actual assault on

Photo 18 Informal group portrait of a number of Japanese soldiers gathered on a hillside, most likely in Papua. The photograph was collected by an Australian soldier who labelled it 'Buna 1943' (AWM P04149.001).

Moresby to be supported by a simultaneous assault from the sea by part of the Kawaguchi Detachment.

The US landing on Guadalcanal on 7 August 1942 would affect these plans. More importantly, the turn of events on Guadalcanal would ultimately force the Army to make a major commitment to the South Pacific area. By late September and early October, as a result of successive failures to retake Henderson Field on Guadalcanal and a shifting to the defensive along the Kokoda Trail, the Army was involved in increasingly serious land campaigns on both New Guinea and Guadalcanal, but it is important to note that as of mid-November, all of the units actually committed to the area, or about to be committed there, were still units that had already been sent, or were scheduled to be sent, to the area as part of Operation FS or the initial overland effort to take Port Moresby. These units included the South Seas Detachment and 41st Regiment on New Guinea, and the Kawaguchi Detachment, 2nd Division and 38th Division on or en route to Guadalcanal.

The Guadalcanal campaign did ultimately force the Army to transfer some of its combat air units from Manchuria to the South Pacific. This meant that the Army had made a strategy level commitment to the war in the South Pacific. In late August 1942, the Navy had asked the Army to send Army air forces to bolster the Navy's air forces in the Solomons and New Guinea, which were overstretched and barely at strength. The Army refused because that would require air units to be pulled out from Manchuria. In addition, the Army stressed that Army air forces were already overcommitted in all theatres – not only in Burma and other areas of the Southern Resources Area, but also in China, Manchuria and the Home Islands. Furthermore they argued that Army air forces were not suited for overwater operations, and that the infrastructure to support air forces in the South Pacific was nonexistent. Finally, the Army pointed out that many air units, especially fighter units, were in the process of refitting to more modern aircraft and required more time both to familiarise themselves with and to receive adequate numbers of the new fighters and bombers. Air units in such a state of transition might have sufficed for the air war being fought against the Chinese, but the Army feared that they would be ineffective in an air war against the Australians and Americans, whose air forces were thought to be both qualitatively and quantitatively superior to those of the Chinese.[26]

Underlying this resistance was the suspicion felt by many in the Army General Staff regarding the Navy's true motives for asking for the Army's assistance in air operations. Most of the members of the Army

General Staff had not been fully informed about the extent of the Navy's losses at Midway and furthermore had continuously been told that the Navy was still winning everywhere. These staff officers suspected that the Navy air forces were stronger than the Navy was admitting, and believed that the Navy only wanted to conserve its air forces at the expense of the Army.[27]

By mid-September, however, the Operations Section of the Army General Staff had begun to lean in favour of committing significant Army air units to the South Pacific and by late September, now that the Army had decided to commit the 2nd Division, part of the 38th Division and heavy artillery units, many in the Army General Staff began arguing for support by the Army's own air forces as well.[28]

By mid-October, the dire condition of naval air forces in the Solomons forced the Navy to appeal even more strongly for Army air support; by then, the Operations Section of the Army was leaning more in favour of responding to the Navy's request, and was conducting feasibility studies of sending its air forces south.[29]

Upon the failure of the 2nd Division's offensive in late October to recapture Henderson Field, the Army and Navy sections of IGHQ concluded that the loss of air superiority over the Solomons was one of the causes of the failed counter offensive. The re-establishment of local air superiority over Guadalcanal became a major pre-condition for the next scheduled attempt to retake Henderson Field. As a result, the Army finally decided in mid-November to commit significant combat air forces to the South Pacific.[30] The air units actually began to arrive in December 1942, starting with the 6th Air Division, which was followed by more bomber and fighter units. While these saw only limited action in the Solomons, they would play a major role in the New Guinea campaign in 1943 and 1944.

The Army increased its commitment at the strategic level in another way in November 1942, when it strengthened its command structure in the South Pacific by activating the 18th Army, to handle operations in New Guinea. This freed the 17th Army to concentrate on the Solomons. Further, the Army activated the 8th Area Army, to command the 17th and 18th Armies, and the air units which would shortly be deployed in Rabaul.[31]

It was also only at this time that the Army made the decision to occupy Wewak, Hollandia, Madang and other areas along the northern coastline of New Guinea, as well as Tuluvu on the western tip of New Britain.[32] The Army needed these places to create a new line of communications, especially to ferry aircraft to and from New Guinea. The Army had previously used the Navy's route, which ran from the Philippines through the Palaus, Truk and then Rabaul, but the long overwater stretches were problematic for the Army, especially its aircraft. The new route ran from the Philippines through Timor, and then to New Guinea.

Finally, in late 1942, the Army began to pull ground units out of its primary areas of interest, namely China and elsewhere on the Asian mainland, and to commit them to the South Pacific. These divisions included the 51st and 41st Divisions, which were serving in South and Central China respectively, and ended up playing major roles in the fighting on New Guinea. The 20th Division, which also played a major role in the New Guinea campaign, was pulled from garrison duty in Korea. The 6th and 17th Divisions, which would be stationed in Bougainville and Rabaul respectively, also came from Central China. The redeployment of these divisions to Rabaul, Wewak and Madang began in late 1942. The problem would remain, however, of how to deploy these reinforcements in sufficient force to the Lae and Salamaua area, which, after the end of Japanese resistance in the Buna area, would become the next major area of conflict between the Japanese and the Australians and Americans.

It is important to note that this sort of commitment on a strategic level by the Army to the war against the Australians and Americans in the South Pacific was made only in late 1942, or approximately a year after Pearl Harbor. Until then, the war with the Australians and Americans was perceived to be largely the Navy's war.

After the decision to withdraw from Guadalcanal was made on 31 December 1942, another debate took place between the Army and Navy over where the next battles should be fought. The Navy insisted on the southern and central Solomons, mainly New Georgia, chiefly to keep the Americans as far away from Rabaul as possible. The Army, on the other hand, wanted to specify eastern New Guinea as the next 'main battlefield'. In part, this was because the Army wanted to avoid a repeat of the Guadalcanal campaign, in an area that was beyond Japan's logistical and air support capabilities.[33] The Army also recognised the greater strategic danger to Japan that would be posed by the loss of New Guinea, which would open the way for an Allied counter offensive to the Philippines and into the heart of the Southern Resources Area – the Dutch East Indies – which would directly endanger the very natural resources that had been the primary objective of Japan's war against the Allies.[34] Institutional interests were also a factor. The Army argued for the identification of New Guinea as the next 'main battlefield' because New Guinea obviously had a greater land mass compared to the Solomons, and therefore seemed to offer a better opportunity for ground operations and the retaking of the initiative vis-à-vis the Americans.[35]

In the end, the Army and Navy reached a compromise of sorts. New Guinea was identified as the 'main battlefield', but the Navy was also permitted to defend its forward positions on New Georgia, albeit mostly with its naval landing forces and with minimal Army support.[36] The Army was now truly committed to the fighting in the South Pacific. Having lost Buna by this time, the Army identified the Lae and Salamaua area to be the next vital location on New Guinea to be held, and tried to rush the 51st Division and other reinforcements to the area. While its initial effort was relatively successful, the shocking losses in the battle of the Bismarck Sea in early March 1943 forced the Japanese to abandon their efforts to send reinforcements to Lae en masse, by convoys of transports. Thereafter, reinforcements arrived at a trickle. From July through September, the Australians and Americans began their offensive against Salamaua and Lae, and ultimately forced the Japanese to abandon both by late September. Much tedious and bloody fighting would be required along the north coast of New Guinea through the end of the war, which ended with the remnants of the Japanese 18th Army hemmed in near Aitape, and virtually isolated from the main action of the war, which had gone on to the Central Pacific, Philippines, Iwo Jima and Okinawa.

THE DIFFICULTIES FACED BY THE ARMY IN THE SOUTH PACIFIC

The IJA faced a number of problems in conducting its 'unplanned war' in the South Pacific. First, the Army was designed for operations on the Asian mainland, so its equipment, logistics and doctrine, among others, were not designed for the mountainous terrain nor the tropical climate of New Guinea. The Army's capability to construct air bases is a good example of this. The Army did have a number of units whose mission was to construct air bases for operations on the Asian mainland. These units typically were equipped with manual shovels, scoops and pickaxes, and a few rollers. They typically numbered around 100 men, with a major or captain in charge. The premise was that they would be able to conscript local labour, and that they would be working on flat ground, such as the plains of Manchuria.

From August 1942 onwards, faced with the increasingly dire situation in the Solomons, the Army carried out studies and experiments regarding the construction of air bases in the terrain and climate of the South Pacific. It was determined that some of the equipment it had for clearing coniferous and deciduous forests could also be used to clear palm groves, although it was unknown how effective they would be for clearing jungle growth. Tractors used to haul heavy artillery were deemed suitable for pulling rollers to flatten runways, and for pulling trees down. Some trucks in civilian use were determined to be possibly effective, but these were largely discounted, because there were too few of them to make any major difference.[37]

As a result of these studies and experiments, a new airfield construction unit was established, equipped with some of the forest-clearing equipment that had been tested, along with the usual shovels and pick-axes, and sent south. The Army was unable, however, to quickly devise a more effective solution to this problem. It did decide that this problem had to be studied further, and set up a school in Toyohashi, Japan for this purpose. However, the Army would never attain the degree of mechanisation necessary to quickly build large numbers of air bases in the South Pacific, or to build air bases large enough to handle the numbers of aircraft necessary for the scale of air operations there. This would hamper Army air operations in New Guinea, and would be one of the underlying causes of the massive defeats suffered by the Army air forces at Wewak in August 1943 and Hollandia from late March to early April, 1944. This situation cannot be blamed fully on the Army's lack of foresight. The Army's capabilities for building air bases were probably adequate for a war in Manchuria, but were lacking for the war in New Guinea, which, as explained earlier, had not been contemplated by the Army virtually until it actually happened.

Not only was the Army hampered by the fact that it was not well set-up for fighting in the South Pacific, but it also faced problems because its operations staff had very little prior knowledge about the geography, topography, climate and other natural features of the area.[38] A good case in point is the plan to take Port Moresby by marching overland, via the Kokoda Trail. The Army decided to undertake this operation in May 1942, but the Operations Section of its General Staff had virtually no useful maps of the area for the planning of the operation. The operation was therefore initially titled a 'Research Operation', and was to be conducted by an engineering unit. The objective was to survey the Kokoda Trail, in order to determine whether an actual operation by infantry units along the trail was feasible. As it turned out, a full operation by infantry units was ordered even before the 'Research Operation' could be launched, so the Army ended up committing infantry and other units to the Kokoda Trail from late July, without full knowledge of the local conditions.[39]

Finally, the entire campaign in the South Pacific caused shipping losses that Japan could ill afford, and which affected Japan's later war efforts. It is difficult to derive specific data on the exact effect losses in the South Pacific had on Japan's entire shipping situation; for example, how the losses suffered by a specific convoy to Wewak affected Japan's overall logistical capabilities. However, many of the officers involved recollected that the shipping losses incurred in Japan's efforts to transport forces to and resupply the New Guinea and Solomons area in 1943 and 1944 worsened the overall shipping situation for Japan. Not only did such losses affect Japan's ability to transport resources from the Southern Area back to the homeland, but they also affected major operational decisions.

For example, in early June 1943, the Army operations staff considered pulling the front back from eastern New Guinea and the Solomons to a more defensible line much further west, which could be supplied more adequately and which would be within Japan's capabilities for conducting air operations, but this plan was not adopted, in part because it was determined that the Japanese Army could not secure enough shipping to pull all of its forces back from the existing front line.[40] The change in

Photo 19 A consequence of Japanese operations in the South Pacific. A Japanese Mitsubishi A6M3 (Zero) Navy type model 32 fighter aircraft damaged and abandoned near the Buna airstrip, Papua (AWM P01097.035).

Japan's strategic situation, which worsened rapidly from July through August 1943, due to the increasing pressure against Salamaua and the American assault on New Georgia, would eventually force Japan to set up its main line of resistance further westwards. In other words, from mid to late September 1943, the concept of the 'Absolute National Defense Zone', would be adopted, the eastern boundaries of which would be a line running along the Marianas through central New Guinea. The adoption of this zone meant that the Japanese 8th Area Army and its subordinate 17th and 18th Armies were effectively abandoned (in fact, each was ordered to fend for itself thereafter), but the hope was that the Absolute National Defense Zone would be more defensible in terms of Japan's logistical capabilities, and that this move would give Japan a little breathing space in order to refit its air forces and prepare for a major counter offensive. As it turned out, this was not good enough for Japan, and the Zone would be breached unexpectedly quickly, at Hollandia in April 1944 and in the Marianas in July 1944. For the purposes of this chapter, however, it is important to note that not only offensive operations, but even this sort of strategic with-drawal was hampered by Japan's critical lack of shipping, which was brought about in part by the campaigns in the South Pacific.

CONCLUSION

Such were the Army's views of the Pacific War, the process by which it became heavily involved in the war in the South Pacific, and some of the problems it encountered as it fought its 'unplanned war' there. The threat of a ground invasion of the Australian mainland had largely receded by early March 1942, at least from the Japanese perspective, when the Army convinced the Navy that an invasion of Australia at that time was not a good idea. Many more months of hard fighting would take place in New Guinea and the Solomons, however, before the ground war would truly move away from Australia.

Notes

1   See Chapter 7 for a discussion of these issues from the Japanese Navy's perspective.

2   Kumao Imoto, *Dai- tōa Sensō Sakusen Nisshi* (Operations Diary of the Great East Asia War), Fuyo Shobo, Tokyo, 1998, pp. 33–4. (Reprint of Kumao Imoto, *Sakusen Nisshi de tsuzuru Dai- tōa Sensō* (The Great East Asia War as written in an Operations Diary), Fuyo Shobo, Tokyo, 1979.) Edward Drea, *Japan's Imperial Army: Its Rise and Fall, 1853–1945*, University of Kansas Press, Lawrence, pp. 125–7.

3   See Fumitaka Kurosawa, *Taisenkanki no Nihon Rikugun* (*The Japanese Army during the Interwar Period*), Misuzu Shobo, Tokyo, 2000, pp. 250–94.
4   Ibid., p. 274.
5   The Army had, however, conducted research itself on the terrain and other aspects of New Guinea prior to the Pacific War. See Peter Williams, *The Kokoda Campaign 1942: Myth and Reality*, Cambridge University Press, Melbourne, 2012, pp. 23–34.
6   Takushiro Hattori, *Dai-tōa Sensō Zenshi* (*Complete History of the Great East Asia War*), Hara Shobo, Tokyo, 1965, p. 151.
7   Imoto, *Dai- tōa Sensō Sakusen Nisshi*, p. 345.
8   Hattori, *Dai-tōa Sensō Zenshi*, p. 167.
9   Bōeichō Bōei Kenshūsho Senshishitsu (ed.), *Tōbu Nyūginia Hōmen Rikugun Kōku Sakusen* (*Army Air Operations in Eastern New Guinea*), Asagumo Shinbunsha, Tokyo, 1967, p. 25.
10 Takeshi Hoshikawa (ed.), *Rekishi Gunzō Shiriizu Taiheiyō Sensō 5: Shōmōsen Soromon Nyūginia no Shitō* (*Sculpture of History, the Pacific War, vol. 5: War of Attrition: Battles to the Death in the Solomons and New Guinea*), Gakken Publishing, Tokyo, 2009, p. 19.
11 Hattori, *Dai-tōa Sensō Zenshi*, p. 185.
12 Ibid., pp. 194–5.
13 Imoto, *Dai- tōa Sensō Sakusen Nisshi*, pp. 115–17. Hattori, *Dai-tōa Sensō Zenshi*, p. 164.
14 Imoto, *Dai- tōa Sensō Sakusen Nisshi*, pp. 315–16.
15 Ibid., pp. 155–6.
16 Bōeichō Bōei Kenshūsho Senshishitsu (ed), *Minami Taiheiyō Rikugun Sakusen (1) Pōto Moresubi Ga-tō Shoki Sakusen* (*Army Operations in the South Pacific (1) Early Operations against Port Moresby and Guadalcanal*), Asagumo Shinbunsha, Tokyo, 1968, pp. 121–2.
17 Ibid., p. 125.
18 Ibid., pp. 126–8.
19 Ibid.
20 Ibid., p. 137. Bōeichō Bōei Kenshūsho Senshishitsu (ed.), *Dai-honei Rikugunbu 4 Showa 17 nen 8 gatsu made* (*Army Section, Imperial General Headquarters, vol. 4: Until August 1942*), Tokyo, 1968, p. 55.
21 Hattori, *Dai-tōa Sensō Zenshi*, p. 151.
22 Ibid., p. 299.
23 *Dai-honei Rikugunbu 4*, p. 49.
24 Harumi Ochi, *Nyūginia Kessennki* (*Record of the Decisive Campaign in New Guinea*), Kōjinsha, Tokyo, 2011, p. 51.
25 Hattori, *Dai-tōa Sensō Zenshi*, p. 302. It should be noted that a Japanese 'Army' normally consisted of two to four divisions, and was therefore the equivalent in size to an Australian or American corps.
26 *Tōbu Nyūginia Rikugun Kōku*, pp. 26–7.
27 Ibid., p. 35.
28 Ibid., p. 32.
29 Ibid., pp. 34–5.
30 Ibid., p. 40.

31   A Japanese 'Area Army' consisted of two or more armies, which, as explained above, were the size of an Australian or US corps. An 'area army' was therefore equivalent in size to an Australian or US 'army'.
32   Hattori, *Dai-tōa Sensō Zenshi*, pp. 379–80.
33   Ibid., p. 413.
34   Ibid., p. 407. Hiromi Tanaka, *Makahsah to tatakatta Nihongun: Nyūginia-sen no Kiroku* (*The Japanese Forces That Fought with MacArthur: A Record of the New Guinea Campaign*), Yumani Shobo, Tokyo, 2009, p. 130.
35   Hattori, *Dai-tōa Sensō Zenshi*, p. 407.
36   Ibid., pp. 387, 407.
37   *Tōbu Nyūginia Rikugun Kōku*, pp. 43–4.
38   According to postwar claims made by many Army General Staff officers; for example, Hattori, *Dai-tōa Sensō Zenshi*, p. 324. Recent research indicates that the Japanese Army General Staff may have known, or should have known, more about the area. See Williams, *Kokoda Campaign 1942: Myth and Reality*, Cambridge University Press, Melbourne, 2012.
39   Tanaka, *Makahsah to tatakatta Nihongun*, p. 65.
40   'Sanada Shōshō Nikki Tekiroku Sono 2' (Abridged Record of Major-General Sanada's Diary No. 2), archives of the NIDS Library, National Institute for Defense Studies, Tokyo, Japan.

FURTHER READING

Bergerud, E. M., *Touched with Fire: The Land War in the South Pacific*, Penguin Books, New York, 1996.

Bergerud, E. M., *Fire in the Sky: The Air War in the South Pacific*, Westview Press, Boulder, Colorado, 2000.

Collie, C. and Marutani, H., *The Path of Infinite Sorrow: The Japanese on the Kokoda Track*, Allen & Unwin, Sydney, 2009.

Drea, E. J., *MacArthur's Ultra: Codebreaking and the War against Japan, 1942–1945*, University Press of Kansas, Lawrence, 1992.

Drea, E. J., *Japan's Imperial Army: Its Rise and Fall, 1853–1945*, University Press of Kansas, Lawrence, 2009.

Tohmatsu, H. and Willmott, H. P., *A Gathering Darkness: The Coming of War to the Far East and the Pacific, 1921–1942*, SR Books, Lanham, Maryland, 2004.

Williams, P., *The Kokoda Campaign 1942: Myth and Reality*, Cambridge University Press, Melbourne, 2012.

Willmott, H. P., *The War with Japan: The Period of Balance, May 1942–October 1943*, Scholarly Resources, Wilmington, Delaware, 2002.

CHAPTER 7

JAPANESE STRATEGY AND INTENTIONS TOWARDS AUSTRALIA

Steven Bullard

VIEWS ON AUSTRALIA

Many Japanese books published in the years leading up to 1942 provide a glimpse of how Japan viewed Australia in the critical period leading up to the opening of war in the Pacific. Several from the pre-war period provide an overview of Australian society: its industry, economy, agriculture and the like, with the aim of developing and strengthening Australia as a trading partner. After 1936, when Australia instituted a trade diversion policy, which favoured British over Japanese markets for Australian wool, several works began to be more critical of what they perceived to be a growing anti-Japanese sentiment in Australia. Central to this was criticism of the so-called White Australia Policy. For example, a work published in 1939 entitled *Present Day Australia (Saikin no Gōshū)*, portrayed Australia as maintaining childish ideas concerning Japan, desperate to keep out the 'coloured man', and locked into believing the 'crazy idea' that Japan was bent on a southward advance.[1]

After the start of war in the Pacific, there was an increase in the number of books published in Japan related to Australia, with a peak during 1942.[2] Some were free of wartime ideology, such as an anthropological account of Australian Indigenous peoples or an economic study of the sugar industry. Others were published with the aim to support Japan's war effort, and included studies of Australian transport and communications infrastructure, agriculture, mineral wealth, harbours and so on. Some of these books argued for the inclusion of Australia in the Greater East-Asia Co-prosperity Sphere, a proposed pan-Asian economic bloc led by Japan, even though the literature of other Japanese nationalists generally did not include Australia in the scope of regional Asian cooperation.[3]

One of the more militant proponents of thinking to incorporate Australia into an Asian sphere was Madarame Fumio, a young school teacher, who published his *History of the Invasion of Australia (Gōshū shinryaku-shi)*, in 1942. Madarame considered Australia to have been an Asian country invaded by the British, and joining the Greater East-Asia Co-prosperity Sphere was the only way to return the country to the rightful owners – Asians.[4]

While these works were generally not specific concerning the means by which this incorporation should take place, many contained a veiled warning. In the case of one work from 1942, however, the threat was less open to interpretation:

> Those without power are replaced by those with power. This is how the progress of humanity has developed. I sincerely hope that Australians wake up to this basic truth. If they do not, they will not be able to avoid the same fate as the original inhabitants.[5]

Such a statement may have contained an ominous resonance in Australia in early 1942, gripped as it was with the manifest reality of a seemingly unstoppable Japanese military. But the attitudes expressed in some of these works do not relate to the course of the war and the military strategies that these Japanese adopted. Like the various and divergent themes and approaches in popular publications, it is almost impossible to find among Japanese military planners a coherent and simple policy with regard to Australia. This also illustrates the inherent problem in attributing intentions to a country, making problematic such questions as: 'Did "Japan" intend to invade Australia during the Second World War?' Such attributions need to be clarified, the context of statements examined and an author's motivations scrutinised.

With this in mind, this chapter will explore the reasons behind Japanese military encroachment into areas of Australian strategic interest during 1942, particularly with regard to mainland Australia. It will do this by examining the context and background of key proposals and decisions taken by military planners within Imperial Headquarters and the Japanese Combined Fleet. Let it be said at the outset, however, that this chapter looks only at Japanese military intentions, not at how these intentions were perceived or understood in Australia. Nor does it look at how Australia responded to these perceptions; these issues are covered in other chapters of this book.

JAPAN MOVES SOUTH

Australia came to figure in Japanese military planning because of the complex circumstances that led to Japan adopting an interest in regions to the south.[6] The southern advance policy was promoted by the IJN, and reflected the long-standing rivalry between the Navy and the Imperial Japanese Army.[7]

In simple terms, the Navy pressed throughout the late 1930s for a southern advance, to secure natural resources vital to the future of Japanese economic (and naval) development, while the Army became more and more entrenched in a protracted war in China. By July 1940, in light of German successes in Europe and what was seen to be the imminent fall of Britain, the Army had agreed in principle with the Navy on the necessity of adopting a southern strategy as a means to solve their problems in China. By November 1941, the Japanese government took the decision to embark on a war in the south, while simultaneously striking at the US Pacific Fleet in Pearl Harbor to buy it time.

JAPANESE STRATEGIC POLICY MAKING

Before moving on to examine how Australia figured in Japanese strategies for the conduct of war in the Pacific, it is worth making brief comment on the process and organisations by which strategic decisions were reached in the Japanese military. The most important institutions for developing military policies during the Second World War were the Ministry of War and the Ministry of the Navy, both organs of the civilian government but headed by serving military personnel, and the Imperial General Headquarters. Over all institutions sat the Emperor, as supreme commander of Japan's military forces.

The Ministry of War and Ministry of the Navy managed administrative matters related to the armed forces, but operational command of the armed forces was controlled by Imperial General Headquarters. Further, this headquarters had direct access to the Emperor, without the need for intervention by the civilian government. The Army and Navy maintained separate general staff offices within Imperial Headquarters, each with a similar staff structure and departments to manage operations, plans, logistics, intelligence, communications, training, troops movements and so on.

At this time, owing to long-standing rivalries, the Japanese Army and Navy general staffs developed strategies and plans separately. This process involved a certain level of informal and semi-formal exchange at various levels, but the mechanism by which these resulting separate strategies were brought together was the so-called Imperial Headquarters – Government Liaison Conference, or simply the Liaison Conference. There, Army and Navy staff officers presented and debated plans and policies with other government representatives. The resulting policies, often filled with compromise and thinly veiled contradictions, were then presented before the Emperor for approval.[8]

The process of formulating strategy was complicated by the growing influence of Admiral Yamamoto Isoroku and the staff of the Combined Fleet. Yamamoto's success in forcing the Navy General Staff to accept his plan to strike against the US Fleet at Pearl Harbor gave the Combined Fleet a disproportionate influence on naval strategy, and ultimately on overall war strategy.[9] The Japanese Army Chief of Operations, Major-General Tanaka Shin'ichi, lamented at this time that 'the Navy has lost control of its strategic leadership'.[10]

AUSTRALIA IN PRE-WAR PLANNING

On 15 November 1941, Japanese high command ratified a document that would become the clearest statement of strategic policy for the conduct of war against the Allied nations. Called the 'Draft proposal for hastening the end of the war against the United States, Great Britain, the Netherlands, and Chiang', it specified a policy for Japan to embark on a speedy campaign to secure the future of the country, and to 'destroy the will of the United States to continue the war'. Australia is mentioned in this document in the context of Japanese efforts to force Britain out of the war and to destroy the United States' will to fight. This was to be achieved 'by means of political pressure and the destruction of commerce'.[11]

In other words, Australia was not identified as a strategic objective in pre-war planning, but Japanese high command was aware of the role Australia would play in the opening stage of operations. The Japanese command expected, for instance, that Australian air and naval bases would be used by Allied forces, and they recognised that Australian forces would join Allied troops 'sooner or later'. However, the Japanese Navy was confident that these forces would not prevent Japan securing their designated targets in southern areas.[12] As the course of events was established, that proved to be the case.

The Japanese Navy had in the pre-war period also given some consideration to operations in the south, which would follow the completion of the first stage of the war. The Navy General Staff envisaged a primarily defensive operation, with a naval force protecting key occupied areas in the

South Seas and Bismarck Islands, including Rabaul, then capital of the Australian-mandated territory of New Guinea. This naval force would patrol the area to protect transport routes, and seek and destroy any enemy fleet that encroached into the region.[13]

In addition, the Navy felt it would be necessary during this second stage to 'raid and destroy' Allied forward bases in the region. This was considered essential to counter Allied air strength from Port Moresby and bases in the north of Australia, such as Townsville.[14] According to the post-war reminiscences of Commander Watanabe Yasuji (a Combined Fleet staff officer), the Combined Fleet questioned the Navy General Staff on orders issued for the operation to clarify the clause 'raid and destroy enemy forward bases'. Subsequent development of these plans led to a decision to occupy certain forward bases, rather than just raid and destroy them. The scope of these operations was refined and included locations in Fiji, Samoa and Australian New Guinea, but bases in northern mainland Australia were not included in these pre-war deliberations.[15]

Nevertheless, there was awareness in the Navy that Darwin and other air bases across northern Australia would be a threat to the Japanese position in New Guinea and the Netherlands East Indies, and that measures would be needed to deal with this threat after the end of the first stage of the war. The Army was also aware of this necessity, but its pre-war planning for the second phase of the war was less developed than that of the Navy. Even so, Chief of Operations Tanaka had listed 'Port Darwin' among those areas where troops may need to be stationed for defensive purposes after the end of the Southern Operations.[16]

To summarise, the concept of operations as developed in the pre-war period was for Japanese military forces in the first stage of operations to secure vital resources in the southern region to foster industry and support the war in China. The Japanese Navy would also strike at the US Pacific Fleet in Hawaii and US forces in the Philippines to keep them out of the war long enough to secure their objectives. The second stage would protect these areas by securing a defensive line through the central Pacific, Rabaul, Solomon Islands, New Guinea, Java, Malaya and Burma. Allied forces would then expend themselves against this defensive barrier, with defeats and losses in a decisive naval battle deemed enough to force the US to lose its will to fight, allowing a negotiated peace from which Japan would keep its newly obtained overseas resources. Though the first stage basically succeeded, events would prove that a defensive line could not be secured over such a vast area, and that Allied resolve would not bend for anything other than complete victory over Japan.

IMPERIAL HEADQUARTERS' ATTITUDES TOWARDS AUSTRALIA IN SECOND-STAGE OPERATIONS

From the moment war began in December 1941, Japanese planners had continued to develop strategies for the second stage of operations. With the first stage progressing faster than even the most optimistic planners had imagined, however, there developed serious differences of opinion about how the war should proceed. It is in the context of this debate between the Navy General Staff, the Army General Staff and the Combined Fleet over the direction of war in the second stage that the issue of an invasion of Australia emerged.

Admiral Nagano Osami and his officers in the Navy General Staff had come to recognise that the Allied counter attack would not come through the Marshall Islands in the Central Pacific, as was thought before the war, but that the United States would use Australia as a base and strike at Japanese positions from the south.[17] Representative of this thinking was Captain Tomioka Sadatoshi, head of the Operations Section in the Navy General Staff. He reminisced that in this period, 'what bothered him most was Australia'. He knew that the United States would apply its formidable industrial might to the war effort, but if this power was allowed to spread through Australia and strike north, then Japan would be hard-pressed to maintain its newly acquired territory and resources.[18]

The Navy General Staff felt that Australia had to be neutralised as a base for an Allied counter attack. To achieve this, Tomioka and others pressed for the adoption of operations in the second stage to blockade the supply route between the United States and Australia. This was to be achieved by occupying key locations in the South Pacific, namely Fiji, Samoa and New Caledonia, the FS Operation.

But Tomioka went further. He also included the occupation of key locations in northern and northeastern Australia as essential to his plans. It was felt that the Japanese fleet could destroy the Australian fleet, such as it was, in these waters, and that an Army contribution of three divisions would be sufficient to hold key areas.[19] While admitting in the postwar period that such a strategy was perhaps reckless, Tomioka felt at the time that it was essential to maintain the offensive and strike at Australia while the conditions were optimal.[20]

It is important to note that the invasion plans of the Navy General Staff as proposed by Tomioka were dissimilar to the ideas of Madarame and other ideologues, who were calling for a return of Australia to Asia, its rightful owner. Tomioka did not plan for Japan to subjugate Australia, or even to occupy all of the country, only key locations in the north and

Photo 20 Admiral Nagano Osami (US Naval History and Heritage Command).

northeast of the mainland. The plans proposed were a strategic measure designed to achieve a specific outcome – the preservation of Japan's newly acquired territory to the north of Australia and a quick end to the war.

The Army General Staff was not blind to the dangers of Australia as a base for an Allied counter attack, but it vigorously opposed an expansion of the war into the Australian mainland. The Army was still preoccupied with China, where it had been bogged down since 1937 in a campaign it had hoped would be over quickly. The Army had committed 11 divisions of Japan's total strength of 51 divisions to the Pacific theatre, and it was expected that around half of these would be withdrawn at the end of the first stage of operations, to allow it to continue to prosecute the war in China and possibly mount an offensive against Russia.[21]

Chief of Staff General Sugiyama Gen wrote to his counterpart, Nagano, in late January 1942 outlining the Army's position. He stressed that future operations needed to establish a state of self-sufficiency and unassailability,

Photo 21 Captain (later Rear Admiral) Tomioka Sadatoshi (University of Pittsburgh Archives).

increasing the country's ability to protect itself and carry out operations to hasten the end of the war. Even so, the Army had agreed to support the Navy's blockade of Australia in the Pacific, without landings in Australia, in return for Navy support for operations in the Indian Ocean. These western operations would protect the flank of the Army in Burma from the British fleet, allow the Army to link up with an anticipated German advance to the near east, and cut China's supply lines through Burma.[22]

In what looks like a further concession, but was perhaps a measure to keep the persistent Navy General Staff officers off its back, the Army agreed on 23 January to consider the possibility of an attack on Port Darwin for defensive purposes, but stressed that this would only involve a temporary landing of troops, not an invasion.[23]

COMBINED FLEET ATTITUDES TO AUSTRALIA

Meanwhile, Yamamoto and staff of the Combined Fleet were pressing ahead with plans and preparations of their own. Yamamoto's Chief of Staff, Rear Admiral Ugaki Matome, reflected in early January on whether future operations should focus on Australia, India or Hawaii.[24]

Ugaki and his staff were aware of the need to study operations against Australia, and were in principle perhaps as enthusiastic as their colleagues in the Navy General Staff on the desirability of invading Australia and removing it from the equation.[25] While accepting that some in his staff

Photo 22 Admiral Yamamoto Isoroku (US Naval Heritage and History Command).

favoured operations in the south, partly as a means to keep the Army from attacking Russia, Ugaki concludes his above-quoted musing by leaning to a policy of 'maintaining the resource areas necessary for the country's self-sufficiency'.[26] To achieve this, the Combined Fleet ultimately did not look to the south, but to the east and west.

Yamamoto had embarked on his bold plan to attack Hawaii to strike a crippling blow to the US Pacific Fleet. He likened his plan to the battles of Hiyodorigoe and Okehazama, two famous episodes in Japanese history where a force of inferior numbers attained a decisive victory by means of a surprise attack from unsuspected quarters.[27] The failure to destroy any of the US aircraft carriers at Pearl Harbor, however, made Yamamoto's victory somewhat superficial.[28] The presence of US carriers in the South West Pacific as early as February and March, while these debates about future operations were continuing, was a vivid reminder of the continuing potential for the United States to wage war in the Pacific. It was also a portent for future operations.

Consequently, on 9 December, the day after the Hawaii raid, Yamamoto instructed his staff to research operations to take Hawaii and Ceylon. While the invasion of Hawaii had obvious motivations, the reasons behind the proposal to go west to Ceylon are less clear. First, it would buy time to prepare bases and air strength for a second attack on Hawaii, in the absence of surprise and given the obvious build-up of strength that would occur. Second, it would also have the added bonus of strengthening Japan's position in the India and Burma theatres, destroy the British Fleet in the Indian Ocean, break Allied shipping in the region and bring pressure to bear on India and Australia, potentially forcing them out of the war.[29]

By mid-January, the Combined Fleet presented a proposal to move through the Central Pacific to invade Hawaii and destroy the US Fleet in a decisive battle.[30] Yamamoto was faced, however, with opposition from the Navy staff and the Army, who had already reached agreement on the FS Operation, and the Hawaii invasion was temporarily shelved. By late January, the Combined Fleet were favouring campaigns first to the west, to attack Ceylon and the British Fleet in the Indian Ocean, and then to return to the east after destroying, but not occupying, Darwin, Fiji and Samoa.[31]

THE DEBATE INTENSIFIES

The debate over Australia intensified through February 1942. Tomioka opposed Yamamoto's eastern or western offensives, as he had opposed the Pearl Harbor operation, and would later oppose the Midway operation.

He continued to press for invasion of parts of northern and eastern Australia, simultaneous with the occupation of Fiji, Samoa and New Caledonia. The imminent fall of Singapore gave further encouragement to Tomioka, who expressed to his Army counterparts that the time was right to strike with a token force and make a clean sweep of Australia's forward bases. It is recorded in the Army's war diary that dealing with the debate was becoming troublesome.[32]

During this period, there were further proposals for invasion of Australia from several unlikely sources. The first was from General Yamashita Tomoyuki, the commander of the 25th Army and 'Tiger of Malaya'. He is said to have approached General Tōjō Hideki after the fall of Singapore with a proposal to lead an invasion force of two divisions to Australia. He proposed to land one division in Darwin to press south through the red centre towards Adelaide and Melbourne, and to land another on the east coast to 'leapfrog its way from port to port down toward Sydney'.[33] This was obviously a plan well at odds with any plans discussed by Imperial Headquarters or the Combined Fleet, and one subject to similar criticisms brought to bear against Navy General Staff proposals.

Yamashita was never popular with Tōjō, and if he was perhaps hoping to curry favour with his prime minister through this highly ambitious plan, the scheme did not work: several months later he was reassigned to command the First Area Army in Manchuria, a newly created unit that was effectively a garrison and reserve force. He did not return to a prominent post, commanding the 14th Area Army in the Philippines, until after Tōjō resigned as prime minister in July 1944.

A further overly ambitious plan was presented on 20 February by the commander of the 2nd Carrier Division, Rear Admiral Yamaguchi Tamon, during several days of table manoeuvres for proposed Indian Ocean operations. It is discussed here in some detail as this 'blueprint' has been put forward in recent debate as a further example of a senior officer supporting the invasion of Australia.[34]

The proposal included several stages of operation. Stage one was to establish a greater East Asian sphere, the second to bring the surrender of Britain, and the third to bring the surrender of the United States. Stage two would see key locations in India taken by the end of May, including Ceylon, Calcutta and Bombay. By the end of June, Fiji, Samoa, New Caledonia, New Zealand and Australia would be captured. If possible, Australia would be coached into joining the Greater East-Asia Co-prosperity Sphere. In the first phase of stage three, the Aleutians would be taken in August or September, Midway, Johnston Island and Palmyra in

November and December, and Java in January 1943. Phase two of stage three involved attacks on the west coast of the United States and the Panama Canal, and the occupation of Californian oil fields, should conditions allow. Air units sent to California would then be able to attack major cities and military installations across North America.[35]

The editors of Japan's official history included this plan as an example of the 'extremist aggressive doctrine held by some in the Navy at the time', and judged that it showed 'great errors of understanding of the actual conditions for war preparations'. Further, there was no consideration of how these vast territories would be held once captured, and no indication of any Army involvement in the execution of the plan. The evaluation of the Navy general staff at the time was that the proposal was only fit for an undergraduate table exercise.[36] Given the unrealistic objectives and methods of this exercise document, regarding it as evidence for support of an invasion of Australia is problematic.

Meanwhile, with debate over future operations threatening to get out of hand, Army Chief of Staff Sugiyama wrote several times to his naval counterpart, Nagano, seeking a speedy resolution. He outlined again Army plans to establish a position of self-sufficiency, to increase the country's position and hasten the end of the war. He felt that any plan to 'deal with' all or even a part of Australia would develop into a war of attrition that would spread across the whole country – a development Japan could ill afford.[37]

A COMPROMISE SOLUTION

By the end of February, the issue of invasion had reached a head. The Army had by then undertaken substantial research into the Navy's plans, and concluded that the proposed operation would exceed the limit of Japan's military and national resources, and was neither a necessary or effective means to end the war, attain a position of self-sufficiency, nor have a dire effect on Britain or the United States. The Army further judged the operation would require 10 or 12 divisions of troops, which were unavailable. It also pointed out that the 2 million tonnes of shipping it felt necessary to transport and support the operation was simply not available.[38]

On 4 March, after repeated failed attempts to reach a compromise at a junior staff level, departmental heads from the Army and Navy General Staffs agreed on a course of action at the residence of the Navy minister.[39] This agreement led to a new policy document, entitled 'Outline of war leadership to be hereafter adopted', which was ratified at a liaison conference on 7 March and then presented to the Emperor by Prime Minister Tōjō,

Sugiyama and Nagano five days later. The outline contained something for both the Army and Navy. It maintained the essence of pre-war plans to shift to a defensive position to protect newly acquired gains, as sought by the Army, but also contained the phrase 'taking active measures if such opportunity should arise', thus satisfying the Navy's desire for offensive measures.[40]

By this compromise, invasion of Australia was, to quote historian Henry Frei, 'put on the back burner for good'. The 'outline of war leadership to be hereafter adopted' did not mention Australia specifically, but an outline of future Army operational guidance presented to the emperor by Sugiyama on 19 March specified the position agreed by the Navy concerning the 'Australia Operation'. This admitted the great value of an invasion of Australia, but conceded that it would require too many troops, would weaken the national offensive strength, and would invite attack from the Soviet Union in the north.

The compromise seemed to give the Navy hope by leaving room to revisit the issue after certain conditions were met: namely after the anxiety over the Soviet Union was resolved, after the Chungking regime had surrendered, and after the situation in general had markedly improved.[41] This was not a simple shelving of the question for later revisiting, for as events would prove, these conditions were never met. In truth, this wording was perhaps an exercise in face-saving, as none present would have been optimistic enough to expect all these conditions to be fulfilled, especially concerning a resolution in China after so many years of heavy resistance. In a final concession, the Army agreed to 'undertake research to consider the necessity of a temporary invasion of places like Port Darwin if circumstances allow'.[42] This was hardly a solid statement of intent.

CONCLUSION

In a sense, however, all this heated debate and carefully worded compromise was rendered academic by the overriding desire of Yamamoto to destroy the US carrier fleet in an early decisive battle. In April, Yamamoto, under threat again to resign as he had done prior to acceptance of the Pearl Harbor attack, forced on the Navy General Staff his plan to capture Midway, a small US outpost in the Pacific, in the hope of luring the US carriers to their destruction. The Army was initially opposed to this plan, as expected, but the Navy threatened to carry it out without Army troops. The Army eventually came around to the plan, however, in no small part because of the psychological impact of the first US air attack against the Japanese homeland on 18 April, the so-called Doolittle raid.

In the event, Japan's defeat at Midway was disastrous: four aircraft carriers, hundreds of aircraft and over 3000 personnel were lost. Though there was much hard fighting to come, the defeat at Midway tipped the scales towards the Allies and ensured that Japan could no longer dictate the overall tempo or location of offensive operations in the Pacific. The FS Operation, the keystone of Navy General Staff plans to isolate Australia, was postponed on 7 June as a direct result of the defeat at Midway, and cancelled altogether on 11 July.[43]

Given the great distances in northern Australia, there is no doubt that a small invasion force may have been able to secure a foothold in northern Australia in early 1942, but to what end? And this might only have been possible after a series of counterfactual turns of history: if Port Moresby had been taken, if local forces had been in a position to mount an invasion, if central headquarters had sanctioned such a plan, if Midway had not been lost, and so on. Further, there is some doubt whether Japan could have supported a force in the islands of the South Pacific sufficient to effect a complete blockade of the supply lines between the United States and Australia, thus negating the whole rationale for the FS Operation.

By mid-1942, the limit of Japanese control spanned a huge part of the globe, but drawing a line between the key locations Japanese forces had occupied did not make for a secure perimeter. The Doolittle raid on 18 April proved that. Neither did colouring the area within the perimeter mean that supply lines would be or remain secure. These would be even more at risk by extending a major front further south. Further, Japanese merchant shipping, which would come under increasing pressure from Allied attack, would struggle to supply sufficient raw materials for Japanese industry, let alone support further operations. In early 1942 Japanese military planners considered, but did not plan or have the capacity to embark on, an invasion of Australia; regardless of the desire to do so by some Japanese officers, regardless of perceptions in Australia at the time, and regardless of the rhetoric of some contemporary Japanese publications. The course of the war ensured they could never reconsider.

Notes

1   Dōmei Tsūshinsha (ed.), *Saikin no Gōshū* (*Present Day Australia*), Dōmei Tsūshinsha, Tokyo, 1939, pp. 92–6.
2   Based on a survey of the holdings of the National Library of Australia, Canberra, and the National Diet Library, Tokyo (http://opac.ndl.go.jp, accessed 8 April 2012).
3   Henry Frei, *Japan's Southward Advance and Australia: From the Sixteenth Century to World War II*, University of Hawaii Press, Honolulu, 1991, p. 197.

4   Madarame Fumio, *Gōshū shinryaku-shi* (History of the Invasion of Australia), Ōbunsha, Tokyo, 1942, pp. 275–6.
5   Nanpō Sangyō Chōsakai (ed.), *Gōshū* (Australia), Nanshinsha, Tokyo, 1942, p. 156.
6   See Chapter 6.
7   Aizawa Kiyoshi, 'Japanese Strategy in the First Phase of the Pacific War', in National Institute for Defense Studies, *Strategy in the Pacific War: NIDS International Forum on War History: Proceedings*, National Institute for Defense Studies, Tokyo, 2009, p. 35.
8   Hattori Takushirō, *Daitōa Sensō zenshi* (History of the Greater East Asian War), 2nd edn, Hara Shobō, Tokyo, 1965, pp. 138–43.
9   Jonathan B. Parshall and Anthony P. Tully, *Shattered Sword: The Untold Story of the Battle of Midway*, Potomac Books, Washington, D.C., 2005, p. 24.
10 Bōeichō Bōei Kenshūjo Senshishitsu (ed.), *Daihon'ei kaigunbu: rengōkantai 2: Shōwa 17 nen 6 gatsu made* (Imperial Headquarters Navy Department no. 2: up to June 1942), vol. 80, Senshi Sōsho, Asagumo Shinbunsha, Tokyo, 1975, p. 314 (hereafter abbreviated BBKS, vol. 80).
11 Nobutaka Ike (ed.), *Japan's Decision for War: Records of the 1941 Policy Conferences*, Stanford University Press, Stanford, 1967, pp. 247–9.
12 Ike, *Japan's Decision for War*, pp. 153, 232–3.
13 BBKS (ed.), *Nantō hōmen kaigun sakusen 1: Ga Shima dakkai sakusen kaishi made* (Navy Operations in the South East Area no. 1: Up to the Start of the Withdrawal from Guadalcanal), vol. 49, Senshi Sōsho, Asagumo Shinbunsha, Tokyo, 1971, p. 29.
14 Doi Kazuo (staff officer, 4th Fleet), 'Statement Concerning Southern Operations', 18 January 1950, in '*Minami Taiheiyō hōmen chinjutsu tsuzuri*', *Chūō Keisen Shori 112*, National Institute for Defense Studies Library, Tokyo.
15 BBKS, vol. 49, p. 34.
16 BBKS, vol. 80, p. 314.
17 BBKS, vol. 49, p. 352.
18 Tomioka Sadatoshi, *Kaisen to shūsen: hito to kikō to keikaku* (The Opening and Ending of War: People, Organisation and Plans), Mainichi Shinbunsha, Tokyo, 1968, pp. 116–17.
19 BBKS, vol. 80, pp. 312–3.
20 Tomioka, *Kaisen to shūsen* (*The Opening and Ending of War*), p. 117.
21 Frei, *Japan's Southward Advance and Australia*, p. 164.
22 BBKS (ed.), *Daihon'ei rikugunbu 3: Shttōwa 17 nen 4 gatsu made* (Imperial Headquarters Army Department no. 3: Up to April 1942), vol. 35, Senshi Sōsho, Asagumo Shinbunsha, Tokyo, 1968, pp. 469, 477–8.
23 BBKS, vol. 80, p. 314.
24 Donald M. Goldstein and Katherine V. Dillon (eds), *Fading Victory: The Diary of Admiral Matome Ugaki, 1941–1945*, University of Pittsburgh Press, Pittsburgh, 1991, p. 68.
25 BBKS (ed.), *Middouei kaisen* (The Naval Battle of Midway), vol. 43, Senshi Sōsho, Asagumo Shinbunsha, Tokyo, 1971, p. 26.
26 Goldstein and Dillon, *Fading Victory*, p. 68.
27 BBKS, vol. 80, p. 300.

28 Parshall and Tully, *Shattered Sword*, pp. 24–5.
29 BBKS, vol. 43, p. 25.
30 Goldstein and Dillon, *Fading Victory*, p. 75.
31 BBKS, vol. 80, p. 323.
32 Gunji Shigakkai (ed.), *Daihon'ei rikugunbu sensō shidōhan kimitsu sensō nisshi* (Imperial Headquarters Army Department War Direction Group Secret War Diary), vol. 1, Kinseisha, Tokyo, 1998, p. 222.
33 David Bergamini, *Japan's Imperial Conspiracy*, William Heinemann Ltd, London, 1971, pp. 898–9.
34 See Bob Wurth, *1942: Australia's Greatest Peril*, Pan Macmillan, Sydney, 2008, pp. 136–7; and Bob Wurth, 'Know Thy Enemy & Thyself', *Australian Army Journal*, vol. VI, no. 1, 2009, p. 15.
35 BBKS, vol. 80, p. 304–6.
36 Ibid, pp. 304, 307.
37 BBKS, vol. 35, p. 470.
38 Ibid, p. 474.
39 Ibid, pp. 512–3.
40 Yashiro Noriaki, 'Japanese Strategy in the Second Phase of the Pacific War', in National Institute for Defense Studies, *Strategy in the Pacific War: NIDS International Forum on War History: Proceedings*, National Institute for Defense Studies, Tokyo, 2009, pp. 82–3.
41 BBKS, vol. 80, p. 338.
42 Ibid.
43 Steven Bullard (trans.), *Japanese Army Operations in the South Pacific Area: New Britain and Papua Campaigns, 1942–43*, Australian War Memorial, Canberra, 2007, pp. 100–8.

FURTHER READING

Frei, H., *Japan's Southward Advance and Australia: From the Sixteenth Century to World War II*, University of Hawaii Press, Honolulu, 1991.

Goldstein, D. M. and Dillon, K. V. (eds), *Fading Victory: The Diary of Admiral Matome Ugaki, 1941–1945*, University of Pittsburgh Press, Pittsburgh, 1991.

Goldstein, D. M. and Dillon, K. V. (eds), *The Pacific War Papers: Japanese Documents of World War II*, Potomac Books, Washington, D.C., 2004.

Ike, N. (ed.), *Japan's Decision for War: Records of the 1941 Policy Conferences*, Stanford University Press, Stanford, 1967.

Iriye, A., *The Origins of the Second World War in Asia and the Pacific*, Longman, Harlow, 1987.

National Institute for Defense Studies, *Strategy in the Pacific War: NIDS International Forum on War History: Proceedings*, National Institute for Defense Studies, Tokyo, 2009.

Parshall, J. B. and Tully, A. P., *Shattered Sword: The Untold Story of the Battle of Midway*, Potomac Books, Washington, D.C., 2005.

Stanley, P., *Invading Australia: Japan and the Battle for Australia, 1942*, Viking, Camberwell, 2008.

Willmott, H., *The Second World War in the Far East*, Cassell, London, 1999.

CHAPTER 8

The Air Raids on Darwin, 19 February 1942

Image and Reality

Alan Powell

In the early morning of 19 February 1942 the Japanese Navy's 1st and 2nd Carrier Divisions, under command of Vice Admiral Nagumo Chuicki – with the four aircraft carriers *Akagi*, *Kaga*, *Soryu* and *Hiryu* – deployed its attack force for the first raid. The carriers reached their launching point some 350 kilometres northeast of Darwin and sent off 188 aircraft – 36 fighters, 71 dive bombers and 81 level-bombers. At 9.57 a.m. the first of them struck the wharf, the shipping and the town. Of the 55 vessels of all sizes in the harbour on that morning[1], eight were sunk or run ashore, including the US Navy destroyer *Peary*, the transports *Meigs*, *Mauna Loa* and *Portmar*, the tanker *British Motorist*, the coastal traders *Zealandia* and *Barossa* – and the liner *Neptuna*, filled with munitions that were still burning and exploding at the wharf half an hour after the raiders had gone. Apart from the loss of 88 sailors in USS *Peary*, the greatest loss of life that day occurred on the wharf, where a whole span collapsed, and aboard *Neptuna*. The town was heavily strafed, although a police count showed that only 17 bombs fell there[2] and property damage was moderate. But the shock to Darwin residents was great, especially as the single bomb that destroyed the Post Office killed nine of the staff, including six women.

By 10.40 a.m. the raiders had departed. Eighty minutes later, 54 land-based Japanese bombers from Kendari and Ambon pattern-bombed the RAAF base, destroying nearly all the aircraft on the ground there, burning out the two hangars, the main store and severely damaging several

Photo 23 A large crater in the middle of what remains of the Darwin Post Office and Post Master's residence, after the first Japanese air-raid on 19 February 1942. The Post Master, his wife and daughter, and members of the postal staff, including four female telephonists and two postal officers, were killed during the raid (AWM P02759.004).

other buildings. To complete the destruction of that day, out at sea the Japanese air armada sighted the Filipino blockade runner *Don Isidro*, reporting her presence to Vice Admiral Nagumo, who sent out a flight of aircraft to destroy the ship. This they did, driving her ashore as a burned-out wreck on Bathurst Island and, for good measure, the final act was the sinking of a second blockade runner, the *Florence D*.

The bombing of Darwin on that day was the only time in our history that the full weight of modern war has fallen upon mainland Australia. As such, it is well covered in Australian historical literature. Almost immediately the raid was made the subject of a Royal Commission, headed by Justice Charles Lowe,[3] while no less than three popular books, all written by journalists, have covered the subject,[4] nor has it been overlooked by the professional community of historians.

The raids were covered in the relevant Navy and RAAF volumes of the official Australian Second World War histories as well as in Paul Hasluck's *The Government and the People*.[5] Historians such as Tom Lewis,[6] Bob Alford[7] and Robert Rayner[8] have discussed the parts played by the separate Armed Services. Pam Oliver[9] and Peter Stanley[10] have meticulously covered the strategic background. Three of my books discuss the raids in the context of broader themes.[11] Personal reminiscences abound and so do magazine and newspaper articles to the present day.[12] There are even kits on *Australia's Frontline: The Territory at War*[13] for Northern Territory schoolchildren.

Thus, we know a great deal about the two raids of 19 February 1942. Yet, the historical record is not perfect and a number of controversies have not been settled – not the least of them being the contrast between the reality of the raids and the evolving image of them that has been presented in the literature during the past 70 years.

It is well established that in early 1942 the Japanese high command had no plans to invade Australia. The 19 February raids were a tactical move to prevent interference with Japanese plans to take Java and the southeastern islands of the archipelago, particularly Timor, where the landing was planned for 20 February. Perhaps the most surprising aspect of this move was the sheer scale of the attacks, 'a sledgehammer to crack an egg', in the words of the attack leader, Commander Fuchida Mitsuo.[14] In Bob Alford's words, the result was 'overkill': a combined total of nearly 115 000 kilograms of bombs dropped on Darwin, two and a half times the number of bombs and 83 per cent of the tonnage dropped on Pearl Harbor on 7 December 1941.[15] As Douglas Lockwood notes, Fuchida was dissatisfied with the role allocated to the Carrier Task Force and argued that no more than a single carrier should have been sent against a secondary target such as Darwin.[16] So why then use two carrier divisions to neutralise the place? It may be that the whole force was used for no better reason than that it was immediately available and could be used without disruption to plans for its later strategic role. In the end we do not know, either because the relevant Japanese documents no longer exist or, more likely, because they have not yet drawn the attention of Japanese war historians and English-language translators.

There's a similar problem, too, with Japanese sources for the raids themselves. Nearly all of the references to the raid originate in the post-war National Institute for Defence Studies (NIDS) series, volume 26, first published in 1969. Part of this document has been translated and appeared in this author's 1988 book *The Shadow's Edge*,[17] and Tom Lewis's and Peter Williams's *Through Japanese Eyes*.[18] Apart from a 1997 NIDS monograph[19] the NIDS volume 26 appears to be the only significant Japanese source so far consulted in Australian accounts of the Darwin raids. This volume lists, with only mild exaggeration, the damage done to shipping, wharf facilities, the town and the RAAF Base – but makes no judgements of how well the effects of the raids stacked up against the aims.

This lack of Japanese source material leads us into a number of puzzles. For example, the 11 naval oil tanks in Darwin, built in the 1930s without thought of air assault and defended only by makeshift machines – gun posts – were wide open to attack. They should have been a prime target. Yet, not one oil tank received a direct hit and only one suffered minor splinter damage. This question was given more substance less than four weeks later when the Japanese destroyed no less than five of the tanks in a minor raid on 16 March, and two more on 16 June. This led the RAN to fear that the port would become unusable and they authorised the driving of oil tunnels into the cliffs below the town of Darwin, a venture that was eventually abandoned unfinished after costing the then-enormous sum of £700 000.[20] The tunnels haven't been an entire waste, though, now being one of the town's most significant tourist attractions. Similarly, the HMAS *Coonawarra*, a vital naval communications station just across the road from the RAAF base, should have been a major target, but was not directly attacked and suffered only minor collateral damage.

Another question relates to the ships sunk in the harbour. As noted earlier, there were 55 vessels in port that day, at least 25 of which could be expected to provide significant targets for the attacking air armada. How was it then that an overwhelming force, manned by pilots who were probably the world's best naval fliers at the time and who, despite the valiant efforts of the defenders, were faced with very light opposition, could sink no more than eight vessels, two of which were quickly refloated? The Defence Studies volume quotes a raider's report to higher authority as claiming 11 ships sunk and stating that 'besides these ships, there were ... some other small ships, but we did not attack them'.[21] The surviving ships included two RAN sloops, *Swan* and *Warrego*, plus five corvettes, all of which were significant military targets. Of these seven ships only *Swan* suffered significant bomb damage and casualties.

From an Australian point of view, the raids were devastating, but did Admiral Nagumo and his staff really believe that, too? Commander Fuchida's remark, at least, suggests that they thought the target hardly worthwhile and their actual estimates of their success are still unknown. *Through Japanese Eyes* implies that documents relevant to answering that question may exist; but why should Japanese historians of the Second World War bother to seek the answer to a minor tactical question when they have so many fields of major enquiry to investigate?

From an Australian perspective, there is also a list of unanswered questions. The big question, of course, is could – or should – the Australian government and the military have done more to aid northern defence? Considering Cabinet Secretary Sir Frederick Shedden's remark that ministers 'ran around like a lot of startled chooks', and other evidence

Photo 24 Darwin, 19 February 1942, the SS *Neptuna* explodes at Stokes Hill Wharf, sending a column of debris and smoke hundreds of metres into the air (AWM P05303.022).

of panic in government ranks,[22] do we really know the full effects that the twin catastrophes of Singapore's fall on 15 February and the Darwin attacks on 19 February had on government action in the immediate aftermath?

A host of other questions remain unanswered. General Archibald Wavell's US, British, Dutch and Australian (ABDA) Command Headquarters staff in Java knew of the presence of the Japanese carrier force in the Timor Sea as early as 17 February[23] and as Darwin was the principal Australian mainland base under Wavell's ABDA command why was the town never informed of their presence? This question goes hand in hand with a question about Father John McGrath's warning from Bathurst Island that was apparently lost in the labyrinth of the Darwin command system.[24]

Other critical questions include, why did the Naval Officer in Charge, Captain Penry Thomas, choose to double-berth and unload ships on both sides of the main wharf, although, as he admitted to the Royal Commission,[25] he fully expected an air-raid on the port that day? What was the total number of deaths caused by the raids? Estimates range from the Royal Commission's minimum figure of 243 to the wildly inflated figure of 'over 1000' perpetuated by contributors to the Darwin Defenders book, *Darwin's Battle for Australia*.[26] Recent meticulous research by Northern Territory Library staff under the supervision of Research Services manager John Richards has set the figure at 230.[27] This is authoritative, but, as John Richards has pointed out, there can never be absolute certainty.[28] Was there a failure of military and civil leadership in the town both before and after the raids? This is a major question that still needs further investigation. How many aircraft did the Japanese lose and who shot them down? Japanese and Australian estimates do not tally and neither do those of various Australian and American sources.[29] And finally, did the Japanese intentionally bomb the hospital ship *Manunda*?[30]

These questions are also shrouded by the supposed controversy over the degree of government censorship in the immediate aftermath of the raids. There were certainly delays, conflicting views among military and government sources and confusion over details though, as Peter Stanley says: 'The common view that the government suppressed details of the raid is simply false'.[31] Nor does there appear to have been any significant public reaction to the news – until Paul Hasluck, then Minister for Territories, put the cat among the pigeons when he told the Northern Territory Legislative Council in 1955 that 19 February was 'the anniversary of a day of national shame: Australians ran away because they did not know what else to do. It was a panic evacuation'.[32]

Hasluck's allegation seems to have been responsible for much of the Australian public's subsequent interest. As noted in *The Shadow's Edge*, Australians at large did not and still do not accept that they could become the flotsam and jetsam of war as easily as anyone else. To a nation that had never known war on its own soil and built a legend for a whole people on the image of a chosen few who fought on foreign ground the reaction to the bombing of Darwin was intolerable.[33] All three journalists who have written books on the bombing of Darwin take note of it.

Douglas Lockwood's *Australia's Pearl Harbour*, first published in 1966, republished many times and lately renamed *Australia Under Attack*,[34] is probably the most influential of them and certainly the most durable. In 1942, Lockwood was the Darwin correspondent for the Melbourne *Herald*. He was in Darwin on the day of the raids and his vivid description of them has never been equalled. He gave due acknowledgement to the courage of the AA gunners, Navy and civilian rescuers on the harbour, police and ARP men on shore, set against the utter disaster of the attacks. His is a well-balanced account, except that his journalistic instinct for a good story got away with him in his account of the post-raid exodus from the town popularly known as the 'Adelaide River Stakes'.

Lockwood records an account of the sanitary truck – the nightcart – leaving town with eight prominent citizens on the roof as it hurtled down the dirt track to Adelaide River. The twist to the story is that the truck overturned on a corner, spilling the contents into the bush and that, while the driver and passengers were heaving the truck back onto its wheels, a military police patrol came by and stopped to ask what the matter was only to be told, 'We're just having a stocktaking, mate!'[35] Alas, the tale is almost certainly apocryphal, as Lockwood well knew, but there is something quintessentially Australian about it. Lockwood's book was, and still is, by far the most likely and enjoyable account of the raids and it contains a lot of shrewd analysis, but it has not done much to dispel the 'panic' image generated by Paul Hasluck.

In 1980 another journalist, Timothy Hall, took up the subject in his book *Darwin 1942: Australia's Darkest Hour*.[36] The title sets the theme. Hall positively revelled in accusations of panic. 'People ran everywhere like a flock of sheep and panicked', he notes 'by the time the second alarm sounded the general stampede was on'. What really happened, says the cover summary, 'was a combination of chaos, panic and, in many cases, cowardice on an unprecedented scale'. The writer of that got the date

Photo 25 Parts of the engines were all that was left of two RAAF Wirraway planes in a hangar at the Darwin aerodrome after the Japanese bombed the area on 19 February 1942 (AWM 026980).

wrong, too, placing the raids on 18 February, a day too early.[37] Hall claimed to have had access to the evidence of the Lowe Report, which had been denied to Lockwood, but there is very little indication of it in the text and none at all in his chapter on the exodus from the town. So, while his overall and very dramatic emphasis on panic and stampede may have sold books, it does not help us to clarify what actually happened that day. The latest general history of the raids, by yet another journalist, Peter Grose, was published in 2009 under the unexplained title *An Awkward Truth*.[38] It is well written, summarises much of the known information about that day and raises some interesting questions, but provides no new answers.

In understanding the reality of the raids' aftermath, the Lowe Report evidence proves to be vital. Justice Lowe had promised all witnesses that their evidence would remain confidential. Thus, they spoke openly and their comments, taken together with other oral evidence, pointed overwhelmingly to exodus, but not panic. These people were simply refugees in their own country, plodding away from war in a fashion as old as war itself.[39]

It is likely that these three books (and, particularly, Lockwood's ever-green account) have been a strong factor in public perception of the events of 19 February 1942 and thus on the ways in which they have been commemorated. Possibly, too, they have been a factor in discouraging professional historians from pursuing a close examination of the overall topic. The point of all this is that, 70 years after the event, we still lack an in-depth and authoritative account of the 19 February raids.

What we do not lack is annual commemoration of them in Darwin and in some ways these events have become a microcosm of Australian political changes and attitudes to war during the past 70 years. These changes over time are revealed through the local Darwin newspaper reports of the commemorative events seen at 10-year intervals. In 1952, local feeling about the Japanese was still raw. The editor of the union newspaper, *The Northern Standard*, set the tone:

> Tomorrow marks the tenth anniversary of the day when the Japanese, in a treacherous sneak raid, blitzed Darwin. Many Territorians have tragic memories of their families, their friends or their fellow-workers shot down before their eyes ... as Japanese machine guns raked the streets and Japanese bombs shattered Darwin's buildings and homes.[40]

On this day the service at the Darwin cenotaph was one of 'simple dig-nity'.[41] Union men and their families gathered at the main wharf to cast wreaths into the water in silent memory of their lost comrades, a custom still carried out today. Minister for Territories Paul Hasluck, in a message read by NT Administrator Frank Wise noted that 'This is a day on which all Australia should recall the perils of the past and the vows made that never again would we be caught unprepared and that never again would we neglect any part of our great national heritage'.[42] The Territory's sole Member of Parliament, Jock Nelson, urged the government to make 19 February a national commemoration day because, he said, it 'usually goes unnoticed in the south'.[43] As a closing note to the sense of personal loss so keenly felt that day, the new *Northern Territory News* published a list of local civilians killed in the raids.[44]

Ten years later, the situation had changed. Darwin's population, about 6000 people in 1952, had grown, mainly through defence spending, to about 12 000 in 1962. This diluted the number and influence of those with personal memories; and local attitudes towards the old enemy had significantly changed, for two main reasons: pearls and salvage. In 1953, against bitter RSL and union opposition, the Commonwealth Government allowed the return of Japanese divers to the north Australian pearling industry. By 1956, 58 Japanese, plus 24 Ryukuans, worked in pearling out of Darwin[45] and there were no protests; business beat bitterness. The second factor was the presence of the Fujita Salvage Company. In 1959, this Japanese company gained the contract to raise and carry off to Japan the scrap metal from the ships their compatriots had sunk 17 years earlier. This they did, with great efficiency, over the following three years. They also paid court to local businesses and carefully cultivated good social relations with the people of Darwin, even donating crosses made from their *Zealandia* salvage to the new Memorial United Church. In July 1960, Dame Pattie Menzies, wife of the Prime Minister, officially opened the church; Paul Hasluck was on hand and Mr Katshshiro Narita, Japanese Ambassador to Australia, spoke in apology for the past and hope for the future.[46]

Small wonder then that the 1962 commemoration ceremony was in a much lower key than that of three years previously, given the distinct possibility that the attendance was already being eroded by growing disaffection with the Vietnam war. Five hundred people had attended the cenotaph service in 1959, 'about 200' in 1962, according to the meagre half-page that *The Northern Territory News* would spare for it.[47] Administrator Roger Nott and Mayor Cooper gave short speeches, largely unreported; there were no messages from the Commonwealth and the ceremony was notable mainly for taking the form which thereafter became conventional: a standing guard at the cenotaph with arms reversed, laying of wreaths by service and civilian personnel, speeches by dignitaries, a RAAF fly-past, sounding of the 'Last Post' and observance of two minutes' silence.

In January 1972 former Leader of the Opposition Arthur Caldwell called for the release of the Lowe Report evidence.[48] This raised a flurry of press interest.[49] During the previous decade, the Northern Territory economy had received a tremendous boost from government spending on defence, education, health, welfare services and infrastructure, raising the 1972 population of Darwin to over 40 000;[50] this increase, together with the publicity generated by Caldwell's comments, might have been expected to provide a good turn-out for the 30th-anniversary commemoration ceremony. It did not. About 100 people attended; there was no Commonwealth representation and Supreme Court Justice Foster was the sole official speaker, warning (if the single paragraph devoted to his speech by the local press is to be trusted) of the dangers in being unprepared, thus harking back to the principal theme of earlier years.[51] No doubt few of those who came to live in Darwin during the previous 10 years had any personal connection with the wartime town and Darwin already had a well-deserved reputation for high population turnover and thus lack of interest in Northern history, but these factors alone seem inadequate to explain the dismally poor attendance at the cenotaph ceremony. At that time, in the late years of the Vietnam conflict, anti-war activism in Australia had reached a high pitch: Anzac Day ceremonial attendances suffered and for the same reason, it seems, so did attendance at the bombing of Darwin commemorations.

The year 1982 was a very different story. The anti-war movement still flourished throughout Australia: in the Territory, the balance of 19 February publicity and ceremonial swung the other way, long before the renaissance of Anzac Day. The coming of Territory self-government in 1978 made the difference. The new Country Liberal Party government, led by dynamic Chief Minister Paul Everingham, energetically pushed everything that promoted national consciousness of the Northern Territory – and the bombing of 19 February 1942 was an experience shared by no one else. Vigorous promotion of the 40-year commemoration ceremony saw attendance rise remarkably. The NT Administrator, Commodore Eric Johnson, read a long message from Governor-General Sir Zelman Cowen (himself a young naval officer in wartime Darwin) and added his own comments, as did guest of honour Air Chief Marshal Sir Frederick Scherger. The Territory government subsidised the return of veterans for the occasion, including Robert G. Oestreicher who, as a young lieutenant in the US Army Air Force, had flown his P40 fighter against the attacking

Japanese that day. Press reports of the principal speeches suggest a subtle shift of emphasis from 'panic' towards heroism, and even pouring rain during the ceremony did not noticeably dampen the renewed spirit of the occasion.[52]

Since then, Territory governments have consistently followed a vision[53]: the bombing of Darwin was unique and its anniversary should be recognised throughout Australia as a special day and, to that end, the 50th anniversary, 19 February 1992, was commemorated with special care and in a manner that would draw national and international attention. A younger generation had, tentatively, begun to take up the traditions of Anzac Day, and new publications drew attention to the north Australian war. The first edition of *The Shadow's Edge*, which was (and still is) the only publication dealing with all aspects of that war, came out in 1988, followed by a second edition on 1992.[54] The first edition of Bob Alford's *Darwin's Air War* appeared in 1991.[55] At least two other publications on maritime aspects were published in 1992[56] and, on 18 February 1992, the popular magazine, *The Bulletin*, printed a lengthy article and survivor's stories, including, significantly, a sympathetic account of the suffering endured by the long-resident Murikami family when they were arrested along with all others of Japanese descent and sent south to internment.[57]

The Territory's Country Liberal Party government, thoroughly entrenched after 14 years in power, and under the firm control of Chief Minister Marshall Perron, set up an organisation, *Frontline Australia*, to organise a commemorative pageant during most of the previous year, using a theme based on mention by Australia's wartime Prime Minister, John Curtin, of the 'Battle for Australia'. Under Director Andrew Coward, Frontline Australia arranged reunions, historical displays, exhibitions, concerts, speeches and promotion of school information kits. Darwin's Today's Territory television production company produced a documentary *The Battle for Australia* and NT Conservation Minister Mike Reed emphasised the tourist potential of the project by authorising the development of wartime historical trails, with documentation available through offices of the Conservation Commission, Tourist Bureau and National Trust. The *Sydney Morning Herald* published an article under the heading 'Forgotten Heroes of Darwin'[58] and the Territory government provided generous subsidies to ensure that as many as possible of those who had served in the Territory during the Second World War returned for the bombing anniversary.

The line-up of speakers at the 19 February commemoration ceremony reached the heights of power and dignity. Sir Zelman Cowen, reprising his role of 10 years earlier, was on hand. So were Prime Minister Paul Keating and the Leader of the Opposition, Dr John Hewson. In a reminder of renewed government interest in northern defence, Hornet fighters from RAAF Base Tindal flew overhead, four RAN ships laid wreaths over the sites of sunken wrecks in the harbour and no less than 13 new plaques were unveiled on the memorial wall – all reported under the heading 'Nation Honours War Dead'.[59] Even George Bush (Snr), President of the US, had his say, sending a message dedicated to the 'courageous individuals' who died in the sinking of USS *Peary*.[60]

'Today is … a day on which we should look to the past with pride and therefore to the future with confidence', editorialised the *Northern Territory News*.[61] The Japanese were also present. After the anniversary, businessman 'Tony' Mitani presented a cheque for $30 000 to complete the purchase of Jaimes Baines vast and lurid painting, 'Bombs Over Darwin', so that it might, 'in sincere apology to the world',[62] hang in the Darwin Aviation Heritage Centre. The trend towards emphasis on heroism, pride and apology was blunted only by fiery journalist Frank Alcorta, who warned that north Australia, in real terms, was no better defended than it had been in 1942,[63] and by local tourist bodies who feared, with good reason, that the $1.5 million spent on promoting the Territory's war service year was not enough to counter the current market depression.[64]

In 1999 Tom Lewis published a dispassionate analysis of the raids, with emphasis on the maritime aspects.[65] But a few months later, John Bradford's book *In the Highest Traditions* resumed the trend towards highlighting heroism rather than disaster.[66] A newly incorporated group, Darwin Defenders 1942–45, began to publish a newsletter at that time and in 2005 turned out a book of reminiscences aiming 'to overcome the results of 53 years of government censorship and discrimination against Darwin Veterans and to set the record straight by publishing their stories before they are lost forever'.[67] Since the major aim of this organisation was (and still is) 'to ensure that the people of Australia will never forget those who left their friends, families and all that was dear to them, endured hardships and dangers and were prepared to sacrifice their lives to protect their country when Australia was attacked by the Japanese in 1942',[68] it was not to be expected that they would emphasise the negative aspects of Australian behaviour on 19 February 1942, and they did not. However, they did add materially to the 60th-anniversary commemoration by being instrumental in bringing veterans and their families to Darwin for the event; according to the *Northern Territory News*, more than 800 of these people came north for the occasion.[69] In the early months of a new Labor administration, which allowed less time for organisation and on an occasion seen to be generally less significant than the half-century commemoration, due notice was taken of the comment by a Darwin Defenders organiser that he did not think his members would come again because 'the average age is 80 and this is their swan song',[70] and much of the press coverage was taken up by the recounting of personal stories.

This year, 2012, the 70th anniversary of the bombing, saw a now long-serving Territory Labor government under Chief Minister Paul Henderson, determined to lay claim to an honourable and lasting place for Darwin in Australian history. 'The bombing of Darwin', he said, 'was a defining moment in the history of our nation, but still too few Australians fully appreciate the magnitude and significance of what occurred on that February day in 1942'.[71] Thus, he said, his government aimed to make 19 February a National Day of Remembrance and to have the bombing of Darwin included in the national school curriculum. His government put $10 million into building a new 'Defence of Darwin Experience', a 'multimedia showpiece' next to the Darwin military museum 'to ensure the stories of that time are recorded' – and, no doubt, to boost the flow of tourists to the Top End. If any further excuse was needed to explain particular emphasis on the 70th anniversary, it was that this really would be the last 10-year occasion on which survivors could gather in Darwin, and Minister of Veterans' Affairs Mark Vail led a party of 26 veterans and war widows to attended the cenotaph ceremony.[72] The official program of happenings on and around that date listed nearly 40 events, ranging from five separate commemorative ceremonies, a wide range of exhibitions, concerts, talks, a new play, a black-tie ball attended by 1000 people, the 'world premier' of a History Channel documentary on the bombing, a film festival, book launches, a commemorative AFL match and, most imaginatively of all, 'A Minute's Warning: A one-off wearable art production showcasing creations inspired by the bombing of Darwin'.[73]

All this did have much of its intended effect. The Prime Minister, Julia Gillard, promised to designate 19 February as a 'new national day of commemoration'.[74] Moreover, she was on hand for the main events, along with the Leader of the Opposition and the Governor-General. Very unusually, both the main commercial TV channels, Seven and Ten, sent teams to cover events in Darwin, and the ABC made good use of its Darwin-based TV and radio staff, so the occasion lacked little in media support. At the date of writing, inclusion of the Darwin raids in the revised national history syllabus is not certain but it would be a surprise if it were not. So Jock Nelson's 1952 wish for a national commemoration day that will not go unnoticed in the south has finally come about and the Territory government, it seems, has achieved the goals set out by the Chief Minister. Of course, there's a lot more to it than that.

Apart from the five commemorative ceremonies, nearly all of the planned events were principally concerned with tourism, commercial opportunity and/or politics. Fundamental to the latter is the constant struggle of Territory governments to make northern voices heard, the voices of a tiny minority of Australians scattered over one-sixth of the continent, in southern halls of power – read Canberra – and the quest for statehood. In the search for due notice, the bombing of Darwin commemorations give leverage far beyond their perpetuation of ritual.

What happens when the survivors of 1942 are no longer with us? As the US has recognised, the world's power centre is moving from the Atlantic to the Pacific and Indian Oceans, and in the future Darwin will again, in war or peace, be in Australia's front line. It is a safe bet that Territory governments are never going to allow their fellow Australians to forget it. Roll on the 80th!

Notes

1   Personal communication, John Richards (Manager, Research and Reference Services, Northern Territory Library) to author, 23 November 2011. This total includes 25 vessels large enough to be classed as ships; the rest of the total is made up of smaller vessels, ranging down to pearling luggers.

2   Alan Powell, *The Shadow's Edge*, 3rd edn, Charles Darwin University (CDU) Press, Darwin, 2007, p. 87.

3   *Commission of Inquiry Concerning the Circumstances Connected with the Attack Made by Japanese Aircraft on Darwin on 19th February 1942, before His Honour Mr Justice Lowe, Commissioner, First Report*, Commonwealth Parliamentary Paper, presented 5 October 1945.

4   Douglas Lockwood, *Australia's Pearl Harbour*, Penguin Books, Ringwood, 1975; Timothy Hall, *Darwin 1942*, Methuen Australia, Sydney, 1980; Peter Grose, *An Awkward Truth*, Allen & Unwin, Sydney, 2009.

5   G. Hermon Gill, *Royal Australian Navy, 1939–1942*, Australian War Memorial, Canberra, 1957, pp. 588–96; Douglas Gillison, *Royal Australian Air Force, 1939–1942*, Australian War Memorial, Canberra, 1962, pp. 423–32; Paul Hasluck, *The Government and the People, 1942–1945*, Australian War Memorial, Canberra, 1970, pp. 128–9, 140–4.

6   Tom Lewis, *A War at Home*, passim, Tall Stories, Darwin, 1999. Lewis has also written a novel (*Darwin Sayonara*, Boolarong Publications, Brisbane, 1991) relating to these events.

7   Bob Alford, *Darwin's Air War, 1942–1945*, The Aviation Society of the Northern Territory, Darwin, 2011, pp. 29–39.

8   Robert Rayner, *The Army and the Defence of Darwin Fortress*, Rudder Press, Plumpton NSW, 1995, pp. 187–218.

9   Pam Oliver, *Raids on Australia*, Australian Scholarly Publishing, Melbourne, 2010.
10 Peter Stanley, *Invading Australia*, Penguin Australia, Melbourne, 2008.
11 Alan Powell, *Far Country*, 5th edn, CDU Press, Darwin, 2009; Alan Powell, *The Shadow's Edge*; Alan Powell, *Northern Voyagers*, Australian Scholarly Publishing, Melbourne, 2010.
12 See, particularly, Powell, *The Shadow's Edge*, bibliography, for relevant examples.
13 *Australia's Frontline: The Territory at War*, compiled and published by the Northern Territory Department of Education, Darwin, 1992.
14 Quoted in Alford, *Darwin's Air War*, p. 39.
15 Ibid.
16 Lockwood, *Australia's Pearl Harbor*, Penguin, Ringwood, 2005, p. 210. Lockwood interviewed Fuchida some 20 years after the war.
17 See Powell, *The Shadow's Edge* (2007), p. 286.
18 Tom Lewis and Peter Williams (transl. Haruki Yoshida), *Through Japanese Eyes*, Darwin Military Museum, Darwin, 2010.
19 Captain Teruaki Kawano, *The Japanese Navy's Air Raid against Australia during World War Two*. See Alford, *Darwin's Air War*, pp. 207–8, 228. This source was apparently not used by Bob Alford. There is no indication that this and other (unspecified) Japanese sources accessed by Alford have significantly altered the raid accounts constructed from Western sources.
20 Powell, *The Shadow's Edge*, p. 138.
21 Lewis and Williams, *Through Japanese Eyes*, p. 21.
22 For Shedden's comment, see Powell, *The Shadow's Edge*, p. 93. See also David Horner, *High Command*, Allen & Unwin, Sydney, 1982, pp. 182–3.
23 See Lieutenant Bobb B. Glenn, diary, 17 February 1942, in possession of author.
24 See Powell, *The Shadow's Edge*, pp. 75–8.
25 Quoted in Powell, *The Shadow's Edge*, p. 74.
26 Rex Ruwoldt (ed.), *Darwin's Battle for Australia*, Darwin Defenders 1942–1945 Incorporated, Clifton Strings, Victoria, 2006: See forewords by Commodore D.H.D. Smyth, p. 6; Air Commodore M. J. Rawlinson, p. 8; editor's comment, p. 215.
27 Plus or minus three doubtfuls.
28 John Richards et al., Roll of Honour, www.ntlexhibit.nt.gov.au/exhibits/show/bod, 2012.
29 See for instance, Lewis and Williams, *Through Japanese Eyes*, pp. 9, 10, 22; interview with Matsuo Fuchida cited in Lockwood, *Darwin's Pearl Harbor*, p. 22; Lowe Report, p. 1; Powell, *The Shadow's Edge*, pp. 90–91; Alford, *Darwin's Air War*, p. 36; R. G. Oestreicher, interview transcript (interviewer Alan Powell), 19 February 1982, Northern Territory Archives Service, Darwin.
30 See Powell, *The Shadow's Edge*, p. 80; Lockwood, *Australia's Pearl Harbor*, pp. 57–60.
31 Peter Stanley, *Invading Australia*, p. 127.
32 Paul Hasluck, quoted in *Northern Territory News*, 29 March 1955.

33 Powell, *The Shadow's Edge*, p. 90.
34 Lockwood, *Australia under Attack*, New Holland, Sydney, 2005. Reference in this article is to the 1992 edition of *Australia's Pearl Harbour*.
35 Lockwood, *Australia's Pearl Harbor*, p. 158.
36 Hall, *Darwin 1942*, p. 132.
37 Ibid, summary, inside front cover.
38 Peter Grose, *An Awkward Truth*, Allen & Unwin, Sydney, 2009.
39 See Powell, 'The Darwin 'Panic', 1942', *Journal of the Australian War Memorial*, no. 3, October 1983, pp. 3–9; Powell, *The Shadow's Edge*, pp. 89–90.
40 *The Northern Standard*, 18 February 1952.
41 A London visitor's comment, *The Northern Standard*, 18 February 1952.
42 Ibid.
43 Ibid.
44 *The Northern Territory News*, 15 February 1952.
45 Alan Powell, *Northern Voyagers*, p. 338.
46 *The Northern Territory News*, 26 July 1960.
47 Ibid, 22 February 1962: See also issue of 20 February 1959.
48 *The Northern Territory News*, 11 January 1972.
49 See *The Northern Territory News*, 10, 11 January 1972.
50 Powell, *The Shadow's Edge*.
51 *The Northern Territory News*, 21 February 1972.
52 Ibid, 19 February 1982.
53 It must be noted that the author has benefitted considerably from government promotion of the Territory's past at that time. Coincidentally, my book on the history of the Northern Territory, *Far Country*, was first published in 1982. Chief Minister Everingham promptly presented me with a well-publicised special award and bought 500 copies of the hardback edition for distribution to all the VIPs he could think of. The Japanese ambassador got one; I'm not sure about the Queen!
54 Powell, *The Shadow's Edge*, Melbourne University Press, Melbourne, 1988 & 1992.
55 Alford, *Darwin's Air War, 1942–1945*.
56 Pat Forster and Ted Egan, *The Navy in Darwin, 1941–1943*, Museums and Art Galleries of the Northern Territory (MAGNT), Darwin, 1992; Sophie McCarthy, *World War II Shipwrecks and the First Japanese Raid on Darwin, 19 February 1942*, MAGNT, Darwin, 1992.
57 'Australia's Unqualified Disaster', *The Bulletin*, 18 February 1992.
58 *Sydney Morning Herald*, 25 January 1992.
59 *Northern Territory News*, 19 February 1992.
60 George H. W. Bush, to 'all those gathered in Darwin . . .', 16 January 1992.
61 *Northern Territory News*, 19 February 1992.
62 Mitani, quoted in *Northern Territory News*, 17 November 1992.
63 Alcorta, 'Opinion', *Northern Territory News*, 18 February 1992.
64 *Sydney Morning Herald*, 25 January 1992.
65 Lewis, *A War At Home*.

66 John Bradford, *In The Highest Traditions: RAN Heroism, Darwin, 19 February 1942*, Seaview Press, Henley Beach, 2000.
67 Ruwolt (ed.), *Darwin's Battle for Australia*, 'Dedication'.
68 Ibid, p. 5.
69 *Northern Territory News*, 19 February 2002.
70 Bob Kershaw, quoted in *Northern Territory News*, 19 February 2002.
71 Paul Henderson, quoted in *Northern Territory News*, 19 February 2012.
72 Department of Veterans' Affairs, Annual Report 2001–2002. www.dva.gov.au/aboutDVA/.../ar_2001_2002-outcome3.pdf
73 '70th Anniversary: Ceremonies and special events', *Northern Territory News*, 10 February 2012.
74 Hon. Julia Gillard, quoted in *Northern Territory News*, 19 February 2012.

FURTHER READING

Grose, P., *An Awkward Truth*, Allen & Unwin, Sydney, 2009.
Lewis, T., *A War At Home*, Tall Stories, Darwin, 1999.
Lewis, T. and Williams, P. (eds) (transl. Haruki Yoshida), *Through Japanese Eyes*, Darwin Military Museum, Darwin, 2010.
Lockwood, D., *Australia Under Attack*, New Holland, Sydney, 2005.
Oliver, P., *Raids on Australia*, Australian Scholarly Publishing, Melbourne, 2010.
Powell, A., *The Shadow's Edge: Australia's Northern War*, 3rd edn, CDU Press, Darwin, 2007.

PART 4

THE WAR ON AUSTRALIA'S DOORSTEP

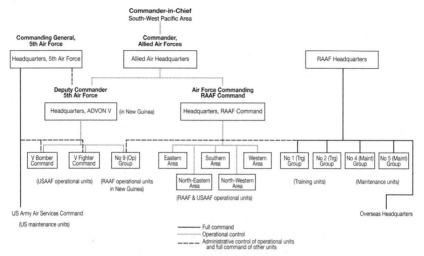

Chart 4 RAAF Command organisation, 1942

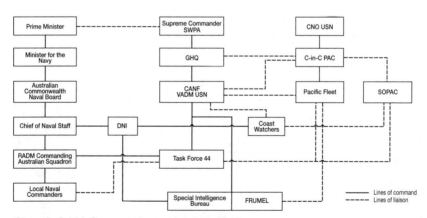

Chart 5 RAN Command organisation, 1942

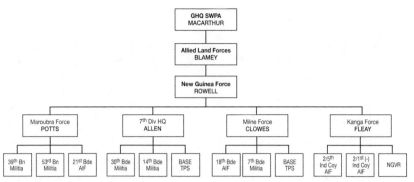

Chart 6 New Guinea Force Command organisation, Kokoda and Milne Bay, 1942

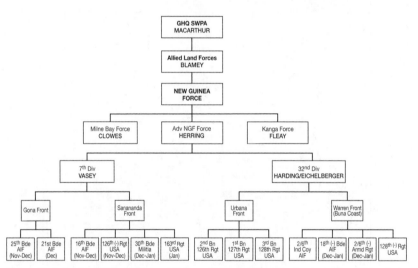

Chart 7 Advanced New Guinea Force Command organisation, Beachheads, 1942

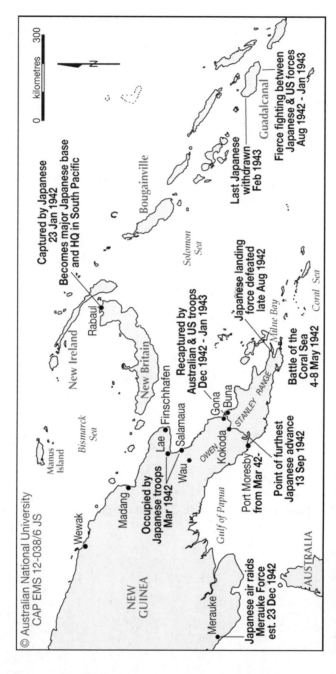

Map 6 Allied Operations: Timor to Guadalcanal, 1942

CHAPTER 9

VANQUISHED BUT DEFIANT, VICTORIOUS BUT DIVIDED

THE RAAF IN THE PACIFIC, 1942

Mark Johnston

When the RAAF was created in 1921, the threat that had been the chief justification for its creation was Japan. Yet, when Japan finally went to war with Australia, 20 years later, the RAAF was not ready for that challenge. What might be called a thin blue line of Australian airfields had been drawn on a great arc running from Malaya and Singapore, the supposed British forward defence of Australia in the west, via the Dutch East Indies through mainland New Guinea to New Britain and New Ireland in the East. The Australian aircraft that flew to those airfields early in 1942 were for the most part inferior to their Japanese opponents in quality and quantity. Japan's entry into the war imposed additional burdens on an air force already straining to meet its commitments to help the Royal Air Force in the war against Germany. There were extra burdens in the way of commonplace, boring but vital work – such as escorting ships from Australia to the outlying islands where the Australian government hoped to contain and then defeat the Japanese. Work such as hunting for Japanese submarines, and reconnaissance work over enemy bases and potential landing places. The air battles were most glamorous and decisive, but it is important to note that in 1942 the air force undertook an immense amount of unglamorous, unsung and indispensable work.

'NO SHOW AT ALL'

By New Year's Day 1942, the RAAF had already been heavily engaged against the Japanese for more than three weeks. Hours before the Pearl

161

Harbor raid began, Hudson aircraft of No. 1 Squadron RAAF had been fighting a Japanese invasion force at Kota Bharu, in northern Malaya. They had sunk a ship and inflicted many casualties that day, but had not been able to prevent the Japanese from coming ashore. In the weeks following, No. 1 and the three other Australian squadrons in Malaya, together with fewer than a dozen RAF squadrons had tried, against odds of about 4-to-1 to contest air superiority over Malaya and Singapore and to stem the Japanese advance on the ground. Losses among the Australian fighter squadrons, Nos 21 and 453, had been so heavy that in late December the two had amalgamated. Their losses owed much to the inadequacy of their aircraft, the Brewster Buffalo. Even after jettisoning enough equipment to make the aircraft 500 kg lighter and dubbing it the Super Special Buffalo, its performance was inferior to that of the Zero and Oscar fighters opposing it. It is testimony to the skill of the Australian Buffalo pilots that they had shot down 17 enemy aircraft in December, and in January would shoot down another 13 using what one of them called 'apologies for an aircraft'.[1]

An Australian sergeant working with No. 27 RAF Squadron acknowledged in late December with many others that 'The Jap has done really remarkably well, and ... we very much underestimated his strength'.[2] He did say, too, that 'Man for man, I'm certain that our chap is far superior to the Jap'[3], but that was not really the point. By mid-January the three Buffalo squadrons based in Singapore could muster just 28 aircraft between them to oppose some 150 Japanese fighters and 250 bombers. Sergeant Norm Chapman, a Buffalo pilot, confided to a mate that 21/453 Squadron had 'no show at all', illustrating that fact by describing how, while Chapman flew along straight, a Zero had recently looped around his Buffalo.[4] Chapman was killed in action the following day when he and his mate, Henry Parsons, were jumped by four Oscars while escorting Hudson bombers. Parsons swore to avenge Chapman and got a chance the next day while escorting Wirraway aircraft that had been withdrawn from a training unit to act as ersatz bombers. Parsons took on the Oscars that attacked the 'Wirras', but like his mate Chapman, was killed. The Wirraways got through to attack enemy barges and launches at Muar. They sank none, and every Wirraway was hit by return fire.

While these Wirraways, which had mainly New Zealand pilots and Australian observers, were trying vainly to stem the seemingly unstoppable Japanese advance in Malaya, even worse odds were facing RAAF Wirraway crews in New Britain, at the other end of that thin blue line mentioned earlier. The Japanese had decided to make Rabaul their main

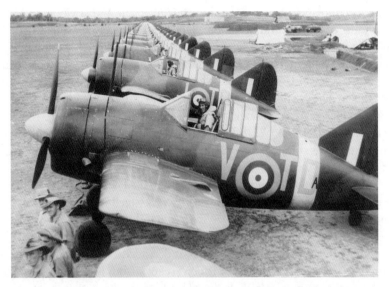

Photo 26 A line-up of RAAF Brewster Buffalo aircraft of 453 Squadron on Sembawang airfield, Malaya, c. November 1941. The Buffalo was completely outclassed by modern Japanese aircraft such as the 'Zero' (AWM 100117).

base in the South Pacific, and the tiny Australian garrison of 1400 men had no hope of thwarting their armada. The Australian RAAF commander at Rabaul, John Lerew, famously signalled headquarters in Latin the words used by doomed gladiators in the Roman arena: 'We who are about to die salute you'. He personally did not die at Rabaul, though he did take great risks. Two other officers who were destined to achieve great things but also to die in 1942 were at Rabaul during this period: Squadron Leader Arch Tindal and Flight Lieutenant Peter Turnbull. Tindal piloted a Wirraway in a fruitless attempt to catch enemy Nell bombers as they flew away from their first raid on Rabaul, while Turnbull, who was grounded and recovering from a car accident, narrowly escaped death when a Hudson exploded nearby while he was trying to save a burning Wirraway. Others were not so lucky.

On 20 January 109 Japanese aircraft flew from the aircraft carriers *Shokaku* and *Zuikaku* to attack Rabaul. Facing them and their veteran crews were just 10 Wirraways. Two 'Wirras' were on a standing patrol to meet any intruders. One was quickly shot down, taking the lives of its crew. In the other, George Herring and Bert Claire were soon tailed by three Zeros. While trying unsuccessfully to hit them, Claire found time to marvel at their manoeuvres. He missed, but they filled the Wirraway with holes, wounding both pilot and observer. Herring managed to crash land and he and Claire had just leapt clear when the Zeros finished the job. Flight Lieutenant Wilfred Brookes, commanding the Wirraways, approached the wreck to see if he could help, and saw that 'two bedraggled forms covered in blood rose from the ground and proved to be Herring and Claire'.[5] Herring would later serve in Kittyhawks, while Claire returned to Rabaul in 1943 in a Beaufighter. However, on this fateful 20 January, within just seven minutes the Australian squadron was, in the words of an official report, 'wiped out for all practical purposes'.[6]

Lerew now had just three aircraft and signalled headquarters, 'Will you now please send some fighters?' The answer, which reflected an unprecedented degree of sympathy, came: 'Regret inability to supply fighters. If we had them you would get them'.[7] A huge Japanese invasion fleet of 22 warships and transports approached and landed on the night of 30/31 January. Lerew and most other airmen escaped from the island, but many of the garrison were not so lucky. The Japanese turned Rabaul into a formidable base, which would be the main Allied objective in the South West Pacific for the following two years.

Before Rabaul became a Japanese base, a solo but epic Australian sortie had obtained an overview of an even bigger Japanese base, at Truk. On 9 January Bob Yeowart flew a Hudson to this island in the Caroline Islands. He and his crew survived enemy ack-ack and fighters and returned with nearly 300 precious films of photograph. It is typical of the danger of operations in that period that although Yeowart survived the war, his three crewmen would all be dead by July 1942, killed in two separate incidents. Yeowart was fortunate to survive not only this mission but also many others, including flying his Hudson as a 'fighter escort' to an Empire flying boat that in February evacuated government officials and planters on many stops between Buna and Samarai. The memory of this task with its prospect of meeting Zeros later horrified Yeowart. Yet, such a confrontation was a daily prospect for many pilots and crews in 1942.

With the fall of Rabaul, the mainland of New Guinea became the focus of the RAAF's air fighting in the region. In the meantime, though, Singapore had fallen on 15 February. The RAAF forces in that region were by then based in the Dutch East Indies, which also fell to the Japanese that month. One island in their path was Ambon. The senior RAAF Officer there was 28-year-old Wing Commander Dallas Scott, a former Melbourne Grammar school captain, junior Victorian boxing champion and a commercial pilot who before the war had flown

Lockheed 14s, the predecessor of the Hudson. His senior position required him to desist from flying, and it troubled him to send his Hudson crews on 'suicide' missions that cost many lives. By the end of January, Scott had persuaded his senior allied commanders to allow him to withdraw his precious aircraft to Darwin. He had retained just two Hudsons at Ambon for reconnaissance and to take out the last of the personnel.

On 30 January these 28 airmen were waiting to board for Darwin when it was discovered that during an air-raid an enemy bullet had damaged the main fuel line on one of the two aircraft. Scott ordered 17 of the 28 aboard the undamaged plane and, after it took off, went to work with the remaining airmen on fixing the other aircraft. Their equipment proved inadequate, so they headed across the island towards a prearranged rendezvous point. On the way Japanese troops intercepted and captured them. Dallas Scott and his brave group were executed amid frenzied Japanese activity that entailed the killing of more than 300 defenceless prisoners. Among them was Corporal Eric Gaskin, an armourer who had given up a place in the last Hudson to a younger man, declaring his own life 'a bit of a mess anyway'.

Of course, the campaigns of which Ambon was part were a 'mess'. As one Australian soldier reminisced soon after the fall of Ambon, '… one day we heard there was a Jap convoy heading this way … Most of the boys played cards to try and take their minds off it'. Of the day following the Japanese landing he wrote, 'Daylight came and we wondered how long we had to live'.[8] He would die in Japanese captivity. Scott and the men he commanded in death were just a few of many thousands of Australian victims of a catastrophic series of campaigns in Southeast Asia in early 1942. Why those operations turned out so badly is a complex issue, but it was a heartrending subject for the relatives of those airmen who died in the campaign. In 1949, the mother of Norm Chapman, one of those unlucky airmen, received a letter from the Department of Air, informing her that her only son's body had still not been found, but that he would be commemorated on a memorial yet to be built in Singapore. 'To me', she replied, 'it will be a constant grief at the loss of our gallant and worthy son, but also that he, with others, were so poorly equipped, directed and eventually abandoned. Australia, the land of his birth sent these lads to their death'. She hoped that the memorial would 'prove more worthy than the treatment they received whilst trying against superhuman odds, to preserve the freedom of their loved ones'.[9]

The bombing of Darwin on 19 February was part of the same 'mess'. It was the nadir of the RAAF's history, partly because it offered no airborne resistance to this first air-raid on Australia, although Arch Tindale was one of those who fought and died on the ground that day, partly because some of its men fled the scene ignominiously. However, the dominant theme of the RAAF's effort in the Pacific in this early period was defiance against great odds. In Malaya and Singapore, for example, the RAAF squadrons shot down a very creditable total of 33 Japanese aircraft, with a further nine probables, before the campaign ended on 15 February.

New Guinea

In New Guinea, Catalinas and Hudsons became the RAAF's main strike aircraft, taking the fight to the enemy at Rabaul. For example, in February 1942, five Catalinas launched a raid on Rabaul harbour. The Australians were greeted by enemy night fighters, operating for the first time. One of the intercepted Cats took cover in the convenient smoke of a live volcano overlooking the harbour, but the crew of another, piloted by Flight Lieutenant Godfrey Hemsworth, had to fight for their lives against a Japanese fighter. Hemsworth, a pre-war civil airline pilot, had been characterised by his squadron leader, C. W. Pearce, in 1941 as a competent pilot but marked by the 'Quantas' [sic] outlook in that he will not take the slightest risk in flying in case it will jeopardise his position with Quantas Airways after the war'.[10] Sergeant Douglas Dick, flying his first operational flight, fired at the fighter with the two Lewis guns in the port 'blister' on the side of the aircraft. So accurate was he that the enemy plane eventually spiralled uncontrollably towards the water, in which other crews saw it crash. Counted officially as a 'probable', this aircraft was the first Japanese fighter claimed in aerial combat in New Guinea. The Japanese pilot had given nearly as good as he got, for Hemsworth now found himself trying to control an aircraft with gunfire damage to its tail, its wings, its fuel tanks, oil lines and propeller. While putting the heavy Catalina into an evasive dive, Hemsworth had to shut down the associated engine. The crew also jettisoned their bombs and all gear that was dispensable. Despite the loss of one engine and the fact that petrol was pouring into the aircraft from one of the fuel tanks, Hemsworth kept the Cat aloft for five hours before making a perfect 'let down' in darkness near Salamaua, an Australian base under enemy threat. He waited only until temporary repairs allowed him to take off on two engines again. His aircraft was incapable of flying over the mountains to Moresby, so he flew around the coast at a height of just 15 metres. On alighting at Port Moresby Harbour, Hemsworth had spent 25 and a half hours on this one operation, 14 of them on one engine and in an aircraft containing more than 100 bullet holes.

He and the other Catalina crews in this period faced extraordinary strain. Quite apart from the fatigue, the tension inherent in their 'milk runs', as they called their long flights, was immense. All their flying time except the small percentage they spent within a narrow area of about 100 kilometres around Moresby was over hostile territory, in a slow-moving aircraft with little chance of returning to base if it was seriously hit.

Throughout 1942, Rabaul was a launching pad from which Japan sought to take the main island of New Guinea. The key to that island was Port Moresby, where in March and April Australian aircraft of No. 75 Squadron engaged in a Homeric struggle against Japanese aircraft seeking to establish air superiority. The Australians, led by Squadron Leader John Jackson, were generally less experienced than their opponents. Moreover, their P-40 Kittyhawk fighters were in most respects inferior aircraft in dogfights against the Japanese Zero fighters. Nevertheless, over the 44 days before being relieved by US fighters, the Australians gave more than they received.

Prior to the squadron's arrival, Port Moresby's garrison had suffered many raids and dubbed the promised aerial reinforcements the 'Tomorrowhawks' or 'Neverhawks'. However, four Kittyhawks finally arrived on 21 March, only to be fired on and damaged by trigger-happy Australian gunners. Later that day two of the P-40s took off and success-fully intercepted a reconnaissance plane, to the unbounded joy of the troops who were watching en masse. The next day the squadron, which had now arrived, added further glory to its name by launching a surprise raid on the Japanese base at Lae and destroying about a dozen aircraft. Jackson was then given the option of withdrawing his squadron to the greater safety of Horn Island, in Torres Strait, but he knew the value of his unit to morale in Moresby and chose to stay.

In succeeding weeks the Kittyhawk pilots struggled against heavy odds to send aircraft against every raid they could or to escort US Dauntless dive-bombers in raids. Jackson was shot down north of the Owen Stanleys on 10 April, and was missing for more than a week. Two locals rescued him and accompanied him through a hair-raising Japanese chase. He was flown back to Moresby in a Dauntless, and lost a fingertip when an enemy air raid interfered with his landing.

Yet, fate had something grim in store for Jackson. He was reprimanded by two senior officers at Moresby, whose own contribution to the morale and well-being of their front-line airmen seems doubtful. These officers criticised Jackson for ordering his men to avoid head-on confrontations with enemy fighters. Jackson knew that dogfighting the far more manoeuvrable Zeros in a conventional manner was foolhardy, but with these chastisements ringing in his ears he tried to lead as his 'superiors' demanded. The result was his death on 28 April in what the squadron called 'the last attack'. By the end of that day, 75 Squadron was virtually spent and it was relieved by two US squadrons on 30 April. For the loss of 12 pilots killed in action, 75 Squadron had destroyed between 22 and 35 enemy aircraft, with many more possibles and up to twice as many damaged. Among the pilots raiding Moresby was Saburo Sakai, the most famous Japanese ace of the war. He acknowledged the courage of his opponents, for 'regardless of the odds, their fighters were always screaming into [the] attack'.[11] Those pilots had damaged the myth of Japanese invincibility, and did so in view of many Allied troops whose morale needed boosting. The pilots' lives tended to be dominated by illness, danger, uncertainty and fear of death and, it must be said, fear of disgrace. I'll give two examples of the human cost of the 44 days.

During one of many raids on the Japanese base at Lae, Sergeant David Brown's Kittyhawk made a forced landing after being hit by AA fire. With a pistol in one hand and a knife in the other he tried to escape over a hill, but was confronted by a section of Japanese troops. Menaced by their machine gun, he surrendered. He was visibly upset when they confiscated a photograph of his fiancée, though this was reportedly later returned to him. His captors flew him to Rabaul. The National Archives holds a copy of a RAAF Casualty Section letter written to Brown's father in 1950 informing him that his son's body had been found in a mass grave with 10 other RAAF members executed by the Japanese Navy at Rabaul. It reported that 'After the execution a Japanese officer addressed his men and spoke of the fearless manner in which all the prisoners met their deaths and said that he hoped the Japanese would be prepared to die for their country as bravely as their enemy had done'.[12]

Two days after Brown was shot down, Pilot Officer 'Bink' Davies was also hit in a dogfight, and last seen spinning uncontrollably earthwards. Ten years after the war, Davies' elderly father approached the squadron's former medical officer, Bill Deane-Butcher, still clinging to the futile hope that his son had somehow survived, disabled in a remote village, waiting for his father to save him.

Thanks to the heroics of 75 Squadron men like Jackson, Brown and Davies, the Allies maintained air superiority over Port Moresby. Then the battle of the Coral Sea saved Moresby from a Japanese amphibious invasion. One of the pilots who spotted the Japanese invasion fleet headed for Moresby was Godfrey Hemsworth, whom we last saw negotiating his damaged Cat through the long flight from Rabaul. He was reporting seeing enemy vessels southeast of the Louisiades, when he suddenly stopped to say that he was under attack from enemy fighters. The Cat was shot down. Its crew were captured by a Japanese destroyer and never heard of again.

The Allies won a strategic victory in the Coral Sea battle, but the Japanese sought next to make an overland crossing to Moresby from beachheads in northern Papua, around Buna. This was the prelude to the Kokoda campaign. The new Supreme Commander of Allied Forces in the SWPA, General Douglas MacArthur, was angered by the Allied air forces' inability to stop the Japanese landings at Buna in July. The Australians had little role in the attempts to do this, but the efforts of one RAAF pilot are well worth retelling here. Pilot Officer Warren Cowan's No. 32 Squadron Hudson was the only Australian aircraft involved in Allied raids on the landing force on 22 July. Ordered to shadow the enemy cruiser force, he inflicted little or no bombing damage, but made an impression on the nine enemy Zeros that encountered him.

Among the nine Japanese pilots was Saburo Sakai. As the Zeros caught up to the Hudson, he was astonished to see it desist from fleeing and turn to fight. Using extraordinary manoeuvres, Cowan was able to exploit his pursuers' eager crowding in for the kill. One manoeuvre involved applying full power to one engine while simultaneously pulling power off the other, a practice that allowed Cowan to amaze his attackers with the speed of his turns. After making four ineffectual head-on passes, Sakai managed to knock out the rear-gunner, and thereby deprive Cowan of information about the Hudson's tail. Within minutes they had set the Hudson's plane alight, and watched the doomed aircraft clip trees and explode in flames.

The Zero pilots were reportedly full of the story of this tenacious Hudson for weeks afterwards. Cowan, 31, a clerk working in wool classing before the war, was married with two children. On receiving a telegram that Warren was 'Missing, believed killed', his wife Betty 'howled [her] eyes out', as she later put it, but clung to hope that he had survived.[13] Her main worry was that the Japanese would mistreat him. Near the scattered wreckage natives discovered and buried the remains of Cowan and his crewmates, Pilot Officer David Taylor, Sergeant Russell Polack and Sergeant Lauri Sheard. For Saburo Sakai, who survived the war, the Hudson pilot of July 1942 was one of the most memorable of the 200 opponents he faced, and he sought to discover his identity. With the help of several Australian historians, Cowan was identified. In motivational speeches he gave after the war, Sakai would often mention this dogfight of 22 July. He wrote in a letter, 'I have encountered many brave pilots in my life but Warren F. Cowan stands alone'.[14] He wrote to Cowan's widow and even to the Australian Minister for Defence Industry, Science and Personnel, suggesting that Cowan be awarded the highest possible medal for bravery.[15]

In August 1942, the Japanese made a landing on the eastern tip of New Guinea, at Milne Bay. Australian infantry and some US troops confronted them, but it was RAAF fighter aircraft that proved, in the words of two Australian Army generals, 'the decisive factor' in the great victory that followed. Ably assisted by Hudsons flying reconnaissance, the key aircraft were P-40s. These were aeroplanes of No. 75 Squadron, under John Jackson's brother Les, and of 76 Squadron, under air ace Peter Turnbull until his death in a crash, and then under Keith 'Bluey' Truscott, air ace and champion Aussie rules footballer.

In the course of the week-long battle, the two squadrons fired 196 000 machine-gun rounds and wore out 300 gun barrels against ground targets and landing craft. They demoralised the Japanese, who scarcely dared to move from beneath the jungle canopy. After the Army asked them to rake the palm trees for hidden Japanese snipers, the pilots were told that 'palm fronds, bullets and dead Japanese snipers were pouring down with the rain'.[16] Most importantly the flying artillery that the P-40s came to represent disrupted the enemy's supplies by sinking their barges and floating oil drums. Corporal Charles Walmsley of 76 Squadron ground staff was with a group sitting around a radio at Milne Bay and listening to the BBC news as it described the 'great victory' won there. Walmsley's diary records that an infantryman told him that he would never forget 76 Squadron for the way it backed them up in the front lines. 'I can see Bluey Truscott sitting in the mess', continued Walmsley, who could also observe Bardie Wawn and other pilots whose 'glory is famed now'.[17]

By September 1942 the Australians had two squadrons of Beaufighters, aircraft that were even better ground-attack aircraft than P-40s. They were armed with four 20-millimetre cannons and six machine guns, and over the course of the war could also carry bombs or rockets. Beaufighters could cut small craft in half, sink 800-tonne vessels and cut through trees like butter. Some onlookers described 'Beaus' as giving off so much firepower that the aircraft seemed to be halted in mid-air by the recoil. Commanded by the brilliant, swashbuckling but overbearing Brian 'Black Jack' Walker, 30 Squadron's Beaufighters created havoc among enemy barge traffic and at bases such as Lae.

The squadron's attacks on Lae airfield were dramatic and dangerous. Approaching Lae down the Ramu River after a long flight, Beaufighters

Photo 27 New Guinea, late 1942. Beaufighter aircraft of No. 30 Squadron RAAF (pilot Flying Officer R. J. Brazenor; observer Sergeant F. B. Anderson) in flight close to a rocky outcrop in a valley in the Owen Stanley Ranges (AWM OG0001).

crossed in front, behind, above and below each other at high speed and low altitude, all weapons blazing. The Japanese replied, and tracers and exploding flak puffs were visible signs of the thousands of projectiles flying in all directions. Enemy troops fired from or darted between gun emplacements. Japanese aircraft were always a menacing presence too, and any Beaufighter that returned from Lae unscathed was exceptional. Even Black Jack admitted that he did not like attacking Lae, 'because boy! Was it heavily defended!'[18] Anyone who crashed north of the Owen Stanleys was unlikely to survive.

The close, jungle-covered nature of the fighting on the Kokoda Track made it difficult for the RAAF to interfere there, and most of the famous air-supply dropping was done by US air-force units. However, once the Kokoda campaign was over the RAAF made a profound contribution to the Allied campaign to evict the Japanese from their bases in Papua, at Gona, Buna and Sanananda. Here, the Beaufighters did great work, but were joined by two other types that also made extraordinary efforts. One was the Wirraway. This two-seater, initially ordered by Australia as a training aircraft, had been found wanting in the fighter role into which it had been forced at Rabaul. However, on the Papuan beachheads, the Wirraways of No. 4 Squadron performed marvels as tactical reconnaissance aircraft. Flying at treetop height, they were able to pinpoint enemy targets, sometimes by courageously inviting the enemy to shoot at them. Some of their brave crews were lost to this fire, but they contributed to the destruction of many enemy positions. Lieutenant-General Robert Eichelberger, commanding Americans in the area, noted, 'I can't say enough ...[of the] "Wirraway boys"', as the Americans called them. 'Their work has been so bravely done that all the praise we have ever expressed rolled into one great tribute is due to them.'[19] In one incident that has entered RAAF folklore, Pilot Officer Jack Archer and his observer, Les Coulston, were flying reconnaissance and suddenly spotted an enemy fighter below them. Archer impulsively dived towards it, and in a frontal attack, fired a five second machine-gun burst. The enemy aircraft struck the water and burst into flames. Archer was rewarded with six priceless bottles of beer and RAAF immortality.

Two types of aircraft had joined the RAAF Beaufighters on the beachheads. One was the Wirraway, the other the Boston. Known as A-20s to the Americans and Bostons to the Australians, the RAAF had a squadron of these magnificent ground-attack aircraft. Modified to carry four 50-calibre machine guns in addition to the original four 30-calibre machine guns, they had formidable firepower. Initially they were terribly dangerous to fly: three Bostons were destroyed when 20-pound fragmentation bombs they had released detonated close enough to the aircraft to destroy them. Once this problem was identified and overcome, the Bostons proved a menace to the enemy. One American serviceman at Buna recalled the frightening sound of these aircraft, so loud they could be heard from a mile away, and how he made himself thin when their bullets thumped into nearby trees.

The Japanese were even more horrified. In mid-December a Japanese lieutenant among the Buna garrison wrote an unwitting tribute to the impact Australian aircraft were having on this great victory, 'Our planes do not appear ... All aircraft seem to belong to the enemy, so we run for shelter when we hear planes approaching. The only planes we see have white and blue circles [the insignia of the RAAF, which had removed the red circle in the centre as it misled trigger-happy Allied aircrew]'. The Japanese continued, 'There are no planes with the star insignia ... At 1200 hours planes with white and blue circles again observed our positions and dropped leaflets. Such impertinence! If and when our infantry arrives, we will annihilate the enemy'.[20] This was not to be. Another Japanese soldier at Buna wrote on the first anniversary of Pearl Harbor: 'We fear aeroplanes most. See several hundreds of enemy aircraft each day'.[21]

DARWIN

New Guinea was one of the two main centres of Australian air fighting in 1942. The other was of course Darwin, or more precisely the North-Western Area of which it was the hub. When the Japanese launched their first and greatest air-raid on Darwin on 19 February, there were no Australian fighters to oppose them and for most of the rest of that year, US air-force fighters were the only or main defence of the Northern Territory. They did this job super-bly. Attacks were launched on Japanese bases from Darwin too, almost exclusively by Australian aircraft, usually the vulnerable Hudsons. One of the two Hudson squadrons had been established at the war's outset by John 'Sam' Balmer. A pre-war regular air-force officer, Balmer was described by an official RAAF historian as 'one of the RAAF's most brilliant pilots'.[22] In peacetime Balmer and Dallas Scott had together driven an open sports car in races across the continent. By 1942, Balmer was imparting his wisdom to a Beaufort Squadron, No. 100, which launched daring torpedo raids on enemy shipping. Balmer received an OBE for his work with these squadrons and was then transferred to the United Kingdom. He earned a DFC while leading the famous 467 Squadron, but was shot down and killed on a mission in May 1944. There are many stories of his leadership. One concerned a young Lancaster pilot who, about to embark on his 16th mission, refused to go. Rather than dress him down as a coward, Balmer sent him to the Medical Officer, who gave him two weeks' leave. Balmer rang friends who agreed to look after the young man on their farm for two weeks. The young pilot went up again, as did Balmer's reputation. One of his men wrote after his death: 'It was a privilege to have served under a commanding officer of such stature'.[23]

Meanwhile the raids on Darwin continued. A remarkable event occurred there during the Japanese air-raid on 23 November 1942. Leading Aircraftman Des Darcy, of a radar unit outside Darwin, wrote this vivid diary account of that moonlit night's events:

> Here they come again!' and we hear the steady drone once more. We live in an agony of trepidation until they safely pass over us, then bob up to see the display ... the crash of bombs is heard ... Here comes another wave! The searchlights have got them again – three silver butterflies on the fringe of a moonlit cloud. This time no ack-ack sounds. We hear the rattle of machine gun fire – our fighters are upon them. Hurrah! They've got one.

See the small trail of flame behind him. Yes he's leaving the others and sweeping round in a wide circle. The flames are larger now – he's one big burning inferno. Now he's just above the tops of the trees. A flaming fragment breaks off and floats to earth on its own. That's one of his wings. Hurrah! Hurrah! Hurrah! The shouts resound thru' the scrub – from us, and the rest of our lads across the road, from the army and navy camps surrounding us. Good show! One less you'll have to send over, Tojo![24]

Just after 5 a.m. Squadron Leader Dick Cresswell of 77 Squadron had signalled 'Tally-Ho', meaning 'enemy sighted'. In his P-40E he had intercepted and attacked a flight of three Betty bombers, which were perfectly silhouetted against the moon. After a series of attacks one Betty exploded in mid-air. Next morning an airman wrote, 'I think everyone in Darwin cheered as that plane came down'.[25] The 22-year-old Cresswell had just achieved two 'firsts' over the Australian mainland: the first confirmed 'night kill', and the first kill by an Australian pilot. Cresswell personified the handsome, courageous, jovial and flamboyant fighter pilot. He had narrowly avoided failing his pilot's course in 1938. Like other fighter pilots, he was inclined to misbehave on the ground, as suggested by his 1943 court martial for 'conduct to the prejudice of good order and Air Force discipline in that, at the Officers' Mess in Port Pirie ... he fired a shot from a revolver into the floor of the mess in the immediate vicinity of the foot of [another officer]'.[26] On returning from his night victory in Darwin, Cresswell was asked what he felt like. In the tradition of the laconic Australian warrior he replied: 'Breakfast'.

Air Vice Marshal Joe Hewitt said of Cresswell that he was 'a better leader in the air than on the ground'. Unfortunately for the RAAF, that was true of most of its good leaders. From mid-1942, the leadership of the RAAF had been mired in problems that would worsen as the war went on. The senior officer in the RAAF, the Chief of the Air Staff, or CAS, was between 1940 and May 1942 a British officer, Air Chief Marshal Sir Charles Burnett. He had prioritised the provision of Australian aircrew for the war effort in Europe. He nominated as his successor Air Vice Marshal Bill Bostock, an experienced and highly able Australian airman and administrator. Unfortunately for Bostock, his association with the politically conservative and outspoken Burnett scotched his chances with the Labor government, which fixed instead on acting Air Commodore George Jones. He, too, had an excellent record, but was so low in the pecking order that some of his contemporaries and subsequent historians have suggested that his appointment may have been an administrative

Photo 28 Livingstone Airstrip, Darwin, c. 1942. Squadron Leader R. C. 'Dick' Cresswell, commander of No. 77 Squadron RAAF, standing beside his Curtiss P40 Kittyhawk. Painted on the side of the aircraft are the flags of the RAAF, Australia, the United Kingdom and the United States (AMW P01868.002).

error. He was an uninspiring leader, but determined to hang on to his new position once given it, even against his erstwhile mentor, Bill Bostock. That should have been the end of it, but was not. The government promoted Jones, but only to the rank of Air Vice Marshal – equal to, but not higher than Bostock.

Moreover, the RAAF was now part of what was called the Allied Air Forces, under the command of the US Lieutenant-General George C. Kenney. While Jones would have command of all matters associated with RAAF personnel, provision of aircraft, supply and training, Kenney would have operational control of RAAF service squadrons – that is, control of their activities on campaign. Moreover, Kenney disliked Jones but liked Bostock, to whom without even consulting Jones he gave a position entitled 'Air Officer Commanding RAAF Command'. This command controlled all RAAF operational units in the SWPA except New Guinea, which came under US control. This scenario was the genesis of what is known in RAAF history as the 'RAAF Command Scandal' and gave rise to an excellent RAAF publication called 'How Not to Run an Air Force!' This scandal, which was to divide the RAAF and affect its efficiency for the rest of the war, was just one of several ominous developments at the end of the RAAF's finest year.

The others related to the Americans. As late as July 1942, American and Australian officers shared the main command positions in the Allied air forces, with staff officers of the two air forces alternating almost automatically down the chain of command. The creation of RAAF Command in September came at the Americans' insistence that the two forces be separated out, with the Americans part of a distinct force, the soon to be famous Fifth Air Force. This was a sign that the Americans saw the Australians as a force to be kept separate and marginal. The logic of the size of the respective forces – 481 US aircraft and 215 Australian on 10 August – meant that the Australians were destined to be a junior partner.

Thus, while in December 1942 Australian airmen were making a real difference in the major ground operations in Papua, there was a shift in balance against them. A telling event occurred on 27 December at Buna, when US Air Force P-38 Lightnings made their first substantial contribution to the campaign. Twelve Lightnings tackled 20 Japanese fighters and seven dive-bombers and for no loss to themselves destroyed 11 of the enemy. This was a taste of things to come. The P-38 would become the aircraft type credited with shooting down the most Japanese aircraft. Lightnings and other second-generation US aircraft such as the Thunderbolt were superior to the Japanese fighters, the Zero and Oscar, that had so troubled Allied fighters throughout 1942.

This changing aerial balance not only doomed Japanese airpower but also condemned the RAAF to second XI status. The Australians would not receive Lightnings or other advanced fighters that would permit them to participate in the dogfights that would see US fighter pilots rack up great victory tallies against their ageing foes. Nevertheless, 1942 had been a year of great achievement for the RAAF. It had started with little more than a defiant attitude to hold it together against a powerful and expert foe. Its men had created a heritage for the RAAF and made real contributions to victory over Port Moresby, Milne Bay and the Beachheads. On 3 December a frustrated Japanese had written of Allied aircraft over the beachheads 'they fly above our position as if they own the sky'.[27] A year earlier it had been Allied soldiers saying the same, but they would never do so again. 1942 had been the RAAF's finest hour. Its members would suffer disappointments and divisions in the remaining three years of war, but the RAAF had contributed to ensuring that from now on the Allied air forces' star would always be in the ascendant.

Notes

1 LAC J. Shanahan, 453 Sqn, Diary 25 January 1942, AWM 3DRL/6601.
2 Sgt J. K. Woodward, Diary 21 December 1941, AWM PR00158.
3 —diary 13 December 1941, AWM PR00158.
4 E. R. Hall, *Glory in Chaos: The RAAF in the Far East in 1940–42*, Sembawang Association, West Coburg c. 1989, p. 304.
5 'Rabaul – Early activities of 24 Squadron', Interview with Group Captain W. D. Brookes, Office of Air Force History, Roll 460 File 284, p. 6.
6 'RAAF Operations from Rabaul', Sqn Leader W. D. Brookes, 24 Sqn, Report 24 February 1942, Office of Air Force History, Roll 459, File 87.
7 Douglas Gillison, *Royal Australian Air Force 1930–1942*, Australian War Memorial, Canberra , 1962, p. 356.
8 Pte J. Armstrong, 2/21 Battalion, Diary, AWM PR89/165 p, 2.
9 Letter from M. Chapman, 12 March 1949, Chapman casualty file, NAA 163/96/105.
10 Service Record of Godfrey Elland Hemsworth, NAA, A9300, p. 13.
11 Saburo Sakai (with Martin Caidin and Fred Saito), *Samurai*, Dutton, New York, 1957, p. 79. There is controversy as to the authorship and accuracy of this book, but this quotation is consistent with Sakai's other public statements.
12 National Archives of Australia, A705, 166/6/845, Casualty file for David Stuart Brown.
13 'Enemy Lines', *Australian Story*, ABC TV, 1 July 2002.
14 Ibid.
15 Unfortunately, Australian law prohibits such awards retrospectively.
16 Gillison, *Royal Australian Air Force: 1939–1942*, p. 613.
17 Cpl C. Walmsley, Diary 31 August 1942.
18 Brian Walker, *Black Jack: 50 Years as a Pilot, 1935–1985*, Banner Books, Belconnen, 1994, p. 71.
19 In 'Army Co-op', *RAAF Log*, Australian War Memorial, Canberra, 1943, p. 54.
20 Buna Operations, Diary 'presumably of Lt Suganuma', 15 December 1942, Office of Air Force History, Roll 459, File 158, pp. 1–2.
21 Ibid., Diary 'of unknown persons', 7 December 1942.
22 George Odgers, *Mr Double Seven: A Biography of Wing Commander Dick Cresswell, DFC*, Air Power Development Centre, Tuggeranong, 2008, p. 11.
23 Colin King, *Song of the Beauforts*, Self published, Keperra, c. 2004, p. 323.
24 LAC D. Dacy, Group 45 RAAF, Diary 23 November 1942, AWM PR00782.

25 Walmsley, Diary 23 November 1942, AWM PR00742.
26 Alan Stephens and Jeff Isaacs, *High Fliers: Leaders of the Royal Australian Air Force*, AGPS Press, Canberra, 1996, p. 107.
27 Gillison, *Royal Australian Air Force 1939–1942*, p. 676.

FURTHER READING

Gillison, D., *Royal Australian Air Force: 1939–1942*, Australian War Memorial, Canberra, 1962.

Hall, E.R. (Bon), *Glory in Chaos: The RAAF in the Far East in 1940–42*, Sembawang Association, West Coburg, 1989.

Johnston, M., *Whispering Death: Australian Airmen in the Pacific War*, Allen & Unwin, Sydney, 2011.

McAulay, L., *We Who Are About to Die: The Story of John Lerew, A Hero of Rabaul, 1942*, Banner Books, Maryborough, 2007.

Parnell, N.M., *Whispering Death: A History of the RAAF's Beaufighter Squadrons*, Reed, Sydney, 1980.

Powell, A., *The Shadow's Edge: Australia's Northern War*, Charles Darwin University Press, Darwin, 2007.

Sakai, S. with Caidin, M. and Saito, F., *Samurai!*, Bantam, New York, 1978.

Stephens, A., *The Royal Australian Air Force*, Oxford University Press, South Melbourne, 2001.

Vincent, D., *The RAAF Hudson Story*, volume 1, D. Vincent, Highbury, 1999.

White, O., *Green Armour: The Story of Fighting Men in New Guinea*, Wren Publishing, Melbourne, 1972.

Wilson, D., *The Decisive Factor: 75 & 76 Squadrons–Port Moresby and Milne Bay 1942*, Banner Books, Brunswick, 1991.

CHAPTER 10

A NOVEL EXPERIENCE

THE RAN IN 1942, DEFENDING AUSTRALIAN WATERS

Ian Pfennigwerth

The British agreement of 1909 that made the RAN possible was conditional upon the Australian Fleet being made available to the Admiralty in time of war as part of a worldwide Imperial naval force.[1] When the First World War broke out in August 1914, the Australian Fleet came under the overall command of the British Admiralty, first deployed to frustrate the actions of the German East Asiatic Squadron in the Pacific, and then dispersed across the globe to whatever theatre of operations the British deemed appropriate. At war's end, few major units had spent any time at all on the Australia Station after early 1915. Ironically, threats to Australia's territorial security posed by German commerce raiders had been countered by cruisers of the IJN.

In 1939, this time with some reluctance, the Australian government again honoured the agreement but with qualifications. It was to be consulted before the ships it dispatched to foreign stations were deployed, and RAN units were put under British operational command only on a case-by-case basis. Nevertheless, by mid-1941 Australian warships had been engaged in operations in the North Sea, North Atlantic, Caribbean, Persian Gulf, Indian Ocean and, particularly, in the Mediterranean. This was all valuable experience for the ships' companies in coping with the kind of state-of-the art threat posed by the Germans and Italians, which they could not have gained had they been kept in Australian waters: the corollary being that few had any experience of operations in Australian waters and, more importantly, in the complicated and largely unfamiliar waters to Australia's north and east.

As the December 1941 Japanese assault gained momentum and surged southwards, at the beginning of 1942 the RAN found itself preparing to defend Australian waters and territory against a concerted enemy attack for the first time. Furthermore, it had to do so without the comforting assistance of a powerful and experienced Royal Navy. The demolition of British naval power in Southeast Asia, from the sinking of HM Ships *Prince of Wales* and *Repulse* in December 1941, to the destruction of their last major vessel, HMS *Exete*r, on 2 March 1942, was complete. In February the British had negotiated out of its commitments to a hastily formed Anzac Force of cruisers and destroyers to defend the Coral Sea, and by April they had withdrawn to Attu Atoll in the Indian Ocean to avoid the power of the IJN.

The RAN's new ally – the US Navy – was an unknown quantity. Apart from the skirmishes with the Japanese during the retreat from the 'Malay Barrier', the US Navy's last fleet action had occurred in 1898. To say that there were reservations on both sides of this alliance would be an under-statement. In American eyes, exaggerated suspicions of 'the British' were extended to the Australians, with whose character and capabilities they were totally unfamiliar. For their part, the Australians, with justifiable pride in their achievements in over two years of furious warfare against the best that Europe could offer, had reservations about the effectiveness and battle-readiness of the US Navy. What the Australians could not know was that US Navy command and control policies and practices were concentrated in the hands of the Chief of Naval Operations, Admiral Ernest King, in Washington, D.C. He decided what ships would be sent where and when, and how they were to be employed. Furthermore, long-standing animosities between the United States Army and Navy came into play when the Combined Chiefs of Staff in Washington gave com-mand of most of the Pacific Ocean theatre to naval officers, with the SWPA, including Australia, Papua and New Guinea and the Philippines, declared an Army command, and General Douglas MacArthur its supreme commander.

Unexpectedly, although it was an unpopular decision at the time, and taken without any consultation with the Australian government, this played to the RAN's strengths. Modest though it was in comparison with any potential concentration of Japanese naval power, the RAN was the strongest naval force in the area. That was not saying much but it was enough to convince the US naval commanders that, strategically, the RAN was deserving of material, organisational and operational consideration and that it could not be simply sidelined. It is useful to reflect on what greeted the eyes of Vice Admiral Herbert Leary, the first commander of the Allied Naval Forces SWPA.

Australian Naval Order of Battle in March 1942

For the RAN, the lead up to the declaration of hostilities between Germany and the British Empire on 3 September 1939 had been a time of intense preparation. Having thrown off the shackles of the 'no war for 10 years' policy imposed by the British government on its defence planners and with German and Japanese repudiation of the hard-argued naval arms limitation treaties of the 1920s and 1930s, the Admiralty was released from restrictions on ship numbers, tonnages and capabilities. As the Australian Squadron had been included in these totals, this also meant a relaxation in the possibilities for the RAN, which ushered in the era of modern light cruisers to replace its two First-World-War-vintage survivors and replacements for its old destroyers.[2]

The RAN entered the war with two heavy cruisers of 1920s design, three modern light cruisers, one older light cruiser and a destroyer flotilla of late-First-World-War-vintage – that had served with distinction in the Mediterranean under the derisive German designation of 'The Scrap Iron Flotilla'. There were two sloops of British design but Australian manufacture and assorted minor war vessels. The first of the 60 little ships of the Bathurst class, officially minesweepers but known as corvettes, were under construction, as was another sloop. Orders would shortly be placed for two modern destroyers of the Tribal class and another sloop, while a merchant liner was being converted into an armed merchant cruiser, the first of three.

Wartime service and the passage of time had changed this order of battle by March 1942. Two of the light cruisers had been lost to enemy action, *Sydney* to the German armed merchant cruiser *Kormoran* and *Perth* to the Japanese at the battle of the Sunda Strait, as had two of the sloops and one of the old destroyers. There were now two armed merchant cruisers, the new destroyer *Arunta* had commissioned, and there were 20 of the Bathurst-class corvettes at sea. The addition of one US cruiser and four destroyers rounded out the sum total of MacArthur's surface naval force. There were no capital ships and no aircraft carriers. The SWPA also boasted two squadrons of US Navy submarines that would operate from bases at Brisbane and Fremantle, respectively. While nominally part of SWPA, their operations were largely dictated by Commander Pacific Submarine Force in Honolulu.

RAN ORGANISATION IN MARCH 1942

Although on a much smaller scale, the organisation of the RAN was sufficiently similar to that of the US Navy to cause no concern to the Americans. Navy Office in Melbourne called all the shots. Naval units were assigned to Naval Officers-in-Charge (NOICs) in each state or to the Rear Admiral Commanding the Australian Squadron (RACAS), who exercised his command from one of the cruisers as flagship. All the officers of flag rank were British, seconded to the RAN, but the staff officers assisting the Chief of Naval Staff were increasingly the front-runners from the initial entries into the RAN College, which commenced training in 1913. These men had gained a lot of experience in larger Royal Navy organisations, where they had performed well. If there was a weakness it was that there were so very few experienced people trying to run an increasingly larger and busier Navy, a problem that got worse as the war continued.[3]

Outside the fleet, the RAN had also taken some important initiatives to support its activities. As a participant in the British Pacific Naval Intelligence Organisation, Australia boasted three naval direction-finding stations, essential in intercepting and tracking Japanese naval movements, as well as two high-power communications stations. Intercepted messages were channelled to the RAN-led Special Intelligence Bureau, and the decoded information shared with Australia's allies. Naval intelligence resources were very effectively led and developed by the RAN Director of Naval Intelligence, who also headed the Combined Operational Intelligence Centre in Victoria Barracks, Melbourne, established in 1941 with the specific task of gathering and promulgating information on Japanese activities.

The RAN Second World War organisation that has attracted most attention was the RAN Coast Watcher Service. Established in 1928 around mainland Australia, from 1935 this had been expanded to watching posts throughout Papua and New Guinea and the offshore island groups, including Bougainville and the Solomon Islands. Although the Japanese assault on New Britain and New Ireland resulted in the loss of the posts and the death of their Coast Watchers, sufficient of the network remained to provide very useful reporting on Japanese activities and to allow for the insertion of parties behind enemy lines. Admiral Halsey in the South Pacific Area was famously to declare that the Coast Watchers saved Guadalcanal and Guadalcanal saved the South Pacific. There are grounds for doubt on both claims but the Coast Watchers did have a significant influence on some parts of the Solomons campaign.[4]

Supporting the RAN were a number of ship-building and repair facilities, including the naval dockyard at Garden Island in Sydney, another at Williamstown in Melbourne and commercial docks and ship-yards scattered around the coast. There were, however, none of any consequence north of Brisbane. In the days to come all of these would be heavily involved in the war effort supporting the two navies and stretched to meet the demands placed upon them.

Three other RAN initiatives were both attractive and significant to GHQ in its war planning. The RAN had established its Hydrographic Service in 1920 to tackle the gargantuan task of charting Australian and Australian Pacific mandates' waters. This work was suspended during the Depression, but in 1933 the task of surveying Papuan and New Guinea waters was resumed. RAN hydrography was well supported with expertise, and the collective knowledge of the Service was undoubtedly a treasure beyond price for a command in which amphibious assault was to feature.

The Australians had also given thought to the requirements of amphibious warfare, and had selected Port Stephens, north of Newcastle in New South Wales, as the site for a base at which naval crews and soldiers would be trained in the art and science of getting men and their equipment off ships and onto beaches under enemy fire. MacArthur's staff reacted energetically to that initiative, and the base opened as HMAS *Assault* in September 1942. Work to convert the RAN's armed merchant cruisers into landing ships had already been put in train.

Not least, the RAN had its own Anti-Submarine Warfare (ASW) School in Sydney. Established principally to ensure a supply of trained Australian personnel to man British and Canadian ships in the Battle of the Atlantic, its existence made the task of training the ships and men of the Allied navies in the SWPA in the theory of ASW much easier. The practice was harder to obtain: submarines to act as 'clockwork mice' for Allied escorts were in short supply in the theatre until 1944.[5]

RAN OPERATIONAL EXPERIENCE IN MARCH 1942

As an element of an Imperial Navy, the RAN had reached agreement regarding the interchangeability of Australian and British naval personnel. RAN officers all undertook part of their training with the RN, and thus the RAN had cadres with the necessary skills gained through exchange postings and from exchanges of ships between the RN and RAN to perform most staff and operational functions in either Navy. The cruiser exchanges were excellent training for the Australian ships' companies alongside the best the British could field, and periods spent working with the Mediterranean fleet were particularly advantageous. In a short few years the RAN ships were fighting there, not just exercising.

Their war service in the Atlantic and Mediterranean exposed RAN ships and personnel to all facets of naval and aerial warfare, from shore bombardments, fleet actions and convoy defence to clandestine and special operations. They were to continue to do this throughout the war, and those returning to Australia in ships or following exchange postings were a most valuable resource. Commanding officers might complain as some of their experienced officers and sailors left on postings to other ships or training establishments, but this did help the spread of skills and knowledge in a service now gearing up towards a seven-fold expansion of personnel.[6] This shared experience and knowledge was a precious resource, which could only be envied by the Americans as their own massive expansion in personnel produced large numbers but without the leavening of experienced men, especially in a naval 'backwater' like SWPA.

Importantly in the new operational circumstances, some RAN ships and personnel had experience in fighting the Japanese. Largely as a result of the losses of an inexperienced US Navy in its battles with the IJN in Solomon Islands waters in the months to come, a myth of Japanese invincibility – especially in night fighting – was to grow and be perpetuated, lasting even to this day. However, this had not been the experience of those RAN units that had survived, nor of the US Navy units that had fought in Indonesian waters. A confidence that, ship for ship and man for man, the RAN would perform at least as well as the IJN, was an important national asset and attractive to the Americans. Not all US Navy senior officers would observe this spirit of Australian readiness to compete with the Japanese and employ it appropriately, but it was evident to those who worked more closely with the RAN at the operational level.

In summary, there was much for the Americans to respect about the RAN of March 1942 and a lot that could be turned to advantage in the Allied cause. This was especially so in 1942 when their backs seemed to be against the wall and the American industrial machine had not yet started to churn out a numerical and technological preponderance of military hardware to swamp that of the enemy. It was a good start to the relationship, even though the Americans would observe that RAN equipment was technologically backward and its manpower stretched. In turn, the Australians were astonished at American technological and material superiority.

DEFENDING AUSTRALIA

Although General MacArthur was portrayed as the man who had been sent to 'save' Australia, what most Australians did not know was, first, that the Japanese had neither the intent nor the wherewithal to capture or seriously harass the country. Of course, in March 1942 that was not entirely clear to the Japanese either, although their Army was not planning any assault. Second, as MacArthur expressed it to Prime Minister Curtin, 'though the American people were animated by a warm friendship for Australia, their purpose in building up forces in the Commonwealth was not so much from interest in Australia but from its utility as a base from which to hit Japan'.[7]

However, neither factor was the popular perception of events in either Canberra or Washington. In January 1942 the Japanese had quickly over-run and destroyed Australian garrisons protecting Rabaul, Ambon and Timor, all outposts of importance to the defence of the continent. On 19 February, Japanese bombs first fell on Darwin, seriously affecting the capacity of the township to support Allied naval and air forces (see Chapter 8). Early March brought the news of naval and convoy losses in Sunda Strait and in the Indian Ocean, and on 3 March Japanese fighters operating at extreme range attacked Allied aircraft in Broome. The only apparent success had been the sinking of the mine-laying submarine *I-124* by HMAS *Deloraine* on 20 January off Darwin.

Until Japanese intentions following the success of their 'Stage 1' assaults in the colonial possessions of the 'Malay Barrier' became clear and Allied forces could be concentrated to oppose them, a holding strategy was all that could be adopted. This was particularly so for the Allied naval forces, with a 'front' of over 2000 miles to defend, few bases to support them and fewer ships. Anzac Force now became Task Force 44, a cruiser-destroyer formation under the command of RACAS, Rear Admiral John Crace, an RN officer who had been born in Australia. Apart from training, the task force had little to do until indications emerged that the Japanese were, in fact, planning an amphibious assault on Port Moresby, and that the likely time frame was early May.

THE BATTLE OF THE CORAL SEA, MAY 1942

This electrifying intelligence was coming mainly from a new Allied organisation, Fleet Radio Unit Melbourne (FRUMEL). This was an amalgam of the RAN intercept organisations – now increasingly staffed by the

Photo 29 The RAN's Bathurst-class corvettes HMAS *Deloraine* (front) passing the corvette HMAS *Colac* (in 1944). *Deloraine* sank the Japanese mine-laying submarine *I-124*, one of the few Allied successes in January 1942 (AWM 075414).

Women's Royal Australian Naval Service (WRANS) – the Australian Special Intelligence Bureau, and the remnants of the US Navy signals intelligence (sigint) unit formerly based in Cavite in the Philippines – Station CAST. Since CAST was both larger and better equipped, but not necessarily any better at decoding Japanese messages, the Americans took command of FRUMEL. This was not a 'happy ship', with the US Navy paranoia about the distribution of its product to other than US Navy sources a principal irritant to the Australians, who were more interested in defeating the Japanese. But at this early stage in the relationship the importance of the intelligence being derived from the joint activity over-rode the internal conflict between its components. As days passed, FRUMEL, with assistance from the US Navy in Honolulu, pieced together almost the entire, complex instructions to all the Japanese forces participating in what they designated 'Operation MO'. It was one of the most important penetrations of Japanese codes of the war.[8]

There was some hesitancy about basing Allied responses on sigint information but, so far as this could be verified by other means, such as traffic analysis and photography of Japanese activities around Rabaul,

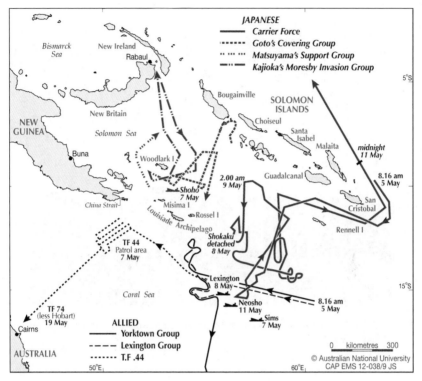

Map 7 The battle of the Coral Sea

it seemed to be accurate. The revelation that two IJN aircraft carriers were to be involved heightened US Navy interest, and Admiral King directed that two of the precious Pacific Fleet carriers were to be detached to form the core of the Allied response. US submarines were deployed to intercept the advancing Japanese covering force, which was first to attack Tulagi in the Solomons before swinging north to support the troop convoy sailing from Rabaul. This would emerge into the Coral Sea through Jomard Passage in the Louisiade Archipelago. The Allied force was designated Task Force 17, under the command of US Navy Admiral Frank Fletcher. Task Force 44 became Task Group 17.3.

Fletcher's tactical plan for defeating the Japanese was unsound and, in keeping with US Navy orthodoxy after the humiliation of Pearl Harbor, his primary targets were the IJN carriers, rather than the troop transports at the heart of Operation MO. He also looked askance at operations with an

Photo 30 7 May 1942. HMAS *Australia* under attack during the battle of the Coral Sea (AWM 044238).

ally that involved sharing confidences. Rear Admiral Crace was sent, unsupported, to wait off Jomard Passage, while Fletcher and the Japanese carrier force performed pirouettes around each other off the Solomons, unaware of the other's presence within striking range. When they did discover one another, the fighting was furious and both sides lost a carrier, large in the US Navy's case, small for the IJN, and damaged one other. Pundits have awarded the fight to the Japanese on points.

This, of course, missed the point of Operation MO, and the part played in the battle by Crace's cruisers. Left out of the picture by Fletcher (who seemed to have forgotten about Task Group 17.3) and under aerial surveillance by the Japanese, the cruisers and destroyers pressed on to their position to block the Japanese convoy. Attacked three times, twice by the Japanese and once by MacArthur's Army Air Force, they beat off the attacks without loss (or were missed completely by US bombs). This stalwart defence, coupled with the misidentification of one of the ships as a battleship by the Japanese and the loss of a carrier, sufficiently rattled the Japanese convoy commander into reversing course and returning to Rabaul. The battle of the Coral Sea had been won. Crace has never attracted much praise for his efforts, but he had achieved his objective and preserved his force in the face of determined Japanese efforts to destroy it. This was more than any Allied-force commander had managed in the five months of the Pacific War, a fact not acknowledged in the official communique.[9]

Prime Minister Curtin spoke for many others when he expressed disappointment that the defeat of the Japanese had not accomplished more slaughter amongst the troop transports. However, the victory at Coral Sea, unbeknown to the Allies at the time, was a serious strategic setback for the Japanese 'Stage 2' plan for the consolidation of its conquests, and precipitated the fruitless attempt to take Port Moresby over the Kokoda Track. In conjunction with its new ally, the RAN had struck a significant blow in the defence of Australia. This was overshadowed by the stunning success of the US Navy against the Japanese at Midway a month later. It would be fair to judge Coral Sea as a turning point in the Pacific War.

DEFENDING THE EAST-COAST CONVOYS

The victory at the Coral Sea is one of the most well-known naval actions of the Pacific War but few Australians know about the next stage of the struggle other than its spectacular opening act. The IJN had devoted considerable time and money to the development of a force of midget submarines, designed to be carried to their immediate area of operations as cargo on larger boats. They proved to be an ineffective weapon, requiring the diversion of scarce resources for delivery and the identification of targets significant enough to warrant the effort. Sydney Harbour was deemed one potential target, so a force of five large submarines, three with midgets embarked, made the long, submerged passage from Truk to launch an attack. This took place on the night of 31 May/1 June 1942 and resulted in the sinking of one naval accommodation ship. All three midgets were lost. Despite the gallantry of the floatplane pilot who flew the previous night over the largest strategic and best-defended area of Australia without being intercepted, and the six crewmen of the midget submarines, the raid was a costly failure for the Japanese. The naval defences of Sydney had been tested and found to be largely effective, although poorly directed.[10]

However, this raid marked the start of a submarine campaign of attrition against shipping on the east coast of Australia, a strategic battle of the greatest seriousness. The Japanese appeared to hold all the cards, with a sizeable and highly regarded submarine fleet, whose boats could operate comfortably for considerable periods from bases at Truk or

Rabaul. Opposing them were a ragtag collection of small and undertrained naval escorts and a still-incomplete maritime surveillance capability mounted by the RAAF. Bulky cargoes, military and civilian, had no option but to be transported by sea as the Australian road and rail systems were already stretched to breaking point. For the nation, this particularly applied to the transportation of coal from the fields in the Hunter Valley to the nation's furnaces and power stations, and iron ore from South Australia to the furnaces at Port Kembla and Newcastle in New South Wales.

The situation for GHQ was no better. Ships moving men, supplies and equipment inbound from the United States or forward to Papua and New Guinea were subject to interdiction at any point in their passage outside the Great Barrier Reef. This was an important consideration as plans to advance to contest Japanese control of the Bismarck Sea between New Britain and the New Guinea mainland reached fruition in May.

The Allies had one card of their own to play. Before the Japanese assault, the Special Intelligence Bureau had been relegated by the British and Americans to the study of 'minor' codes, including the code used by Japanese submarine fleets. The Bureau had made breaks into this so that the reports sent by Japanese submarines following attacks were able, in large part, to be read. Instructions to submarines from the fleet commander were also able to be partially read. These decodes would not always indicate when attacks on shipping could be expected but they did contain significant information about operating areas, weapons states and Japanese views of the results obtained.

One other factor entered the equation: contrary to the practice in other navies, submarines were regarded as an essential part of the IJN Combined Fleet for the execution of a strategy described as 'decisive battle' against the US Navy. Their role was to sink or damage US ships as they approached the battle zone so that a weakened US force would face an attack by the whole might of the IJN. As it transpired, the conditions necessary for the execution of this strategy never occurred during the Pacific War, but the concept meant that Japanese submariners were not adept at sinking merchant ships, nor was the submarine fleet switched to convoy interdiction as a principal role. Submarines were often diverted to other task meaning that while costly of Allied resources the attacks on Australian coastal shipping were sporadic.[11]

The Allied counter to the Japanese submarine campaign called for improvisation. Convoys were introduced and escorts assigned to the role of protecting them. The RAN's corvettes were really no match for the

Japanese I-Class oceanic submarines, and were even out-gunned by them. The RAAF had insufficient practice in ASW to deliver effective attacks, and there was confusion and squabbling about inter-service procedures and responsibilities. The one Allied success by the new destroyer *Arunta* despatched *RO-33* off Port Moresby in August. These measures appear to have deterred the Japanese, because in the following six months they managed to sink only five ships and to damage seven others, incurring only one loss.

Nevertheless the crisis introduced organisational changes that took some time to settle down. Admiral Leary decided that the protection of shipping should be an Australian responsibility with support from the US Navy as feasible. The Australian Chief of Naval Staff now accepted a heavy operational burden as Commander South West Pacific Sea Frontier and, over time, his responsibility would extend as far north as Hollandia in Dutch New Guinea. The organisation and its effectiveness grew over the following two years, but it was initiated in 1942. In its final form in 1944, there were over 100 Allied ships involved in the ASW and convoying effort under CNS's operational command. Out of confusion and scarcity, a strategic weapon had been forged.

MILNE BAY AND THE BATTLE FOR BUNA AND GONA

MacArthur's strategy to push back the Japanese obstructing his advance to the Philippines depended on the seizure of suitable locations to isolate Japanese garrisons and from which his air power could neutralise and then destroy the enemy's capability to respond. This required command of the sea from which to launch his assaults and over which to build up his forces and their logistics support. Milne Bay at the extreme southeasterly point of Papua was selected as the site of the first new air base, and in June orders were issued for its occupation. The 36 km-long fiord was check-surveyed by the RAN Coast Watchers and the first convoy entered on 24 June. Within six weeks there were over 10 000 Australian and US troops at Milne Bay, with RAAF fighter squadrons operating from two completed airstrips and a further runway under construction. All had been got there in convoys escorted by the RAN.

The Japanese, meanwhile, had determined on a land assault on Port Moresby through the Buna–Gona area. They landed on 21–22 July, impeded but not stopped by Allied air attacks, and commenced stockpiling supplies for the advance over the Owen Stanley Range. Recognising that this was not a sustainable route for full development of their initiative, the Japanese decided that Milne Bay needed to be eliminated as a prelude for a second seaward assault on Moresby.[12] Events elsewhere, particularly the defeat of the Combined Fleet's attack on Midway Island and loss of four carriers in early June, curtailed this plan, but Milne Bay was assaulted on 26 August by Japanese Special Naval Landing Forces supported by cruisers. By 7 September the Japanese remnants had been withdrawn in utter defeat. Task Force 44 was on alert to intervene if necessary, but was not called forward, although its destroyers were engaged in the defence.

Various claims are made for this battle. Regardless of their validity, the defeat finally put paid to any hopes of further Japanese attempts to invest Port Moresby by sea which, in turn, certainly doomed to failure the cross-country assault, known to Australians as the Battle for Kokoda. The Japanese would fight tenaciously but in vain. Their fate was sealed when GHQ decided on a strategy to retake Buna, Gona and Sanananda (see Chapter 12).

It is difficult to understate the difficulties that this plan faced. To all intents and purposes, the Japanese controlled the sea approaches to these villages and had control of the air. There was a grave shortage of suitable shipping and escorts, and the waters through which the convoys would have to sail were poorly charted. General Blamey scoffed at naval reservations about this plan, which he attributed to timidity, but there was very little point in having precious ships with their passengers and cargoes hung up on coral reefs for the Japanese to pick off at will. A safe route had to be surveyed without drawing Japanese attention to the fact. This task was carried out by the RAN Hydrographic Service and the Coast Watchers who, between September and the end of October surveyed a passage for ships from China Strait to Oro Bay south of Buna, from where the Japanese defences could be outflanked. The first supplies were ferried forward in small ships and the troops in corvettes. The first convoys – Dutch merchant ships escorted by RAN corvettes – began shuttling equipment and supplies, including tanks, north from Port Moresby in early December.[13] Despite fanatical Japanese resistance, the land battle concluded on 22 January 1943. The threat to Port Moresby by land and sea had been eliminated.

ASSAULT ON THE SOLOMONS

The other part of the Japanese 'Stage 2' plan of most importance to Australia was their determination to seize the southern Solomon Islands and to establish Guadalcanal as a major air base from which to harass communications between the US and Australia and to attack Allied concentrations in

Fiji and New Caledonia. Shortly after the raid conducted on Tulagi as part of Operation MO, the Japanese had commenced this work. To stop it required an Allied assault under the codename Operation WATCHTOWER, authorised on 10 July, by US Marines supported by ships and aircraft from both the South Pacific and SWPA commands, supplemented by a carrier force, again under command of Admiral Fletcher. Admiral Kelly Turner US Navy commanded the amphibious force with the new RACAS, Rear Admiral Victor Crutchley VC RN, as his second-in-command, with Task Force 44 providing the bulk of the surface escort force.

WATCHTOWER involved a significant number of 'firsts' and it was inevitable that there would be problems arising from inexperience, especially on the US side. The difficulties of coordinating cooperation across the boundary between two operational theatres also became apparent during the operation, but there were other command and control problems between US elements of the attacking force. These would determine the course of the battle that ensued.[14]

The plan was simple. The 1st Marine Division would be landed at Tulagi and Guadalcanal to dislodge the Japanese, who were busy constructing their airfield. The transports would be held close to the beachheads and protected by a light force while they were unloaded. To guard against a Japanese surface response a force of seven Allied cruisers and supporting destroyers would block the northward entrance to the operations area. Air defence and air support for the Marines would come from Fletcher's carriers, and an elaborate system of air surveillance would be initiated to warn of the approach of Japanese submarines, ships and aircraft. Early warning of raids launched from Rabaul would be communicated to the force by RAN Coast Watchers in Bougainville, while others with local knowledge would land with the Marines.

The assault went in on 7 August and was a complete success. The Japanese reacted with largely ineffectual bombing raids but they also sailed a naval task group under Admiral Gunichi Mikawa to force a passage into the anchorage and to destroy the transports. This was sighted by patrolling RAAF aircraft on the morning of 8 August but their sighting reports were delayed, and did not reach Turner and Crutchley until the evening. Mikawa managed to make his approach to the area undetected by using the cover of darkness and bad weather. The failure of the US Navy to deploy an aerial surveillance program as well as the decision of Fletcher to withdraw his carriers due to threat of submarine attack meant that the first the Allied cruiser force knew of the presence of the Japanese was when they were fired upon.

Photo 31 HMAS *Canberra* sinking following the battle of Savo Island in the Solomons. (AWM 137295)

By unfortunate coincidence, Crutchley and his flagship HMAS *Australia* had been called into the transport anchorage by Kelly for a conference shortly before the Japanese attack, but the performance of the cruisers and destroyers left on the scene was little short of appalling. Four cruisers were sunk or disabled, with little loss to the Japanese, but Mikawa forgot what he was there to do and turned away without attacking the transports and their fragile screen. HMAS *Canberra* had taken the full brunt of the first broadside without even getting away a shot of her own and was sunk by Allied torpedoes the following morning. In view of his losses and the absence of the carrier air support, Turner decided to withdraw his ships that day, leaving the Marines to fend for themselves.

It was a less than glorious outcome for the first of the many battles that were fought in Solomons waters in the coming nine months. US critics were quick to blame Crutchley for 'faulty' dispositions and failing to tell the US cruiser captains what to do if fired on by the Japanese. Admiral King did not agree, putting the cause of the disaster down to a lack of war-preparedness in his commanding officers. Crutchley kept his command of the joint Task Force until his term as RACAS expired in 1944.

The important point was that the transports had not been destroyed by Mikawa, for their loss would have doomed the Marines to isolation and defeat in detail.

There is an interesting twist to this tale. Ordinarily, the interception and decoding of Japanese messages concerning Mikawa's force in the main naval code by FRUMEL and others would have provided advanced warning for Kelly. However, the Japanese had recently changed the variant of the code in use, which meant that it had to be 'broken' all over again. The submarine code, referred to above, had not changed and was being read. FRUMEL knew where all the Japanese submarines were and what they had been told to do. One might, perhaps, empathise with Admiral Fletcher's apprehension when all he was seeing in intelligence reporting was an onrushing flotilla of Japanese submarines towards the southern Solomons. The importance of sigint as a strategic weapon was confirmed, in this case by its absence.

PREPARING FOR THE ADVANCE, 1942

Men, ships and equipment were poured into the South Pacific area throughout the rest of 1942 as the US struggled to blunt and defeat Japanese efforts to retake Guadalcanal. Some, however, reached Australia, as part of the build-up of forces and capabilities necessary to advance against the Japanese in SWPA. The great need was amphibious capability and material for, although the Australian initiatives in that direction were useful, they were small in comparison with what would be required. MacArthur's amphibious force commander would not arrive until in January 1943.

In October the USN engineered a takeover of FRUMEL, ejecting many of the Australians. There was no shortage of organisations vying for their services, including MacArthur's own sigint organisation, Central Bureau in Brisbane, where he now had his headquarters. One of the other Australian initiatives he had commandeered was the Combined Operational Intelligence Centre, while the Coast Watchers became one arm of the Allied Intelligence Bureau. Both were to remain under RAN command throughout the war. The decision was also made to concentrate all SWPA hydrographic effort in a single task group, to be designated Task Group 70.5 in 1943, again under RAN command. Continued RAN command of the cruiser/destroyer force has already been mentioned.[15]

Necessarily, the exercise of these joint command responsibilities and the participation in other allied activities required a harmonisation of naval codes, communications and operating procedures, in which the larger partner took the lead. 'Americanisation' of the RAN had begun, not just in operational areas but in matters as basic as a decent serviceable uniform to wear in the tropics and in the provision of washing machines to keep them clean, innovations seemingly beyond the RAN. Operational experience had already demonstrated shortcomings in RAN ships regarding air defence and endurance, and the burden of supporting a force deployed on a front line well forward of the base facilities in Australia would weigh heavily on the RAN in the Pacific War. Improvisation and a fighting spirit were not substitutes for adequate ammunition and food. The tentative efforts made to create an afloat support force from Australian resources in 1942 never achieved the adequacy of supply that was the hallmark of the US Navy in the Pacific, and tins of the ubiquitous Australian 'meat and vegetables' would never compete in attractiveness with American frozen chicken and ice cream.

CONCLUSION

In the first three months of the Pacific War the RAN had suffered a number of strategic and material reverses, including the disappearance of its major partner and mentor, the Royal Navy. Nevertheless, it still possessed operational, material and organisational capabilities that were not only essential to the conduct of the war in SWPA during 1942 but proved to be the building blocks on which the incoming US command could develop the strategies and capabilities to advance on Japan. Moreover, its operational readiness and performance made important contributions in the fighting that did occur, especially in the East Coast convoys, the Coral Sea and in Papua and New Guinea. Defending Australia was a new experience for a Navy that had done most of the fighting in its short history well away from the continent, but it learned its task quickly.

In consequence, the story of cooperation between the US Navy and the RAN was one of mutual respect where the American command drew on and developed RAN areas of special expertise. In turn, the RAN learned much about fighting war on an oceanic front and the organisational and logistics demands that made. Far from being a marriage of convenience, it developed into a strong and confident partnership advancing on Japan, such that in August 1945 as the Australian Army was demobilising or employed in mopping-up operations, and the RAAF had made very public its dislike of the mundane tasks it was performing, the cruisers and destroyers of the RAN were in Subic Bay in the Philippines preparing with the rest of the 7th Fleet for the assault on Kyushu.

Notes

1 Arthur W. Jose, *The Royal Australian Navy*, Angus & Robertson, Sydney, 1937, pp. 3–5.
2 P. Cannon, 'The Acquisition of Modified Leander Class Cruisers for the RAN', *Journal of Australian Naval History*, vol. 5 no. 2, pp. 19–46.
3 Ian Pfennigwerth, *The Royal Australian Navy and MacArthur*, Rosenberg, Sydney, 2009, pp. 27–9.
4 George H. Gill, *Royal Australian Navy 1942–1945*, Australian War Memorial, Canberra, 1968, pp. 332–3.
5 David Stevens, 'Southwest Pacific Sea Frontiers', in David Stevens (ed.), *The Royal Australian Navy in World War II*, Allen & Unwin, Sydney, 1996, p. 95.
6 Gill, *Royal Australian Navy 1942–1945*, Australian War Memorial, Canberra, 1968, p. 710,
7 Robert G. Neale et al. (eds), *Documents in Australian Foreign Policy 1937–1949, Vol II: 1939*, Australian Government Publishing Service, Canberra, 1976, pp. 818–20.
8 Frederick D. Parker, *A Priceless Advantage: US Navy Communications Intelligence and the Battles of Coral Sea, Midway and the Aleutians*, National Security Agency, Fort Meade Md., 1993, pp. 30–2.
9 Gill, *Royal Australian Navy 1942–1945*, p. 55.
10 David Jenkins, *Battle Surface! Japan's Submarine War against Australia 1942–44*, Random House, Sydney, 1992, p. 223.
11 David Stevens, 'I-174: The last Japanese Submarine off Australia', *Journal of the Australian War Memorial*, vol. 22, 1993 p. 430.
12 Gill, *Royal Australian Navy 1942–1945*, pp. 119–20
13 Ibid., pp. 45–7.
14 Ian Pfennigwerth, *Missing Pieces: The Intelligence Jigsaw and RAN Operations 1939–71*, Sea Power Centre, Australia, Canberra, 2008, pp. 88–90.
15 Gill, *Royal Australian Navy 1942–1945*, p. 434.

FURTHER READING

Carruthers, S., *Japanese Submarine Raiders 1942: A Maritime Mystery*, Casper Publications, Sydney, 2006.
Coulthard-Clark, C., *Action Stations Coral Sea: The Australian Commander's Story*, Allen & Unwin, Sydney, 1991.
Feldt, E., *The Coast Watchers*, Currey O'Neil, Melbourne, 1981.
Gill, G.H., *Royal Australian Navy 1942–1945*, Australian War Memorial, Canberra, 1968.
Jenkins, D., *Battle Surface! Japan's Submarine War against Australia, 1942–44*, Random House, Sydney, 1992
Jeremy, J., *The Island Shipyard: Shipbuilding at Cockatoo Island 1870 to 1987*, Sydney Harbour Federation Trust, Sydney, 2006.

Lewis, T., *Darwin's Submarine: I-124*, Adelaide, Avonmore Books, 2010.
Loxton, B., *The Shame of Savo: The Sinking of HMAS* Canberra, Allen & Unwin, Sydney, 1997.
Pfennigwerth, I., *A Man of Intelligence: The Life of Captain Eric Nave, Australian Codebreaker Extraordinary*, Rosenberg, Sydney, 2006.
Stevens, D., *The Royal Australian Navy in World War II*, Allen & Unwin, Sydney, 2005.

ON AUSTRALIA'S
DOORSTEP

KOKODA AND MILNE BAY

Karl James

Japan's attacks on Pearl Harbor, the Philippines, Malaya and elsewhere
on 7–8 December 1941 changed Australia's war. Overnight, the war went
from a distant conflict fought against the Germans and Italians in North
Africa, the Mediterranean and in the skies above Europe, to a war suddenly
being waged on Australia's doorstep. In a radio broadcast to the nation on
8 December 1941, Prime Minister John Curtin warned the men and
women of Australia that the forthcoming Pacific War would be 'the gravest
hour in our history'. 'This', he continued, 'is our darkest hour'.[1] This was
not just political rhetoric. Focusing Australia's military effort and modest
resources on the European war had come at the expense of Australia's
home defences that, in December 1941, were in a dire state.

In the weeks and months to come, Australia would rapidly mobilise
and industrialise for war. The Navy grew just as the Air Force expanded
with new squadrons and modern aircraft. The battle-hardened AIF
was recalled from the Middle East and the militia's ranks swelled with
men called up for service. But in early 1942, time was a luxury Australia
did not have. The only island barrier that remained between mainland
Australia and the Japanese was Papua. Here, along the Kokoda Trail in
Papua's imposing Owen Stanley Range, Australian soldiers fought
against a formidable enemy and battled an exhausting terrain. A powerful motivator for the Australian soldiers to enduring these hardships
was the belief that they were fighting to stop the Japanese southern
advance, with one veteran later likening the campaign to 'Australia's
Thermopylae'.[2] Australian forces also fought a desperate action at

Milne Bay, on Papua's southeast coast. This chapter will give an overview of these two campaigns.

Curtin's grim warning of 8 December 1941 proved all too true. The Japanese advanced rapidly, capturing Malaya, Singapore and the Netherlands East Indies in just four months while the Philippines too would soon fall. The shadow of war quickly fell on Australia. With the devastating loss of Singapore, Ambon and Timor, some 20 000 men, virtually all the 8th Division AIF, became prisoners of war. More Australians were captured on Java. Australian mandated territory had also been invaded and occupied with the Japanese overwhelming the forlorn garrison at Rabaul in New Britain during January 1942 and landing in New Guinea at Lae and Salamaua in March. Rabaul subsequently became the major Japanese base in the South Pacific, controlling operations in New Guinea and the Solomon Islands.

Forecasting what he felt was sure to come, Churchillian Curtin described the fall of Singapore as heralding the 'battle for Australia'.[3] Two days later Darwin was bombed in the first of many attacks on mainland Australia, adding to Curtin's fears, but fortunately such a battle was never to eventuate. The Japanese had no firm plans to invade, adopting instead a strategy to isolate Australia from the United States with the Operation FS (Fiji–Samoa).[4] This plan included occupying Port Moresby and the southern Solomons and 'smashing [the] enemy plans for a counteroffensive in the region'.[5] But for many Australians the threat of Japanese raids or an invasion was a genuine fear.

There is no doubt that early 1942 was Australia's darkest hour. But in mid-March, the first glimmer of light began to shine through when the US General Douglas MacArthur escaped from the Philippines, arriving in Darwin on the 17th. A few days earlier the first troop convoys carrying the 7th and then the 6th Division reached Australia from the Middle East followed, at the end of the month, by their controversial commander, General Sir Thomas Blamey. MacArthur was celebrated as the 'savior of Australia'.[6] US forces had been arriving in Australia since December 1941 but MacArthur's arrival was seen as a guarantee of American support. Australia would not face the Japanese thrust alone. MacArthur formed a strong bond with Curtin, but over time the American's relationship with Blamey would prove more difficult.

A further boost to Australia came on 20 April when Darwin received a signal from the Australians on Portuguese Timor announcing 'Force intact. Still fighting. Badly need boots, money, quinine, tommy gun ammunition'.[7]

Photo 32   Militiamen from the 30th Brigade carrying out manoeuvres outside of Port Moresby, July 1942 (AWM 025881).

This was the first news anyone had from Sparrow Force since the Japanese invaded Timor 59 days earlier. For almost two months the Australian high command had presumed that, like their compatriots at Rabaul, they had all been either killed or captured. Instead, Sparrow Force was to go on to wage a successful year-long guerrilla war against the Japanese on the island. Largely conducted in secret, it was not until early 1943 that their exploits were publicised in Australia.

All eyes though were on Port Moresby and Papua. Until 1941, Papua and New Guinea had been backwaters. Little had been done to prepare for their defence beyond raising two under-strength local units, one for Europeans and one for Papuans. In March 1941 a militia battalion was sent to Port Moresby from Australia for 'Tropical Service'. This unit was reinforced in January 1942 by the militia's 30th Brigade but there the amenities and facilities for the troops remained completely under-developed. From February, Japanese air raids became regular occurrences yet there was little opportunity for the brigade to undertake serious training. Soldiers were instead used as a source of labour for working parties and unloading ships. When the AIF's Brigadier Selwyn Porter arrived to take over the brigade in April, he was surprised by the general lack of preparedness. 'It was a sorry story', he commented to a war correspondent. 'There were no plans, the troops were untrained', and brigade headquarters 'consisted of a telephone in the corner of the mess', and there were 'no maps'.[8] Gradually, Port Moresby was reinforced with soldiers, equipment and aircraft. But by the end June, the total strength of Australian and US troops in all of New Guinea was only 15 000.[9]

The Japanese had intended to take Port Moresby by sea but following their losses in the battle of the Coral Sea in May they devised a naively ambitious plan for an overland attack on Port Moresby by crossing the Owen Stanley Range. On 19 May, Allied code-breakers in Melbourne intercepted a Japanese radio message revealing their intention of taking Port Moresby by land.[10] Three weeks later, MacArthur wrote to Blamey, informing him of the increasing evidence suggesting the Japanese were interested in developing a route from Buna, on Papua's north coast, across the mountains, to Port Moresby.[11] A small number of Papuan soldiers were consequently sent to Kokoda to observe the coast. In late June, Blamey ordered further steps to defend the north coast by sending 'white troops' to stop any possible overland Japanese movement.

The operation was codenamed 'Maroubra'.[12] Major-General Basil Morris, the Australian commander of New Guinea Force (NGF) in Port Moresby, doubted that any force could cross the Owen Stanley Range and was more concerned with securing Port Moresby's coastline as he considered the real threat would come from the sea. When he handed over command of NGF to Lieutenant-General Sydney Rowell in August, Morris commented: 'The mountains will beat the Nips and we must be careful they don't beat us'.[13] Despite his misgivings Morris did as he was ordered. On 8 July the first soldiers from the 30th Brigade's 39th Battalion began making the long trek over the unnamed and unmapped track that became the Kokoda Trail.

Ninety-six kilometres long, the Kokoda Trail is a narrow, muddy foot track that runs from Owers' Corner, on the southern side of the Owen Stanley Range, to Kokoda, on the northern side. The terrain is rugged and isolated; the foothills are covered in thick jungle that becomes dense rainforest as the mountains get higher. At its peak the track reaches an altitude of 7000 feet.[14] It is hot and humid during the day and cold at night. It rains constantly, while tropical diseases, such as Malaria, are endemic. Lieutenant Colonel Frank Norris, who commanded the 7th Division's medical units during the campaign, wrote one of the best descriptions of the track:

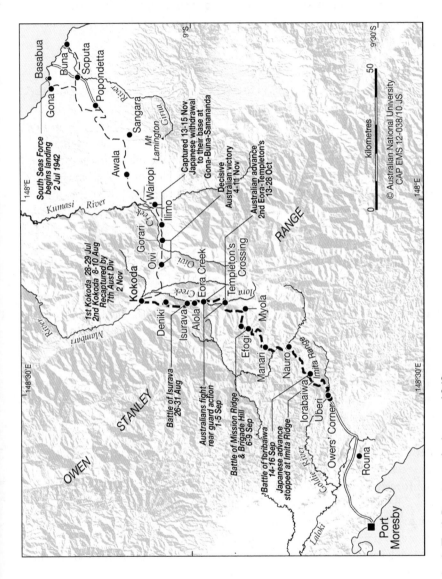

Map 8 Kokoda Trail: Retreat and advance, 1942

> Imagine an area 100 miles long – crumple and fold this into a series of ridges, each rising higher and higher ... cover this thickly with jungle, short trees and tall trees tangled with great ... savage vines. [Through this density] cut a little native track 2–3 feet wide, up the ridges, over the spurs, around gorges and down across swiftly following ... mountain streams.[15]

Contrary to popular perception, the track was well known in the territory. It was first used by Australians in the 1890s and was trekked regularly in the four decades before the war as the overland mail route between Port Moresby and the mines, missions and plantations on the north coast. But this did not make the trek any easier. Already fatigued by the time he reached Uberi, Corporal Albert Long was exhausted by the climb. The constant rain made the track very muddy and, having earlier thrown away his blanket and spare clothes to lighten his load, he was wet through and 'losing weight fast through sweating so much'. By the time he reached at Nauro, Long confessed in his diary to feeling 'more dead than alive'.[16] Writing in his diary at night by candlelight under his ground sheet, Warrant Officer George Mowat, a decorated Great War veteran, described the climb more simply: 'Track slippery [in] some places had to crawl [on] hands and knees. Hills & yet more hills'.[17] The first soldiers from the 39th Battalion reached Kokoda in mid-July. A week later they were skirmishing with the Japanese.

The Japanese invasion of Papua began on 21 July when the Sasebo 5th Special Naval Landing Party came ashore near Buna, along with troops from Yokoyama Advance Party, consisting of infantry and combat engineers who landed at Gona. The first major clash occurred two days later near Awala with the overwhelmed Australians and a handful of Papuan soldiers falling back towards Kokoda. The struggle for Kokoda and its potentially valuable airstrip became the first major action of the campaign. Between 29 July and 10 August, control of Kokoda swung back and forth between the Australians and the Japanese as each side received piecemeal reinforcements. Outnumbered and with food and ammunition running low, the battered 39th Battalion eventually withdrew to Isurava in mid-August where they dug in 'using their bayonets, bully beef tins and steel helmets'. Here, they received a new commanding officer, Lieutenant Colonel Ralph Honner, who later described his first impressions of the battalion, 'Physically, the pathetically young warriors of the 39th were in poor shape. Worn out by strenuous fighting and exhausting movement, and weakened by lack of food and sleep and shelter, many of them had literally come to a standstill'.[18]

Relief was coming. Along with another militia battalion, the first AIF troops were moving up the track to reinforce Maroubra Force. MacArthur had not initially taken the Japanese landings seriously. He believed that once the US Marines landed on Guadalcanal, in the Solomon Islands, in early August, the Japanese would withdraw from Buna. Blamey, however, was not so sure and when the 39th Battalion was first driven out of Kokoda at the end of July, he sent the AIF to Papua. The 7th Division's 21st and 18th Brigades were the first to arrive, respectively reaching Port Moresby and Milne Bay by sea in mid-August. The division's 25th Brigade along with the units from the 6th Division soon followed.

Up until mid-July, immediately before their troops landed in Papua, the Japanese commanders in Rabaul had been contemplating the feasibility of an overland attack on Port Moresby. Their Ri Operation Study was to research the possibility of an overland attack and make the necessary preparations for its implementation. The Japanese command knew little of the conditions in Papua apart from the discovery of a book by a European explorer that referred to a 'Kokoda Road'. Aerial reconnaissance had also suggested a vehicle road existed between Buna and Kokoda.

As such, Major-General Horii Tomitaro's South Seas Force, which had previously captured Guam and Rabaul, was given the task of carrying out the operation.[19] Horii, however, was not enthusiastic. He thought an overland advance would be extremely difficult and ran a high risk of failure. He knew the problem was always going to be supply. Horii's headquarters estimated that his force of about 5000 men would need about 4600 carriers if they were to cross the peak of the Owen Stanley Range in 20 days. Privately, Horii did not think reaching Port Moresby was a possibility. But despite his concerns, when asked he did not strongly object and the operation went ahead.[20] The main body of the South Seas Force, built around the 144th Infantry Regiment, landed at Buna on 18 August and began moving to Kokoda the next day. They were soon joined by the 41st Infantry Regiment, veterans of the Malayan campaign. Although it began as a reconnaissance operation, the campaign quickly developed its own momentum. When Horii arrived at Kokoda on the 23rd, he decided to destroy the Australians at Isurava and then continue quickly across the mountains.

The intensity of the contacts and clashes around Isurava had been building for several days until on 27 August the Japanese attacked with artillery support from a mountain gun. Bitter, close-quarter fighting ensued. Honner later wrote a graphic account of the battle:

Photo 33 Members of the 39th Battalion withdrawing after the battle of Isurava, September 1942 (AWM 013288).

> The enemy came on in waves over a short stretch of open ground, regardless of casualties ... They were met with Bren-gun and Tommy-gun, with bayonet and grenade; but still they came, too close with the buffet of fist and boot and rifle-butt ... [It was] vicious fighting, man to man and hand to hand.[21]

The 39th Battalion hung on long enough to be reinforced by the lead troops from the 21st Brigade's 2/14th Battalion. Fighting continued for another two days until, on 29 August, the Japanese broke through the Australian lines. Twenty-four year-old Private Bruce Kingsbury was one of the few survivors whose platoon had been overrun. Kingsbury immediately volunteered to join a different platoon that had been ordered to counter attack. Firing a Bren light machine gun from the hip, he rushed forward and cleared a path through the Japanese. Kingsbury's charge broke the Japanese attack but just as the rest of his platoon was about to reach him he was shot dead. Despite Kingsbury's bravery, for which he was posthumously awarded the Victoria Cross, Isurava had to be abandoned. This battle set the pattern for the rest of the campaign with Maroubra Force conducting a fighting withdrawal along the Kokoda Trail. Supplies were limited and there was a constant fear, quite rightly, of the 21st Brigade's beleaguered column being outflanked. Soaked to the skin by the constant rain, their feet shrivelled with 'trench foot', most men had not had a hot meal or even a mug of warm tea for days.

In Australia, the series of withdrawals and reverses caused MacArthur to become increasingly alarmed. A senior Australian officer described the atmosphere in MacArthur's GHQ as being 'like a bloody barometer in a cyclone – up and down every two minutes'.[22] Dudley McCarthy, in the official history, went even further, describing MacArthur as 'fidgety'. On 6 September MacArthur told General George Marshall, the US Army chief of staff in Washington: 'The Australians have proven themselves unable to match the enemy in jungle fighting. Aggressive leadership is lacking'.[23]

This crisis in confidence from MacArthur as well as Blamey and other Australian senior officers and politicians partly contributed to the circumstances by which several commanders in Papua were relieved. The first to go was Maroubra Force's commander Brigadier Arnold Potts, the 21st Brigade's much-loved, aggressive but ultimately overwhelmed leader. Potts was relieved in the field even as his men were fighting for their lives. Lieutenant-General Rowell and, later, Major-General Arthur 'Tubby' Allen, the 7th Division's commander, were also sacked. Much has already been written on this issue and the dismissals are still a source of bitterness and resentment.[24]

Throughout the Papuan campaign there was a tension between the expectations of high command. On the one side was MacArthur and, to a lesser extent, Blamey, pushing NGF to counter attack, while the commanders in the field, such as Potts, were struggling to fight a delaying withdrawal, or, as happened later on to Allen, struggling to advance against the Japanese. Potts had not been ordered to block the Japanese advance, as is generally assumed, but rather his task was to 'attack and capture Kokoda' and to undertake further actions in preparation for operations against Buna and Gona.[25] Potts, Rowell and Allen were unable to manage the expectations of their superiors.

When MacArthur fleetingly visited Owers' Corner on 3 October, he met Brigadier John Lloyd whose 16th Brigade from the 6th Division was starting its move up the Kokoda Trail. 'Lloyd', MacArthur told the brigadier, 'by some act of God, your brigade has been chosen for this job. The eyes of the western world are upon you. I have every confidence in you and your men. Good luck and don't stop'.[26] This was a less than subtle statement of MacArthur's expectations.

After weeks of struggling against the Australians, the environment, and their own hunger, the Japanese reached Ioribaiwa in mid-September. Dug-in on the next rise, Imita Ridge, was the 7th Division's fresh 25th Brigade and other units. A few days earlier, the 25th Brigade had relieved the remnants of the 21st Brigade, who now numbered only just over 300 men. When the 21st Brigade marched towards Isurava a month earlier, it had been nearly 1800 strong.[27] The Japanese had also suffered. Ioribaiwa was to be the limit of their advance, leaving, as the Japanese battalion commander Major Koiwai Mitsuo noted, only one more mountain to cross before they reached Port Moresby. At night they could see the glow from the searchlights from the city that was 'their long sought objective'.[28] Horri, however, had initially been ordered to restrict his advance to the saddle of the Owen Stanley Range. His problem was that in the seemingly endless mountains he did not know which peak was the highest. While the Australian maps were vague and inaccurate, Japanese maps were nonexistent. Isurava was only the first in a series of mountain ridges.

It is thought the Japanese suffered about 1000 casualities during their advance, including deaths from both battle and sickness. The remaining men were weary, many were close to exhaustion and starvation as their supply lines, harried by Allied aircraft, broke down. By the start of September the men's rations had been cut to just a handful of rice per day. An incentive for the Japanese to continue on towards Port Moresby was the hope that they would discover supplies abandoned by the Australians or that rations would be carried forward; neither happened. The Australians destroyed their supply dumps before retreating.[29] Many years later, Staff Sergeant Imanishi Sadashige still recalled how the Australians dumped their rations, making holes in biscuit tins and throwing them into the valleys. 'We ended up washing mud off Australian rice and eating it.'[30]

In stark contrast to the Japanese, the Australians maintained a supply line that evolved and slowly improved over time. A reserve of stores for Maroubra Force was built up at the dry lakes of Myola and at Kagi, with supplies dropped by Allied aircraft. Stores were also dropped at Efogi. The backbreaking work was done by the Papuans indentured and conscripted to work for the Australians, immortalised by poet Sapper Bert Beros as 'fuzzy wuzzy angels'.

The Papuans brought up ammunition and supplies, and carried back the wounded on improvised stretchers made from blankets lashed to poles. Six hundred carriers were employed early in the campaign and by the end of October more than 1600 Papuans were working along the Kokoda Trail.[31] A 21st Brigade report later acknowledged the work done by the carriers could not 'be too highly praised'. The report also conceded that the carriers were overworked, often forced to go without rest, and conse-quently sickness and desertion rates were sometimes high.[32]

While the 39th and 2/14th Battalions were fighting at Isurava, a Japanese amphibious force landed at Milne Bay. A horseshoe-shaped bay, the natural deep-water harbour was surrounded on three sides by heavily wooded mountains and a narrow coastal strip, soggy with sago and mangrove swamps. The area was well known for its torrential rain and malaria. The first Australian soldiers and US engineers arrived in Milne Bay in June and began work constructing airstrips, roads and wharves around Gili Gili. The area soon became a large base though conditions were basic. One pilot, Flight Lieutenant Arthur 'Nat' Gould, who had flown in Europe earlier in the war, described his time at Milne Bay as 'dreadful'. The air strips were 'primitive', he remembered 'literally just carved through the coconut trees ... And [the] rain, my goodness me, I don't think it ever stopped raining'. It was 'awful' with 'mud up to your ankles' and enormous mosquitoes. Everyone became ill, including Gould, who suffered from malaria and dysentery. This was not enough to preclude them from flying.

> I'd be sitting up at 20 000 feet in a Kittyhawk [fighter-bomber] on patrol of some sort with diarrhea, you'd just be ... you'd feel it all going down the back of your legs and there's nothing you can do about it for the next hour. You just had to sit in it. So it was pretty unpleasant.[33]

While not the most pleasant of regions, MacArthur realised the bay's strategic possibilities. An Allied airbase at Milne Bay would protect Port Moresby's eastern flank against a Japanese naval attack while also paving the way forward for a move along Papua's coast to Buna and then to New Guinea without having to cross the Owen Stanley Range. Similarly, bombers from Milne Bay could also fly north to attack Rabaul without having to make the dangerous climb over the mountains.[34] The Japanese commanders in Rabaul also realised Milne Bay's significance. They deci-ded the area would make a good jumping-off point for the Navy for an attack on Port Moresby in conjunction with the Army's push across the mountains. As the airstrips had only just become operational, it was thought Milne Bay's garrison would only be small.[35] This new offensive was called Operation RE. In reality, there were nearly 9000 Australians and Americans, including the 7th Division's 18th Brigade, the militia's 7th

Brigade, field and anti-aircraft artillery batteries plus a flight of Hudsons from No. 6 Squadron, RAAF, and Kittyhawks flown by Nos. 75 and 76 Squadrons, RAAF.[36]

Late on the night of 25 August, a Japanese amphibious force based on the Kure 5th Special Naval Landing Party (5SNLP), with some 2000 troops and two light tanks, landed between Waga Waga and Wandala on the bay's north coast, about 11 kilometres east of Rabi and the airstrip at Gili Gili and clashed with Australian militiamen during the night. The next morning, the Air Force's Kittyhawks attacked and destroyed the Japanese's barges and stores, stranding 5SNLP. This set the pattern for much of the battle. During the day, low-flying Kittyhawks bombed and strafed the Japanese positions, suppressing any movement. The Air Force was relentless. One observer insisted that under the Kittyhawks's guns, 'palm fronds, bullets and dead Japanese snipers were pouring down with the rain'.[37] At night, however, the Japanese attacked, wading through the swamps to outflank Australian positions, while the two light tanks, emerging from the darkness and rain with their headlights on, broke through the Australians' lines. Japanese warships also entered the bay on successive nights, when the Air Force could not fly, shelling defences and landing reinforcements. Milne Force's commander, Major-General Cyril Clowes, was very much aware that the Japanese could possibly land another force on the bay's western or southern coastline. He was also hampered by poor communications, the constant rain that turned the muddy tracks into a morass, and a general uncertainty as to the actual strength and intentions of the Japanese.[38] The general feeling, Clowes later commented, 'was one of impotence – that we could do but little to prevent the Jap coming and going at will, as he did, almost'.[39] Conscious his flanks were not secure, the general did not immediately commit his two AIF battalions but kept them in reserve; a decision that led Clowes to being unfairly criticised by MacArthur for being hesitant, who thought he 'hemmed and hawed', and by Blamey, who commented to General Rowell that 'by not acting with greater speed', Clowes was 'liable to have missed the opportunity of dealing completely with the enemy'.[40]

By the time Rowell received Blamey's letter, the fighting at Milne Bay had already reached its climax. During the night of 30–31 August, the Japanese attack on No. 3 Strip, the most eastern airstrip, was beaten back with heavy casualties. Thereafter the Japanese were in full retreat. On 4 September, as Australians fought to clear 5SNLP from the northern shore, 28-year old Corporal John French's section, from the 2/9th Battalion, was held up by three Japanese machine-gun posts. Ordering his

Photo 34 Papua, September 1942. Australian soldiers inspect Japanese Type 95 Ha-Go light tanks bogged and abandoned at Milne Bay. (AWM 026632).

section to take cover, French silenced the first two posts with grenades and then rushed the third, firing his Thompson sub-machine gun from the hip. French was hit but kept going. When the Japanese machine gun ceased firing, his section moved forward and found the machine gunners dead, with French's body lying on the lip of the third pit. French was posthumously awarded the Victoria Cross.

With the battle lost, the surviving Japanese – many of who were ill or wounded, and all were hungry – were evacuated between 4 and 7 September. Of the 2800 Japanese who landed at Milne Bay only 1300 escaped. An estimated 750 were killed during the battle while the majority of the remainder died while trying to escape overland to Buna. The far-lower number of Allied casualties included 161 Australians killed or missing, as well as one American.[41] This number includes several Australians executed by the Japanese after being captured during the battle. A number of Papuans, including Papuan women, were also murdered. Many of those killed were bayoneted to death and some were badly mutilated.[42]

The war was turning against the Japanese elsewhere, too. Buna and the beachheads were coming under increasing air attack but more importantly, the campaign on Guadalcanal was going badly. Such was their concern that on 8 September the Japanese commanders at Rabaul signaled Horii to withdraw his force back to Kokoda. A similar signal was sent a few days later. It is not clear if Horii received these signals or if, continuing to push on towards Ioribaiwa, he chose to ignore them. On 14 September, choking back his tears, it is said, Horii cancelled the offensive. The Japanese began withdrawing two days later.[43] On 28 September Australian patrols discovered Ioribaiwa had been abandoned. Thereafter, the nature of the campaign was very similar to the earlier Australian withdrawal, though the roles were reversed. The Japanese retreat was bitter and demoralising. Okada Seizo, a Japanese war correspondent travelling with the South Seas Force, wrote that the order to withdraw 'crushed' the troops' spirits that until then had only been kept up through 'sheer pride'.[44] Casualties quickly mounted, as more and more men succumbed to tropical diseases and exhaustion due to starvation and malnutrition. Major Koiwai commented that at one point during their retreat, the strength of his battalion was down to 25 men. Very few of those lost had been battle casualties.[45] The Australians even discovered a few isolated cases of cannibalism.[46]

This phase of the campaign is usually described as the 'Australian advance' but really it was a pursuit, as they tried to maintain contact with the retreating Japanese. But the Japanese rearguard remained formidable. At Templeton's Crossing and Eora Creek, they skilfully established defensive positions that held up the Australian advance long enough for the main body of the South Seas Force to reach Kokoda in early October and then the coast. It took the 25th Brigade a week to clear Templeton's Crossing with 50 Australians killed and 133 wounded. By mid-October the brigade had also had 730 officers and soldiers evacuated through sickness.[47] At Eora Creek the fresh 16th Brigade, who had relieved the 25th Brigade, lost between 228 and 300 men killed and wounded in just nine days.[48] The first Australian soldiers reached Kokoda on the morning of 2 November, finding it abandoned by the Japanese. On hearing of Kokoda's liberation, MacArthur sent his 'hearty congratulations' to Blamey, commenting, 'these fine troops must feel a pride and satisfaction at his splendid accomplishment which I fully share'.[49] Given his earlier condemnation, MacArthur's praise was somewhat hollow. Two more vicious actions at Oivi and Gorari would be fought during the second week of November before Australian forces crossed the Kumusi River, bringing the Kokoda campaign to a close.[50]

During the four-month long campaign, more than 600 Australians were killed or died along the Kokoda Trail and over 1600 were wounded. Worse fighting was still to come during the vicious beachhead battles at Buna, Gona and Sanananda. Ultimately, from July 1942 to January 1943, more Australians were to die in Papua than in any other campaign during the war, some 2000 in total. Japanese losses were far greater. An estimated 12 000 Japanese, including General Horii, died in Papua. It is not surprising that Japanese survivors of the 144th Infantry Regiment called New Guinea 'Hell Island'.[51]

The Kokoda campaign was fought on the fringe of a vast war to defeat Japan; Kokoda did not save Australia. The Papuan campaign taught the Australians how to fight in the jungle and, ultimately, how to beat the Japanese – lessons that were put to good effect in New Guinea, Bougainville and Borneo in the years to come. MacArthur later generously commented that it had been the Australian success in Papua that 'turned the tide' in the South West Pacific and that had been the basis for 'all future success'.[52]

Notes

1   *The Argus*, 9 December 1941.
2   Ralph Honner, 'The 39th at Isurava', *Stand-To*, July–August 1956, p. 9.
3   *Sydney Morning Herald*, 17 February 1942.
4   See chapters 6 and 7.
5   Steven Bullard (trans.), *Army Operations in the South Pacific Area: New Britain and Papuan Campaigns, 1942–43*, Australian War Memorial, Canberra, 2000, p. 86. See Peter Stanley, *Invading Australia: Japan and the Battle for Australia, 1942*, Viking, Melbourne, 2008 and Bob Wurth, *1942: Australia's Greatest Peril*, Pan MacMillan, Sydney, 2008, for the emotional debate surrounding the Japanese plans to invade Australia.
6   William Manchester, *American Caesar: Douglas MacArthur, 1880–1964*, Hutchinson, Richmond, 1978, pp. 280–8.
7   *The Argus*, 1 January 1943.
8   Gavin Long, diary no. 8, 6 July 1942, p. 34, AWM: AWM67, 1/8.
9   Most of the Australian troops, the militia's 12 273 and the AIF's 1098, were employed in lines of communication, maintenance, fixed defence and anti-units. The 2208 US troops were mainly 'service' not 'combat' troops. Dudley McCarthy *South-West Pacific Area First Year: Kokoda to Wau*, Australian War Memorial, Canberra, 1959, p. 115.
10 Jack Bleakley, *The Eavesdroppers*, Australian Government Publishing Service, Canberra, 1992, p. 43.
11 McCarthy, *South-West Pacific Area First Year*, p. 114.
12 New Guinea Force war dairy, 22 and 23 June 1942; New Guinea Force Operational Instruction No. 16, 12 June 1942, New Guinea Force Headquarters and General (Air) war diary, June 1942, AWM: AWM52, 1/5/51.

13 Comments on draft chapters of the official history, Major-General B. Morris, p. 8, AWM: AWM67, 3/274.

14 Report on New Guinea operations, Buna–Ioribaiwa, p. 2, AWM: AWM52, 519/6/52.

15 Medical Service, 7 Aust Div during the Papuan campaign, Jan. 1943, p. 2, AWM: AWM52, 1/5/14/45.

16 Corporal Albert Long diary, 5 September 1942, AWM: PR00233.

17 Warrant Officer II George Mowat diary, 27 July 942, AWM: 3DRL 7137.

18 Honner, 'The 39th at Isurava', p. 9.

19 Bullard, *Japanese Army operations in the South Pacific Area*, p. 110.

20 To supply his force with the 3 tonnes of supplies it would need daily, Horii's headquarters estimated that it would need up to 32 000 carriers if they were to reach Moresby. Bullard, *Japanese Army Operations in the South Pacific Area*, p. 114.

21 Honner, 'The 39th at Kokoda', p. 12.

22 David Horner, *Blamey: The Commander-in-Chief*, Allen & Unwin, Sydney, 1998, p. 322.

23 McCarthy, *South-West Pacific Area First Year*, p. 225.

24 See David Horner, *Crisis of Command: Australian Generalship and the Japanese Threat,1941–1943*, Australian National University Press, Canberra, 1978; Stuart Braga, *Kokoda Commander: A Life of Major-General 'Tubby' Allen*, Oxford University Press, South Melbourne, 2004; Bill Edgar, *Warrior of Kokoda: A Biography of Brigadier Arnold Potts*, Allen & Unwin, St. Leonards, 1999; and Rowan Tracey, 'Conflict in Command during the Kokoda Campaign of 1942: Did General Blamey deserve the blame?', *United Service*, vol. 61, no. 2, June 2010.

25 21 Aust. Inf. Bde report on operations: Owen Stanley Range 16 Aug.–20 Sep. 1942, p. i, 21st Brigade war diary, Aug.–Oct. 1942, AWM52, 8/2/2121.

26 16th Brigade war diary, 3 October 1942, AWM52, 8/2/16/18.

27 21 Aust. Inf. Bde report on operations: Owen Stanley Range 16 Aug.–20 Sep. 1942, p. 15, 21st Brigade war diary, Aug.–Oct. 1942, AWM52, 8/2/21.

28 Statement by Major Koiwai Mitsuo, NARA, Washington, D.C., RG331, 104.

29 Bullard, *Japanese Army Operations in the South Pacific Area*, p. 114 and p. 183; John Moreman, 'Advance of the South Seas Force', Australia–Japan Research Project, http://ajrp.awm.gov.au/ajrp/ajrp2.nsf/pages/NT00010DD2?openDocument, <accessed 1 February 2009>.

30 Craig Collie and Hajime Marutani, *The Path of Infinite Sorrow: The Japanese on the Kokoda Track*, Allen & Unwin, Sydney, 2009, p. 116.

31 It has been estimated that as many as 3000 carriers worked the track. Native labour section, Headquarters ANGAU war diary, 31 October 1942, Oct. 1942, AWM52, 1/10/1; Paul Ham, *Kokoda*, HaperCollins, Pymble, 2004, p. 211.

32 21 Aust. Inf. Bde report on operations: Owen Stanley Range 16 Aug.–20 Sep. 1942, p. 24, 21st Brigade war diary, Aug.–Oct. 1942, AWM: AWM52, 8/2/21.

33 Interview Flight Lieutenant Arthur Gould, No. 75 Squadron, RAAF, AWM: S00578.

34 Charles A. Willoughby, (gen. ed.), *Reports of General MacArthur: The Campaigns of MacArthur in the Pacific*, vol. I, US Government Printing Office, Washington, 1966, pp. 50–1.

35 Bullard, *Japanese Army Operations in the South Pacific Area*, p. 168.

36 McCarthy, *South-West Pacific Area First Year*, p. 159.

37 Dougals Gillison, *Royal Australian Air Force 1939–1942*, Australian War Memorial, Canberra, 1962, p. 613.

38 Report by Comd Milne Force on operations between 25 Aug. 1942 and 7 Sept. 1942, p. 3 and p. 7, AWM: AWM54, 579/7/19.

39 Milne Bay operations – 24 Aug.–8 Sep. 42, p. 2, AWM: 3DRL 4143, 34.

40 Horner, *Blamey*, p. 346; Letter Blamey to Rowell, 1 Sep. 1942, AWM: 3DRL 6763, 3.

41 McCarthy, *South-West Pacific Area First Year*, pp. 185–6.

42 Report on atrocities committed by Jap Forces during the recent action at Milne Bay, 10 September 1942, AWM: AWM54, 1010/9/108; Reported atrocities – Milne Bay operations Sep–Oct 1942, National Archives of Australia, Canberra: A6237, Exhibit 50.

43 When the Japanese commander at Rabaul heard that the 144th Infantry Regiment had occupied Ioribaiwa on 19 September, he immediately issued strict orders to withdraw the front line. It took three days for telegrams issued by the South Seas Force headquarters to reach Rabaul. It is unclear how long it took for telegrams from Rabaul to reach the force headquarters, but it must have been three days. Bullard, *Japanese Army Operations in the South Pacific Area*, p. 165 and pp. 184–5.

44 'Lost Troops' by Seizo Okada, pp. 18–19, AWM: MSS732, 1.

45 Interrogation of Major Koiwai Mitsuo, NARA: RG331, 93.

46 On 14 October a patrol from the 2/25th Battalion found a large piece of raw flesh wrapped in green leaves. The next day the bodies of two men killed from the 3rd Battalion were found in old Japanese positions. One body had had both arms amputated while the other had a large piece of flesh cut away from his thigh and deep gashes down the other leg. 25th Brigade war diary, 15 October 1942, Sep.–Oct. 1942, AWM: AWM52, 8/2/25.

47 McCarthy, *South-West Pacific Area First Year*, pp. 274–5.

48 Gavin Long, *The Six Years War*, Australian War Memorial and the Australian Government Publishing Service, Canberra, 1973, p. 232; Mark Johnston, *The Proud 6th: An Illustrated History of the 6th Australian Division, 1939–45*, Cambridge University Press, Melbourne, 2008, p. 141.

49 Signal, MacArthur to Blamey, 2 November 1942, AWM: EXDOC156.

50 The Army battle honour 'Kokoda Trail' gives the dates of the campaign as 22 July to 13 November 1942. See Army Council Secretariat, *The official names of the battles, actions & engagements fought by the land forces of the Commonwealth during the Australian campaigns in the 'South-West Pacific 1942–1945'*, Her Majesty's Stationary Office, London, 1958, p. 11.

51 *Going to the Land below the Southern Cross* (transl. Kazuhiro Monden), p. 1, AWM: PR00297, 11.

52 *Sydney Morning Herald*, 6 March 1945.

FURTHER READING

Brune, P., *A Bastard of a Place: The Australians in Papua*, Allen & Unwin, Sydney, 2004.

Bullard, S. [trans.], *Army Operations in the South Pacific Area: New Britain and Papuan Campaigns, 1942–43*, Australian War Memorial, Canberra, 2007.

Collie, C. and Marutani, H., *The Path of Infinite Sorrow: The Japanese on the Kokoda Track*, Allen & Unwin, Sydney, 2009.

Horner, D., *Crisis of Command: Australian Generalship and the Japanese Threat, 1941–1943*, Australian National University Press, Canberra, 1978.

Horner, D., *Blamey: The Commander-in-Chief*, Allen & Unwin, Sydney, 1998.

McCarthy, D., *South-West Pacific Area First Year: Kokoda to Wau*, Australian War Memorial, 1959.

Paul, R., *Retreat from Kokoda*, Panther Books, London, 1969.

Williams, P., *The Kokoda Campaign 1942: Myth and Reality*, Cambridge University Press, Port Melbourne, 2012.

CHAPTER 12

ANZACS AND YANKS

US AND AUSTRALIAN OPERATIONS AT THE BEACHHEAD BATTLES

Peter J. Dean

AN EASY VICTORY?

The re-capture of Kokoda on 2 November 1942, followed by the battle of Oivi-Gorari (4–11 November), heralded a major victory for the Australians in Papua. To both the US and Australian high commands and their troops it seemed that the main Japanese force in Papua had been defeated and that the clearing of the Japanese from the north coast of Papua, around Gona, Buna and Sanananda, would be a quick and relatively easy objective. Once this area was secured the Allies could then start developing the area for their planned counter attack to retake the Japanese strong hold at Rabaul.

As the 7th Australian Division, under Major-General George Vasey, descended out of the Owen Stanley Range and advanced onto the low-lying ground near the Japanese bases on the coast, Lieutenant-General Edmund Herring opened Advanced New Guinea Force Headquarters (Adv NGF HQ) at Popondetta. This headquarters was to command both the 7th Division and the recently arrived US 32nd Infantry Division.

By this time the plans of the Australian C-in-C, General Sir Thomas Blamey, for the capture of the Japanese beachhead bases was well advanced. His thrust was to be along three axes, the 7th Division driving down from the Kokoda Trail to Gona and Sanananda while two regiments of the US 32nd Division, under Major-General Edwin Harding, advanced to Buna via a combined air, sea and land route. By mid-November the final orders had been set, with the Girua River acting as the boundary between the two divisions. The Allies were reasonably confident of success with General

Douglas MacArthur's General Headquarters, South West Pacific Area (GHQ) estimating that only 4000 Japanese troops occupied the entire area.

Despite this confidence the battlefield on which the Australian and US troops descended in November 1942 was far from ideal. The distance between Buna village, where the pre-war magistrate and government stations had existed, to Gona was approximately 12 kilometres. The terrain included coconut groves and razor-sharp kunai grass sitting on a low-lying, flat plain that was covered in jungles and swamps, which effectively divided the battlefield into three separate operations.

This daunting landscape was largely undeveloped in terms of modern infrastructure and was alive with tropical diseases that made mere survival – let alone combat – difficult. MacArthur acknowledged that of the nine campaigns in which he had fought he had 'not seen one where the conditions were more punishing on the soldier than this one'.[1] The Deputy Chief of the General Staff and acting Chief of Staff of NGF, Major-General Frank Berryman, noted that '... the Jap is, in one sense only, our worst enemy, malaria and other tropical diseases claim far more victims'.[2] Indicative of this is the fact that the 'fresh' US 32nd Division was to suffer a 66 per cent sickness rate. While by the end of 1942 the Australians were to have some 15 575 cases of sickness due to the tropical conditions, including 9249 cases of malaria.[3]

The Japanese positions within this horrendous terrain consisted of heavily fortified bunkers, blockhouses, trenches and weapons pits, situated on the only dry ground in the area. They had made excellent use of the landscape to maximise their defences that one US official report described as 'perfect'.[4] Around the Buna area they had used the swamps to channel the Allied attacks into four restricted areas; Buna village, the 'triangle', a narrow bridge across the air strips and finally through the coconut plantation below Cape Endaiadere. It was, as the US Official History described it, a defensive 'masterpiece'.[5]

FROM OPTIMISM TO DEFEAT – PHASE I

But Allied confidence in Papua was riding high in November 1942. GHQ and NGF had assumed that they had defeated the bulk of the Japanese forces in the Owen Stanleys and that the Japanese forces in the area consisted only of stragglers from two depleted Japanese regiments and a battalion of mountain artillery. Unknown to the Allies was the fact that a considerable number of Japanese troops had not advanced into the mountains, but instead had remained in the beachheads area to develop

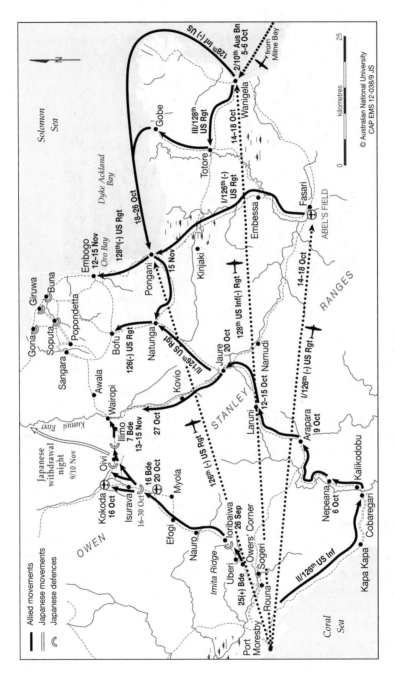

Map 9 The Allied advance in Papua, October–November 1942

Photo 35 Japanese defences in the Beachheads area are described as a masterpiece of defensive warfare. These highly camouflaged positions were almost impossible to see until Allied troops were right on top of them. This one has been damaged by tank fire (AWM 013931).

the Japanese bases. In addition, contrary to the GHQ's assessment, the Japanese had every intention of holding the area indefinitely and as such they had poured in supplies and reinforcements. By the time of Adv NGF's assault in November there were in fact 9000 Japanese troops in these positions, many of them fresh troops, and reinforcements continued to arrive throughout the early stages of the campaign, bringing the defenders' strength up to approximately 12 000 troops.[6]

All of this was unknown to the Australians in the 7th Division's 25th Brigade (AIF) as they closed in on the northern-most Japanese position at Gona Mission. The brigade, under command of Brigadier Ken Eather, was battered and bruised from its fighting in the mountains and could only muster 850 men for action. The brigade launched its first assault on 22 November with small gains being made against the exceptionally strong Japanese defences at the cost of over 100 casualties. Reinforced by the 3rd (Militia) Battalion, the brigade tried again on 24 November, this time supported by an air bombardment of the Japanese positions, but the result was the same.

The failure of the 25th Brigade to take Gona, coupled with its severely reduced strength, meant that Herring and Vasey decided to recall the 21st Brigade (AIF) from Port Moresby. A veteran of the defensive actions against the Japanese on the Kokoda Trail, like the 25th Brigade, this formation was severely understrength, mustering only some 800 men. Over the subsequent days their attacks failed to make any decisive headway.

The efforts of the Australians and Americans further south were not much better. While Eather's men assaulted Gona the depleted 16th Brigade (AIF), reinforced by elements of the 126th US Infantry Regiment from the 32nd Division, had advanced on Sanananda. The troops came up against an advanced Japanese position at the Cape Killerton track junction. After the 16th Brigade pushed back the forward Japanese positions, depleting its remaining strength, the US troops took over the advance. Over the following two days, in bitter fighting, the US troops inched their way forward. Their attacks and Japanese counter attacks continued for a week and by 30 November one of the two main US thrusts had managed to outflank the Japanese positions and establish a road block along the track behind the Japanese position. Their efforts, though, had exhausted their strength and increasing Japanese pressure forced them onto the defensive. As E. G. Keogh noted, despite the 'notable' achievement of the US troops 'all hope of a quick decision north of the [Girua] River had now vanished'.[7]

Further south, beyond the Girua River, great hope had been placed on the advance of the rest of the 32nd US Division around Buna village and the airstrip. While Major-General Warren Harding's troops had suffered a major setback before their attack started, with Japanese aircraft sinking the small ships bringing forward the division's supplies and artillery support, it nevertheless advanced brimming with confidence. Both Harding and his troops firmly believed that they had been sent to Papua merely to 'mop up' the remnants of the defeated and exhausted Japanese troops at Buna. Harding's troops thought that not only would Buna be a pushover, but that they would prove to the world the superiority of the US Army over both their enemy and their Australian allies.

This misplaced confidence meant that when the 32nd Division clashed with the exceptionally well-sited and reinforced Japanese positions at Buna on 19 November the consequences were seismic. Lacking fire support and advancing en masse in a frontal assault on the Japanese defences in the pouring rain, the US troops were butchered. Some broke and others refused to advance; however, with great resolve they rallied and after a brief bombardment of the defences from Allied aircraft they tried again the next day, only to meet a similar fate. The attacks continued on 21

Photo 36 Wanigela, Papua, 15 November 1942. US troops of 128th Infantry Regiment, 32nd Division move up to the Buna front during the first stage of the Battle of the Beachheads (AWM 127507).

November, supported by the recently arrived 2/6th Australian Independent Company (AIF) but this time the air support arrived at the wrong time and a large part of the ordnance landed amongst the attacking US troops 'killing six, wounding twelve, and almost burying seventy others'.[8] The assault was delayed but the next round of air support failed to arrive causing the attack to be delayed a third time, by the time it was launched the troops were both disorganised and disheartened and no progress was made.

The US and Australian troops tried again on 26 and 30 November with much better coordinated air and mortar support but the gains proved to be minor. The attacks at Buna had stalled, with the 32nd Division suffering 492 battle casualties without making a single penetration of the enemy's line. The 'mopping up' of the 'depleted' Japanese at the beachheads had ground to a halt in the face of murderous enemy fire, from well-prepared positions, in difficult country. From here the Allied prospects looked bleak. What was to follow was weeks of continued infantry assaults on the

Japanese positions before the Allies were able to bring forward the necessary forces and equipment to defeat the Japanese.

STRATEGIC CONTEXT

The events of November 1942 saw Australian and US troops make continued frontal assaults with little fire support into heavily defended Japanese positions. Quite rightly, these beachhead battles are often portrayed as one of the darkest episodes of 1942. Most histories paint a grim picture of the events on the northern shores of Papua. A number of these texts have portrayed the gallant Australian soldiers operating at the mercy, not only of their Japanese opponents, but also their incompetent and often 'cowardly' US Allies, while all the time suffering under the mismanagement of the insensitive and inept US and Australian high commands.[9] While there is no denying the horrendous conditions in which these battles were fought, and the suffering that the soldiers endured, of critical importance in understanding the reasons for their sacrifice are the complicated operational and strategic contexts.

Understanding this context is something poorly done in most accounts of the fighting at Buna, Gona and Sanananda. For instance, one of the main criticisms of higher headquarters and in particular of the C-in-C, General Douglas MacArthur, is the constant pressure they placed on commanders at the battlefront to push forward with all possible speed, regardless of casualties. This approach has often been seen as callous and out of touch with conditions on the frontline and generally motivated by the desire of MacArthur and Blamey to salvage their own positions at the expense of the troops. Little consideration is given to the broader circumstances that motivated these senior commanders to push so earnestly for quick and decisive results.

Due to a lack of airpower and naval assets, principally any amphibious ships or troops, MacArthur and Blamey were forced in 1942 to fight a land campaign in a maritime environment. While MacArthur was able to exploit his continually increasing airpower, his lack of an amphibious force and the US Joint Chiefs of Staff and US naval commander in the Pacific, Admiral Chester Nimitz, decision to deny him sufficient naval forces meant that he could not to take full advantage of the defeat of the Japanese invasion force bound for Port Moresby at the Coral Sea in May or the subsequent Japanese defeat at the battle of Midway in June 1942.

The consequence was that neither the Japanese nor the Allies could gain control of the seas around Papua and New Guinea, and this led to the long, drawn-out struggle along the Kokoda Trail between July 1942 and November 1942. MacArthur and the Australian efforts to defeat the over-land attack on Port Moresby along the Kokoda Trail also owed much to the landing of the US 1st Marine Division at Guadalcanal in the neighbour-ing South Pacific Area on 7 August 1942. This operation forced the Japanese at Rabaul to divide their forces and ultimately choose the pursuit of the recapture of Guadalcanal over the assault on Port Moresby.

As a result of the Marines landing at Guadalcanal the Japanese offen-sive in the Owen Stanley Range was reduced in scope and then ultimately cancelled. However, the difficulties that the Australians faced in operating in Papua as well as the determined efforts of the Japanese to delay their advance along the Kokoda Trail meant that operations did not progress at the pace that the US Joint Chiefs of Staff, MacArthur or Blamey desired. This meant that MacArthur was under increasing pressure. The serious-ness of the situation was underlined by a cable from the US Joint Chiefs to MacArthur on 16 October, reminding him that they viewed the situation in Papua as 'critical'. MacArthur's vulnerability was further highlighted two days later with the sacking of Vice Admiral Robert Ghormley, the C-in-C of the US forces in the South Pacific who were fighting the Japanese at Guadalcanal.

Driving much of the anxiety at MacArthur's GHQ was also a constant threat of the reinforcement of the Japanese positions in northern Papua. MacArthur knew that if Guadalcanal fell he would be on the back foot as the Japanese would be able to direct substantial air, land and sea assets from Guadalcanal to Papua. This meant that GHQ was forced to consider, and plan, for the possibility of the need to withdraw and redistribute forces in the advent of the failure of the Marines and the US Navy to hold on in the South Pacific.

The seesawing battle for Guadalcanal continued right through November and December 1942. While the main Japanese land offensive to retake the Henderson Field was defeated on 29 October it was at sea that the struggle for Guadalcanal really hinged and here the US Navy failed to established sea control around the island until late December 1942. Allied success at Guadalcanal was not guaranteed until the Japanese started to withdraw in January 1943. Up until the second week of January 1943 the US feared that Japanese naval activity around the island was a precursor to another assault rather than a withdrawal of their ground forces from the island.

The loss of Guadalcanal would have necessitated the abandonment of the Allied positions around Buna and along the southeast coast of Papua.

This would have included a reversal to a defensive position on the Kokoda Trail based around only one brigade with the remainder of the force withdrawing to Port Moresby. It would also have resulted in a withdrawal from Goodenough Island, Milne Bay and Merauke, a reduction in the air support valuable in Port Moresby and discontinuance of the build-up of Allied forces in New Guinea.[10] Thus, all MacArthur's plans hinged on Guadalcanal. As MacArthur's operations chief Brigadier-General Chamberlin noted just before the Beachhead campaign kicked off:

> the key to our plan of action lies in the success or failure of the South Pacific in holding Guadalcanal. None of [our] ... plans ... has a reasonable chance of success if Guadalcanal falls. Their failure will adversely affect the success of our basic and fundamental mission. If Guadalcanal holds, the success of [our] plan is assured.[11]

Guadalcanal was not MacArthur's only concern during this period. The Japanese had exceptionally large air, sea and ground forces based in Java and Timor to the west of New Guinea and as the campaign at the beachheads wore on MacArthur became increasingly concerned about his left flank. By mid-December GHQ's intelligence section was monitoring the expanded activities of the Japanese to the northwest, which included the occupation of Tanimbar, Kai and Aroe Island and the building of an airfield in eastern Timor. Darwin was still under air attack by the Japanese and this what forced MacArthur to cancel his plans to move the US troops based there to Papua. On 23 December MacArthur wrote to Blamey of these concerns and the possibility of Japanese operations towards the Torres Straight and the south coast of New Guinea and ordered garrison forces into Cape York Peninsula and reinforcements to Merauke.[12] Air-raids on Merauke in early January plus troop and naval build-ups convinced GHQ that an invasion of Merauke was a distinct possibility, resulting in further reinforcements being sent to protect its airfield.[13]

Concerns over Guadalcanal and Japanese intentions from Timor gave the operations at Buna and Sanananda its degree of haste in November and December. While with hindsight this emphasis on speed from MacArthur downwards does not seem legitimate, at the time it remained a critical part of the considerations for the campaign at the beachheads, and these concerns were only exacerbated by GHQ's original underestimation of Japanese strength in the area. When GHQ and the Australians realised that the Japanese were much stronger than expected and that they were attempting to reinforce their positions in November and early December,

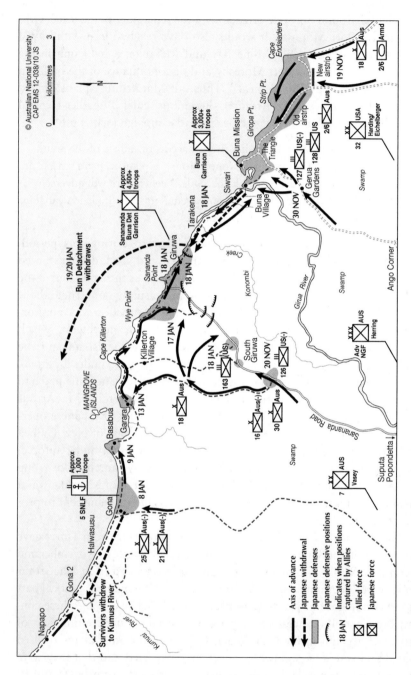

Map 10 The Battle of the Beachheads, November 1942 – January 1943

coupled with their advances from Timor, it gave rise to fears of a Japanese repositioning towards New Guinea and this led to an even greater emphasis on clearing the Japanese out of the beachheads.

AGAINST ALL ODDS

The failure of the US and Australian forces to break through in November 1942 led to a shake-up in the command and troops at the beachheads. Many of the AIF troops in the 7th Division would be relieved by Militia units, the 126th US Infantry Regiment would move from the Sanananda Front to Buna while the poor performance of the 32nd Division meant that MacArthur sacked its commanding officer, Harding, and replaced him with the US I Corps commander, Lieutenant-General Robert (Bob) Eichelberger. Before setting out to take command of the division at Buna Eichelberger was summoned to a meeting with MacArthur, where he was issued with his now infamous order to 'take Buna or don't come back alive'. MacArthur went on to state that 'time is of the essence … Hurry Bob: Our dangers increase hour by hour'.[14]

Despite the reshuffle of troops and the change in command for the 32nd Division, many of the serious problems facing the Australian and US troops at the beachheads remained. MacArthur's naval commander, Vice Admiral Arthur S. Carpenter, was very reluctant to operate his small number of destroyers in the close uncharted waters off Buna and Sanananda. Blamey was scathing of the Navy in this regard noting that these conditions did not seem to be affecting the Japanese Navy and pushing for Carpenter to operate his destroyers under the cover of land-based airpower to support his troops; however, this never occurred.[15] Air superiority throughout the operation was not absolute and the inability of air power to operate effectively at night meant that until late in the campaign the Allies also lacked sea control and could not close off the area to Japanese resupply or reinforcements.

Air power was also having a limited effect on the frontline. Despite the statement in 1942 from the C-in-C Allied Air Forces (AAF) Lieutenant-General George C. Kenney that the 'artillery in this theatre flies',[16] at the beachheads this was to prove entirely optimistic. As Peter Williams has noted, for every bomb dropped in 1942 by the AAF in the SWPA, 16 tonnes were dropped in 1944. The air effort in 1942 was around 6 per cent of what it was in 1944 – the tactical air offensive in the SWPA and at the beachheads was small.[17]

The AAF was providing excellent strategic and operational support but air–ground coordination at the front was poor. On several occasions the AAF bombed friendly units; they often missed targets entirely or aircraft arrived late and delayed attacks. Mitigating this was the fact that, as one Australian battalion noted during the campaign, 'the country just didn't lend itself to air support, which was a waste of time and effort'.[18] The low priority the AAF allocated to the protection of supply lines meant that many Allied coastal tuggers, that were so critical to the tenuous supply line, were run ashore or sunk by Japanese aircraft. The AAF did, however, perform an exceptionally valuable service in the strategic mobility of troops, in maintaining supply lines over the Owen Stanleys and in evacuating the sick and the wounded. Once introduced to the battlefront in late November, No. 4 Army Co-operation Squadron RAAF made exceptionally valuable contribution to intelligence collection and artillery spotting.

The urgency of operations also created massive problems for the overstretched Allied supply lines. There were not enough merchant ships to carry supplies and Port Moresby's infrastructure was underdeveloped. The very tenuous supply line around the north coast of Papua meant that Blamey's forces had to rely heavily on air power. This was very limiting, especially in terms of moving and supplying heavy equipment such as artillery and tanks. For instance, it took 17 planeloads to move just one troop of two 25-pounder artillery pieces to the beachheads area from Port Moresby, including just 306 rounds of ammunition per gun. In Papua air resupply was further hampered by the atrocious weather.

The lack of small ships to bring forward supplies, coupled with the lack of air superiority early in the campaign, made the use of ships on the north coast of Papua a major problem, as Major-General Harding discovered when the supply lugger he was on while moving to the battlefront was sunk by Japanese aircraft, leaving him to swim ashore. To make matters more complicated these small coastal craft were attacked just before Christmas 'by our Beaufighters who knocked out five of the eight plus a portion of the personnel' and if 'this was not enough, some [US] motor torpedo boats attacked our small craft at Haroki … and set fire to one which blew up … [Adv NGF HQ] strongly suspect[s] that this was their first successful action'.[19]

The greatest problem caused by these supply issues was the lack of artillery at the battlefront. The US 32nd Division had only 15 artillery tubes at Buna, including only one US 105-mm howitzer.[20] US doctrine called for an infantry division like the 32nd to field 48 guns of this type while the 7th Australian Division was supposed to have three field-artillery regiments of three batteries each in action. As Herring's command was a corps-level force in normal circumstances he would also have had a regiment, or more, of medium guns in support of his troops. As a point of contrast, the 6th Australian Division went into action at Bardia on 3 January 1941 with 70 guns and howitzers under command. At the beachheads Adv NGF, a corps-level force of over two divisions, had a very limited artillery staff present during the battle and between 12 November 1942 and 4 January 1943 only three 3.7-inch howitzers, four 4.5-inch howitzers, 18 25-pounders and one 105-mm howitzer arrived, a total of only 26 artillery tubes, less than one division's worth in allocation. Significantly, 12 of these guns did not arrive until late December–early January. Brigadier-General Clarence A. Martin, Commander 126th Regimental Combat Team at Buna, summed up the supply situation best when he noted that 'The troops went in on a shoestring, and the shoestring was mildewy rotten'.[21]

THE OFFENSIVE CONTINUES

In order to resume the offensive the 30th (Militia) Brigade had been flown into the beachheads area and its 39th battalion was allocated to the 21st Brigade at Gona. Gona was the smallest of the three main Japanese positions and had been heavily worn down by the Australian attacks in November. The offensive resumed at Gona on 6 December but with similar results to the previous attacks, heavy casualties and little progress. But a second attempt two days later broke through the Japanese defences. That night the Japanese troops attempted to break out of their position but were shot to pieces and the following day after bitter hand-to-hand fighting the last Japanese positions were eliminated. It had cost the Australians some 750 casualties.[22]

The breakthrough at Gona was, unfortunately, not a precursor to a Japanese collapse in early December 1942. On the Sanananda front the Allied position was to stall again. From 2–6 December the 16th Brigade had attempted several attacks to break through to the US positions at the Higgins Road Block, but to no avail. The exhausted and depleted 16th brigade was now relieved by Brigadier Selwyn Porter's 30th Brigade, who attacked on 7 December but with little result. The brigade launched a series of attacks between 10–15 December, supported by the arrival of the 36th (Militia) battalion and the 2/7th Cavalry Regiment (AIF). Although the cavalry made it through to the road block these attacks were generally failures. They continued until 22 December before Vasey called the slaughter to a halt.

The performance of the 30th Brigade in these attacks had been far from satisfactory. In late December 1942 Brigade HQ noted that:

> in the 39 and 49 Aust Inf Bns the bulk of the trained and resolute leaders have become causalities, and those that remain are not up to the standard of the units when they originally arrived here. Seven members of the 39th Aus Inf Bn are under arrest on charges of cowardice; this condition is not peculiar to 39 Aust Inf Bn as similar action could be taken in numerous cases in other units.[23]

The 2/7th Cavalry Regiment AIF also came in for criticism, with Major-General Vasey noting that 'I am not yet convinced that [it is] up to the standard of the A.I.F. Inf Bns ... [it] failed to show that aggressiveness necessary for successful offensive action'.[24] Brigadier Porter reported to 7th Division HQ on 22 December 1942 that the 55/53rd and 36th militia battalions 'are NOT fit for war under the present conditions'. The long duration of the campaign, its slow progress, the frontal attacks and losses through death and disease even broke some soldiers in the hardened and elite AIF units. The composite 2/16th – 2/27th battalion of the 21st Brigade reported on 23 December 1942 that 'two soldiers have been placed under arrest for refusing to take part in a routine [reconnaissance] patrol'.[25] Morale had plummeted.

The 30th Brigade's problems at Sanananda were a result of the severe strain on the Australian and US forces in the SWPA in 1942 that forced commanders to commit troops to battle that were not adequately trained. The Australian militia units were to suffer the consequences in 1942. With the best men and equipment allocated to the elite AIF units the conscripts of the militia were initially provided with only 90 days of training. In January 1942 AIF officers were posted to militia units; however, this was not as effective as it should have been as the troops were largely untrained. 49th Battalion (30th Brigade) was seen as undisciplined and under-trained until late 1942.[26] In 1941 the Chief of the General Staff noted that he considered it 'quite the worst [battalion] in Australia'.[27] Yet, it was soon to depart for service in New Guinea. The battalion's history noted that 'with hindsight, it is unbelievable that Army commanders or a government could have allowed troops as inadequately prepared as the 49th to move to a war zone'.[28]

Level	Description	Unit/formation
A	Efficient and experienced for mobile operations	7th Division AIF
B	Efficient for mobile offensive operations, but not yet experienced	2/7th Cavalry Rgt ↓ AIF
C	Efficient for mobile offensive operations - higher training not complete	—
D	Efficient in a static role. Additional brigade and higher training required	32nd US Division ↓ 7th Militia Brigade
E	Units have completed training. A considerable amount of brigade and high training is required	14th Militia Brigade ↓
F	Unit training is not yet complete	30th Militia Brigade

Chart 8 Australian Army formation capability assessments, 1942

On arrival in Port Moresby the 30th Brigade had been used as labour gangs, leaving little time for training. Of the two other militia brigades in Papua, Blamey considered the 14th Brigade a 'poor show', and while the 7th brigade was regarded as better trained only five of its officers had seen active service before and only one, the commander, had seen action in the Second World War.[29] Still, the 7th Brigade was only rated by the Army as a D-level unit, only 'efficient in a static role'. The 14th Brigade was a level E, 'a considerable amount of training … is required' and the 30th Brigade, the first militia troops to see action against the Japanese, were a level F – the lowest rated, meaning 'unit training is not complete'.[30]

By late December 1942 Brigadier Porter noted that 30th Brigade's, which now included a number of battalions from the 7th and 14th Brigades, 'present state of training has been the cause of a costly series of encounters with the enemy, both in life and material; and, the gain has been negligible'. The problem Porter noted was a 'lack of opportunity' for proper and adequate training rather than the men as 'junior leadership is on a very much higher plane, moreover; there is some knowledge of minor tactics on the part of the personnel'.[31]

DECISION AT BUNA AND SANANANDA

The lack of training amongst the Australian militia units was replicated in the US units at Buna, who were also struggling to deal with the Japanese. Prior to being committed to battle their corps commander, Lieutenant-General Robert Eichelberger, had rated the division as 'barely satisfactory' in combat efficiency and he told MacArthur that the division 'was not sufficiently trained to meet Japanese veterans on equal terms'.[32] His prediction has been borne out by their initial contact with the Japanese at Buna, which had been devastating for the morale of the US troops.

Probably the best analysis of US combat performance in these first few weeks at Buna comes from Major W. B. Parker, a US Army liaison officer sent forward to observe the 32nd Division in action. Parker noted that 'The first opposition from the enemy here [at Buna] was a surprise and shock to our green troops'. He noted the 2/6th Australian Independent Company AIF, serving side by side with the Americans, was 'much better prepared for jungle combat, as far as training and psychological conditioning were concerned, than our troops'.[33]

US tactics, Parker noted, were 'initially bad'; however, they went through 'rapid evolution … our troops first attempted to advance in mass formation … with disastrous results … after a week of fighting the method finally evolved was that of small patrol advances'. However 'the most striking and depressing feature gleaned from our whole observation [was that] our junior leadership in this operation was poor'. Thus, the men have 'no resiliency … no interest in getting back into the fight to win it'. Parker admitted that many of the men and their leaders were frightened and often reluctant to press forward.[34] This report stands as a damning indictment of the training and preparation of the division for combat.

However, it was not to remain all doom and gloom for the US units. Tactical improvements, as Parker noted, came quickly and US leadership improved after Harding was sacked and replaced with Eichelberger. He subsequently sacked a number of senior officers and unit commanders, spent considerable time on the frontline and put enormous effort into reorganising the division and improving cooperation and communication with the Australians. Initially found wanting, in Eichelberger the US troops found their tonic. As his biographer noted, at Buna Eichelberger's philosophy of leadership was the margin 'between victory and defeat'.[35] A proposition supported by a number of Australians from the men of the 2/12th Battalion[36] to Major-General Berryman,[37] the corps chief of staff and Lieutenant-General Herring. At the end of the campaign Herring would note that 'General Eichelberger kept them [32nd Div] going and he proved himself to be a most courageous officer, his effort[s] could not be surpassed'.[38]

Still, Blamey remained unconvinced about the performance of the 32nd Division and in early December he decided that the Buna front needed reinforcement by elite, battle-hardened and experienced jungle soldiers, but such troops were not easy to find in late 1942. The 7th Division was a shadow of its former strength and fully committed to Gona and Sanananda. With the militia units moved forward to bolster the Sanananda front there was no spare infantry in Port Moresby; the 6th Division AIF had already committed its 16th Brigade to Papua while the rest of the 6th Division had been split up with one brigade defending Milne Bay and the other forming the core of the Northern Territory Force. The rest of the militia were either defending the mainland or lacked training and equipment.

With the situation at the beachheads not improving Blamey decided to take a risk. By weakening the defences at Milne Bay he could move the 18th Brigade (AIF), along with tanks from the 2/6th Armoured Regiment (AIF), and additional artillery to Buna. This move was to change the nature of the

Photo 37 Papua, 28 December 1942. Bodies of four dead Japanese, killed in the Buna action, lying beside a large pillbox. These were defended by the Japanese to the last man, and without the Australian-manned Stuart tanks it would have been difficult to have destroyed them quickly. Each pillbox was placed so as to give supporting fire to others in the vicinity. Some had steel and concrete tops. Many pillboxes of this type were crushed in by the tanks (AWM 013933).

fighting on the 32nd Division's front and prove to be the formula to victory. The 18th Brigade was placed under Eichelberger, who gave its commander, Brigadier George Wootten, command of the US troops around the Buna airstrip. He soon launched a coordinated attack on the Japanese defences using tanks, artillery and his 2/9th and 2/10th battalions. In a series of hammering blows Wootten's men and the tanks, supported by US troops, steadily destroyed the Japanese defences around the Buna airstrip.

Wootten's assaults were coordinated with a renewed effort by the rest of the 32nd Division further west at Buna village and on the same day that the 18th brigade cleared Cape Endaiadere the Americans had driven a corridor through to the sea to the east of the village. On 1 January 1943 the Japanese defences had been cut to pieces and on the following day the remaining Japanese attempted to evacuate to Sanananda. The success at Buna in December 1943 was, as the 2/9th battalion's history noted, built on the back of a foundation of training, experience, 'the character of the men ... the iron discipline of the assaulting troops and ... the strength of the command structure of a disciplined fighting unit',[39] factors that had been sorely missing in the previous month. Their success, however, had come at great cost. The 18th Brigade suffered 863 casualties to clear Buna, with a further 2000 casualties being suffered by the men of the 32nd Division. The Japanese left behind 1390 dead.

Herring now moved to concentrate this force on the remaining Japanese defences at Sanananda. Here, Vasey's 7th Division had been reinforced during December by the 163rd US Infantry Regiment, from the 41st US Infantry Division, the last remaining reserve in the SWPA. These troops were considerably better trained and led, and much better prepared for combat than their counterparts in the 32nd Division. They took over from the 30th Brigade and would assault along the axis of the main Soputa-Sanananda track and capture the main Japanese road block. This would be phase one of the main attack to clear the Japanese out of Sanananda.

While still not anywhere near the standard of the 18th Brigade, the 163rd Regiment generally performed well, although Vasey did criticise it for its slow operational tempo. The 2/12th battalion (18th Brigade) recorded that the 'perceived slowness [of the 163rd Regiment] ... may have, in objective terms, been wrongly based given the tenacity of the Japanese defenders'. In addition criticisms of the 163rd were more of a result of it being 'forced take on the mantle and reputation previously generated by earlier American units', noting that it would 'take time ... before this new generation of toughened American infantry units' could overcome the 'earlier mindset of "non-performance" in battle of American infantry'.[40]

The 163rd Regiment was, however, just the warm-up act and the main thrust at Sanananda would come from the tanks and infantry of the 18th Brigade. The 2/9th and 2/12th battalions supported by mortars, tanks and artillery kicked off the brigades attack on 12 January 1943 against fierce opposition. The Japanese had used the long respite between attacks to strengthen their position, and a well-sited anti-tank gun knocked out two of the three supporting tanks, which meant that the infantry assault ground to a halt suffering 140 casualties without securing any Japanese positions.

The failure of 12 January was a bitter pill to Herring, Eichelberger and Vasey as they had pinned their hopes on this attack breaking through the Japanese defences. Vasey believed that with the loss of the tanks to continue the attack against deeply entrenched Japanese positions using only infantry was inviting a repetition of the 'costly mistakes of 1915–1917' and that such attacks were 'unlikely to succeed',[41] an observation that could easily have been made regarding the division's attacks two months earlier. Talk at Adv NGF HQ now turned to a blockade of the remaining Japanese at Sanananda. However the attack of 12 January had exhausted most of the remaining Japanese anti-tank ammunition and, finally cut off from supplies and reinforcements, they started to withdraw from their positions over the following two days.

On the morning of 14 January patrol reports and a prisoner interrogation provided Adv NGF HQ with their first indication of the Japanese withdrawal. Vasey contacted Eichelberger to inform him that the 'bugger's gone'[42], and the 18th Brigade and the 163rd Regiment advanced steadily over the next few days against ever-diminishing resistance. The last Japanese were eliminated from Sanananda on 22 January 1943.

THE RECKONING

Securing the Japanese beachheads at Gona, Buna and Sanananda was supposed to have been a relatively easy task, mainly mopping up the remnants of the Japanese forces that had been defeated in the Owen Stanleys. Instead, what transcribed was the bloodiest campaign of the South Pacific in 1942. The battles of Gona, Buna and Sanananda were to cost the Australian and US forces some 5500 battle casualties, with thousands more evacuated sick. These beachhead battles with their frontal assaults against heavily fortified Japanese positions with little fire support represent some of the darkest episodes of Australia's war in the Pacific in 1942.

The shadows of war that led to this campaign were long and they reached well back from Papua in terms of the lack of training, poor logistical arrangements and inadequate preparation that a significant number of Australian and US units had before going into the front line. The AIF troops of the 7th Australian division went into action at the beachheads tired, worn out, diseased and well below strength. Meanwhile, the Australian militia and the US 32nd Division had everything stacked against them: poor training, poor equipment and supplies, limited fire support, inadequate leadership and a limited understanding of doctrine. As Major-General Vasey noted in January 1943: 'my experiences of the last two months convinces me that for success in jungle warfare, such as is taking place in the Sanananda-Soputa area, the first requisites for success in either attack or defence are high morale, [and] a high standard of tng [Training], both individual and collective'.[43]

The failure to prepare the militia and the US troops for combat resulted from a combination of the systemic problems in the US and Australian armies in the 1920s and 1930s and the strategic pressures facing MacArthur and Blamey in 1942.

There were many failures at Buna and Sanananda: a failure of intelligence regarding Japanese strength, intentions and dispositions; the failure of supply; the failure to apply the correct doctrine and the failure to undertake combined arms warfare. These factors, coupled with the lack of resources available in the SWPA and the strategic circumstances that forced MacArthur and Blamey into fighting a large-scale land campaign in a maritime environment, resulted in high casualties and slow progress.

At the strategic level the question remains as to how much the emphasis on a speedy end to the campaign was driven by the desire to eliminate the Japanese at the beachheads due to the inherent risks of a possible Allied defeat at Guadalcanal and Japanese movements in Timor and northwestern New Guinea versus the threat that the slow progress was having on MacArthur's position as C-in-C SWPA and Blamey's as Commander of Allied Land Forces. This debate will remain controversial but we should not, however, overlook the fact that the Japanese HQ at Rabaul had initiated the campaign in Papua by beating MacArthur to the punch and landing at Buna in July 1942, and they ended the campaign in January 1943 when they chose to withdraw after their defeat at Guadalcanal forced them onto the strategic defensive.

Success at Buna and Sanananda came with the arrival of the fresh troops of the 18th Brigade, who were acclimatised, jungle trained, well led, adequately supplied and supported by armour and sufficient artillery. The absence of these factors, including proper planning, reconnaissance and battle preparation, generally led to disasters for all armies in Papua, AIF, Militia, US and Japanese. With their proper training and proven battlefield experience the performance of the AIF troops was superior to that of the Militia and their US counterparts. But these later two were on par and with more time in the line and additional training these units improved considerably and were to go on to provide excellent service during the rest of the war. Courage was not lacking at the beachheads, but most other things necessary for success in battle were until 1942 drew to a close.

Notes

1 MacArthur, as quoted in David Horner, *High Command*, Allen & Unwin, Sydney, 1992, p. 248.

2 Berryman to Irving, 7 January 1943, Berryman Papers, AWM PR 84/370, item 11.

3 Samuel Milner, *Victory in Papua*, Office of the Chief of Military History, Washington, 1957 p. 372.

4 'History of the Buna Campaign', December 1, 1942 – January 25 1943, G-3 History Division, GHQ, AFPAC, 5 October 1945, AWM 54 581/6/8, p. 8.

5 Milner, *Victory in Papua*, p. 143.

6 Lieutenant-General Yoshiawa Kane, *Southern Cross: An Account of the Eastern New Guinea Campaign*, Tokyo, 1955, US Army Office of Military History, 228.01, HRC, Geo T New Guinea, 314.73.

7 E. G. Keogh, *Southwest Pacific 1941–45*, Grayflower, Melbourne, 1965, p. 225.

8 Milner, *Victory in Papua*, p. 178.

9 See Paul Ham, *Kokoda*, ABC Books, Sydney 2004. Ham's book includes five index entries for American 'cowardice' in these battles. See also Peter Fitzsimons, *Kokoda*, Hodder, Sydney, 2004, p. 443 for a summary of his views of US leadership and battlefield performance.

10 Petersburg Plan, Copy No. 1 on Redistribution of Allied Forces SWPA in the event of a Japanese Success in the Solomon Islands, 31 October 1942, USAHEC, Carlisle Barrack, Pennsylvania.

11 See Chamberlin to Sutherland, 'GHQ Plan of Action', 30 October 1942, NARA, RG407 98-GHQ1-3.2, G-3 Journal and Files Box 574, October–November 1942.

12 MacArthur to Blamey, 23 December 1942, NARA, RG407 98-GHQ1-3.2, G-3 Journal and Files Box 576, December 1942.

13 GHQ G-2 Daily Intelligence Summary 4–5 January 1953 and MacArthur to Rear Admiral F. W. Coster, Senior Naval Officer Royal Netherlands Forces in

Australia, 5 January 1943, NARA, RG407 98-GHQ1-3.2, G-3 Journal and Files Box 578, January 1943.

14 Eichelberger to Edward T. Lauer, 17 October 1953, Leslie Anderson Collection, USAHEC, Carlisle Barrack, Pennsylvania.

15 Blamey to MacArthur, 7 November 1942 NARA, RG407 98-GHQ1-3.2, G-3 Journal and Files Box 574, October-November 1942.

16 Kenney as quoted in *Papua: US Army Campaigns of World War II*, US Government Printing Office, Washington, D.C., 1992, p. 20 www.ibiblio.org/hyperwar/USA/USA-C-Papua/index.html

17 Peter Williams, *The Kokoda Campaign 1942: Myth and Reality*, Cambridge University Press, Melbourne, 2012, pp. 223–4.

18 Ken Clift, *War Dance: A Story of the 23rd Australian Infantry Battalion*, Streamline, Sydney, 1980, p. 333.

19 Berryman to Irving, 24 December 1942, Berryman Papers, PR 84/370, item 11.

20 *Papua: US Army Campaigns of World War II*, US Government Printing Office, Washington DC, 1992, p. 20 www.ibiblio.org/hyperwar/USA/USA-C-Papua/index.html

21 'Clarence A Martin to Samuel Milner, 6 March 1951' Interviews, New Guinea Operations, 1942–1943, RG319, Records of Army Staff Centre of Military History, NARA, Washington D.C.

22 Keogh, *Southwest Pacific 1941–1945*, p. 257–8.

23 Report by Brigadier Porter and Major Sublet on condition of troops under command of 7th Australian Division and Strength State, Sanananda, 1942, AWM 54 581/7/16.

24 Ibid.

25 Ibid.

26 McCarthy, *South West Pacific Area: The First Year*, AWM, Canberra, 1959, p. 44.

27 David Horner, *Crisis of Command*, ANU Press, Canberra, 1978, p. 81.

28 Frederick Cranston, *Always Faithful: A History of the 49th Australian Infantry Battalion 1916–1982*, Boolarong, Brisbane, 1983, p. 168.

29 A. B. Lodge, 'Geese and Swans: The Australian Militia in Papua, 1942–1943', Papers of Brigadier M Austin, AWM 419/4/24, pp. 9–16.

30 Horner, *Crisis of Command*, p. 87.

31 Report by Brigadier Porter and Major Sublet on condition of troops under command of 7th Australian Division and Strength State, Sanananda, 1942, AWM 54 581/7/16.

32 Robert Eichelberger, *Jungle Road to Tokyo*, Viking, New York, 1950, p. 11.

33 W. B. Parker, 'Notes on Operations near Buna, New Guinea, USA Liaison officer 1942', AWM 54 417/1/4, p. 8.

34 Ibid., p. 13, 18.

35 Paul Chwialkowski, *In Caesar's shadow: The Life of General Robert Eichelberger*, Greenwood, Westport, 1993.

36 Alex Graeme-Evans, *Of Storms and Rainbows: The Story of the Men of the 2/12th Battalion A.I.F.*, volume II, 12th Battalion Association, Hobart, 1991, p. 229.

37 Peter Dean, *The Architect of Victory: The Military Career of Lieutenant-General Sir Frank Horton Berryman*, CUP, Melbourne 2011, p. 206.
38 Edmund Herring, 'The Battle of the Beachheads', AMW 581/6/10, p. 4.
39 Gordon Dickens, *Never Late: The 2/9th Australian Infantry Battalion, 1939–1945*, AMHP, Loftus, 2005, p. 236.
40 Graeme-Evans, *Of Storms and Rainbows*, p. 324.
41 'Notes on Situation – Sanananda Area 13 Jan 43', War Diary, Adv NGF HQ, AWM 52 1/5/51.
42 Berryman, Diary, 14 January 1943 AWM PR84/370.
43 Vasey in 'Report by Brigadier Porter and Major Sublet on condition of troops under command of 7th Australian Division and Strength State, Sanananda, 1942', AWM 54 581/7/16.

FURTHER READING

Beregerud, E., *Touched with Fire: The Land War in the South Pacific*, Penguin, New York, 1996.
Brune, P., *A Bastard of a Place: The Australians in Papua: Kokoda, Milne, Bay, Gina, Buna, Sanananda*, Allen & Unwin, St Leonards, 2004.
Gailey, H., *MacArthur Strikes Back: Decision at Buna, 1942–43*, Presidio, Novato, 2000.
Keogh, E. G., *Southwest Pacific 1941–1945*, Grayflower, Melbourne, 1965.
Luvass, J., 'Buna 19 November–2 January 1943: A Leavenworth Nightmare', in Heller, C. E. and Stofft, W. A. (eds), *America's First Battles, 1776–1965*, University of Kansas Press, Lawrence, 1986.
McCarthy, D., *South-west Pacific–first year: Kokoda to Wau*, AWM, Canberra, 1959, www.awm.gov.au/hirstories/second_world_war/volume.asp?levelID=67907
Milner, S., *Victory in Papua*, Office of the Chief of Military History, Washington, D.C., 1957, www.ibiblio.org/hyperwar/USA/USA-P-Papua/index.html
Papua: US Army Campaigns of World War II, US Government Printing Office, Washington, D.C., 1992, p. 20, www.ibiblio.org/hyperwar/USA/USA-C-Papua/index.html

CONCLUSION

1942 IN REFLECTION

Australia's experiences in 1942 were just one small part in a global conflict. While the shadows of war merely touched Australia's shore, millions of people across the globe lived in the darkness that came with Nazi or Japanese occupation. Outside of the Pacific, 1942 also saw a number of critical battles and events. The Allied victory at the second battle of el Alemein (23 October – 4 November 1942) coupled with Operation Torch, the invasion of Morocco, Algeria and Tunisia (8 November 1942), saw the turning of the tide of the war in North Africa, while the battle for the Atlantic continued to see-saw. In Eastern Europe, where the bulk of the German military effort was directed, Hitler's forces suffered a devastating defeat at the battle of Stalingrad (21 August 1942 – 2 February 1943). In the air 1942 also saw the Allied strategic bombing offensive against Germany swing into full action when, on the night of 30–31 May 1942, the RAF launched its first 1000-bomber raid on the German town of Cologne. One thousand and forty-six aircraft rained more than 2000 tonnes of bombs on the city, reducing 13 000 houses to rubble. In the Pacific, tens of thousands of Allied military personnel became prisoners of war of the Japanese, while the Sino-Japanese war in China continued unabated, occupying the bulk of the Japanese Army. Yet, while the Second World War was global in nature, its ramifications were felt most significantly at the local level.

Speaking in Federal Parliament on 27 January 1943, Prime Minister John Curtin reflected on what had been achieved during the year to 'save this country from invasion' and to 'protect our own soil'. The successes were self-evident. 'Nowhere in Australia last night', he continued, 'did people fear that air-raid warnings would interrupt their slumber or work.'[1]

The victories at Coral Sea, Midway, Kokoda, Milne Bay, Guadalcanal and the Beachheads had swung the balance of the war in the Pacific firmly towards the Allies. With Papua secure MacArthur and Blamey could put forth their offensive plans for the reconquest of the SWPA and the defeat of the Japanese.

The country had emerged from the crisis of 1942 much stronger. The fledgling minority government had established itself and the Prime Minister had emerged as a national leader. The government had put in place major reforms to the wartime economy, and had reorientated Australian society to the war effort. The partnership with the United States was cemented and critical victories had been won in the air, at sea and on land. In 1943 the Australian and US militaries were poised to strike at the very heart of Japanese power in the SWPA and by the end of that year the reconquest of central New Guinea would be complete and MacArthur would launch his deep-strike operations that would take him rapidly onto the Philippines in 1944.

For Australia 1942 was and will remain a 'pivotal' year in our history. In the 70th Anniversary year this book has attempted to capture some of the key issues and events of that year and explain their significance and importance, while providing a broader understanding of how these events shaped Australian life and our history. As the 100th anniversary of Gallipoli arrives and its public events aim to commemorate 'all Australian servicemen and women, including those who fought along the Kokoda Track and at Tobruk; those who were held as prisoners of war; those who fought on the seas and in the skies; and those who served from Korea and Vietnam to Iraq and Afghanistan',[2] this critical year in Australia should continue to receive its due recognition in the crowded space that is Australian memory and history of war.

Notes

1   Digest of decisions and announcements and import speeches by the Prime Minister, no. 51, 26 January 1943 to 27 January 1943, Commonwealth Government Printer, Canberra, 1943, pp. 3–4. I am indebted to Dr Karl James for providing me with this quote and allowing me to use it in the conclusion.
2   As quoted on the Anzac Centenary Homepage www.anzaccentenary.gov.au/

INDEX

Note: Page numbers in *italics* refer to maps and illustrations.

242